David Potter is Francis W. Kel[illegible]sor of Greek and Roman Histo[illegible]fessor of Greek and Lat[illegible]dies at the University o[illegible]r's *Crown*, also publish[illegible]

… Collegiate Professor …
… y and Arthur F. Thurnau Professor …
… , in the Department of Classical Stu…
… f Michigan. He is the author of The Victo…
… hed by Quercus.

£2.50

THE EMPERORS OF ROME

THE STORY OF IMPERIAL ROME FROM JULIUS CAESAR TO THE LAST EMPEROR

DAVID POTTER

Quercus

First published as an illustrated edition in
Great Britain in 2007 by Quercus

This updated paperback edition published in 2013 by
Quercus
55 Baker Street
Seventh Floor, South Block
London
W1U 8EW

A CIP catalogue record for this book is available
from the British Library

ISBN 978 1 78087 750 1

12

Text designed and typeset by Ellipsis Digital Ltd, Glasgow

Printed and bound in Great Britain by Clays Ltd, Elcograf S.p.A.

Contents

Prologue

Being Caesar

One murdered his mother. Another fought as a gladiator. Two were philosophers, while yet another is revered as a saint in the Eastern Orthodox Church. What all these diverse personalities had in common was that they were emperors of Rome. Given the extreme behaviour exhibited by many of the holders of this office, it is little wonder that much of the political comment that has come down to us from Ancient Rome focuses on individual personalities. In polemical tones all too familiar to modern ears, Romans lambasted their leaders as lunatics, murderers or imbeciles or lionized them as heroes or geniuses.

Roman political discourse also resembled that of the present day in judging leaders and their achievements by an ideal standard. In the light of this, it is worth considering for a moment what a job description for a prospective emperor might look like. Following the approved practice of human resources managers, in drafting this description we need to consult the best available literature, and keep in mind both the experience of previous holders and the needs of the organization. Aided by ancient works of political theory on kingship, and taking the average age of the incumbents as our yardstick of the level of experience required, we might well arrive at the following profile:

Wanted: *Well-educated man in his late thirties*
Key responsibilities: *Ruling the known world; commanding the world's most powerful army; preserving civilization as we know it*
Applicants should possess:

- *A keen legal mind*
- *Good interpersonal skills, especially in dealing with foreign peoples*
- *An ability to handle an enormous volume of communication and make clear policy decisions*
- *A proven ability in a senior military capacity, while not essential for the role, would be a distinct advantage*

Diverting though this exercise is, two basic problems bedevil any attempt to quantify the role of Roman emperor. First, the job as outlined above is fundamentally impossible, and second the material that we used to construct our job description is misleading. In writing about the 'perfect' emperor, the topic ancient commentators were actually addressing was the purpose of government. Emperors were representatives of the government as a whole, and the individual job description for each one might vary enormously from our norm. Even the notion of an ideal age for a new emperor is specious – in practice they fell into roughly three age brackets: one starting at around the age of 60, one around 40, and one in the early teens. These were largely conditioned by the needs of the age. There were periods when Romans did not need their emperor to do very much at all, and yet other times when his services were in great demand.

Communal power

It was quite remarkable that Romans should opt to be governed by emperors at all. Their state had done very well without a sole ruler and they were generally hostile to anything that smacked of kingship, for historical reasons that will presently become apparent. Moreover, temperamentally they were inclined to individualism, a trait which, when it has manifested itself in other societies, has sat uneasily with autocracy. Yet after hundreds of years of democracy, Romans found that their government could no longer keep pace with the speed of change and the special demands that came with being a superpower. Foremost among these demands was that government should remain responsive to the needs of the majority of the people and not be hijacked by special-interest groups. The government of the Roman Republic failed to do this, and fell victim to men who took advantage of its weaknesses to further their own ambitions. That said, the men who usurped power in this way still found it impossible to do away entirely with the traditions of collective government that had existed for centuries under the Republic. The result was that Roman emperors always remained part of a governing group. What is even more extraordinary, however, and distinguishes the Roman empire from many more modern such polities, was that the post of emperor was not reserved for people of Roman ancestry. Over time, it was filled by men from many different parts of the empire. Some only spoke Latin as a second language, while one was even the son of a freed slave.

At the root of these apparent idiosyncrasies of Rome's imperial system lie certain ingrained Roman attitudes. Notable among these was the great emphasis that Romans placed on an individual's relations with the community at large, plus their tendency to gauge personal happiness in terms of how other members of society saw them. These factors had a crucial bearing on Romans' perception of what it meant to be emperor.

The Roman fixation on communal participation is even enshrined in the official designation of the state – the *res publica populi Romani*, or 'public possession of the Roman people'. To be one of the people – a citizen – was therefore to be co-owner of an extraordinary entity. That said, not all the state's joint owners were created equal; every person's standing was reflected in the level of service that they devoted to the state. Being a wealthy Roman entailed taking an active role in government, holding public office and serving in positions of command in the army alongside one's peers. Middle-class Romans also undertook military service, while their appointed political role was to sanction the position of their social betters by voting them into office and affirming the proposals they put forward to the state's legislative bodies. The concept of serving the state even extended to the poor, who were expected to raise children and affirm the status quo by participating in the rituals of the state. To the Roman mind, there was nothing more abhorrent than the man who tried to shirk the duties that attended his station in life.

Virtus and *domus*

An essential quality required by a Roman citizen was that of *virtus*. Its English derivative 'virtue', defined as 'the quality or practice of moral excellence or righteousness', does not successfully convey the meaning of the Latin concept. To the Romans, the word *virtus*, which was cognate with the Latin term for man (*vir*), denoted specifically male qualities of service to the state. So prevalent was the notion that *virtus* was essential to the community as a whole that women were also expected to demonstrate their own particular form of *virtus* by playing a supporting role to their menfolk. This role required them to maintain a stable environment within the man's home, or *domus*. The *domus* housed the family, who lived under the control and protection of a *paterfamilias*. His role was to represent the group in public and make sure that its members comported themselves in a fitting manner. To this end the *paterfamilias* was granted *patria potestas* – the power of life and death over every member of his family. Being invested with this draconian power meant that the Roman male was not truly a private person even within the bosom of his family. Rather, he was a representative of the community, supervising the actions of women, children and slaves to ensure that their behaviour conformed to the norms of Roman society. The fact that the *domus* was filled with sundry individuals who were subordinate to, and excluded from, the male world of public life meant that it was also a potential threat to the order of society. In Roman thought the back rooms of the *domus* were places where un-Roman activities could occur. The antithesis of open public life was conspiracy, and conspiracies tended to be hatched by slaves and women in places that were out of sight of the community. It was within the *domus* that a man might give vent to unacceptable passions, where he might be dominated by women or slaves, indulge excessively in sex with his subordinates, eat to excess, or waste the resources that should be at the disposal of the state in times of need.

To the poor Roman who could not afford a *domus*, living in one room with a spouse and children in a rickety tenement, or in a hut in the country, the real test of the worth of a prominent citizen was how he behaved within his domestic setting. Did he live up to his public image or disgrace himself when he thought no one was looking? Be nice to your slaves if you are thinking of running for office, one politician advised another – they're the ones the people who hang around the forum will be talking to. It was in reaction to crimes committed within the *domus* that the Romans believed their *res publica* was shaped.

From monarchy to republic

By the time the Romans started writing their own history in the third century BC, it was generally believed that kings had ruled them between the foundation of the city and the end of the sixth century. According to legend, in 509 BC the son of an odious king by the name of Tarquin the Proud (Tarquinius Superbus, reigned 535–510 BC) raped a woman called Lucretia. Lucretia revealed the crime to her brother Brutus before committing suicide. This outrage sparked a popular uprising; Brutus summoned the Roman people to the forum and called on them to depose the royal family, declaring the king and all members of his *domus* outlaws. In their place, he instituted a government based on annually elected colleges of magistrates. The working principle of this system was the devolution of *imperium*, the power to rule that the people had once conferred upon the king. The new government, where *imperium* was not only shared but also subject to checks and balances through legislation passed by the people, was seen as the polar opposite of one-man rule and autocracy, which came to be known simply as *regnum*, or 'royal power'.

The government of the Roman Republic proved astonishingly successful. During the fourth century BC the Romans conquered almost all of Italy south of the Po river. Rome then humbled Carthage, the North African city-state that had long controlled the sea-lanes of the western Mediterranean. The victory over Carthage and its great general Hannibal, which only came after decades of fierce fighting and terrible defeats, was the defining struggle in Roman history. It transformed Rome from a regional into a Mediterranean power and precipitated the rapid defeat of the Greek kingdoms that had dominated the eastern rim of the Mediterranean since the death of Alexander the Great in 323 BC. By 146 BC, Rome had become the greatest power in the region's history. So why, given the signal success of their Republican form of government and their hatred of autocracy, did the Romans even entertain the possibility of imperial rule? This was a question that even the Romans had difficulty answering.

Who was the first Caesar?

The most significant difference between Romans who wrote about the empire and modern authors who make the Caesars their subject matter is that latter-day commentators tend to assert as incontestable fact that the first emperor was Augustus (r. 31 BC–AD 14). Yet the only ancient Roman historian we know of who explicitly dated the start of the imperial system at 31 BC was Cassius Dio (*c.* AD 155–after 229), who was writing almost 300 years after the event. Among the many precursors and contemporaries who disagreed with Cassius was the biographer Marius Maximus, who was also active in the early third century. Maximus' book on the 'next' 12 Caesars (from Nerva to Elagabalus) implicitly takes its point of departure from the famous *Lives of the Twelve Caesars* by Suetonius (*c.* AD 69–130), which ended with the death of Domitian. Suetonius' first Caesar was Julius Caesar. In turn, Suetonius' account of the Caesars also excited opposition from his contemporaries, such as the Greek biographer Plutarch. Plutarch included Julius Caesar in his work on prominent Greeks and Romans who lived before the advent of the empire. Another first-century historian, Cornelius Tacitus (*c.* AD 57–120), chose to begin his account of the development of the imperial system with the death of Augustus.

The lack of unanimity among these historians is mirrored in texts connected with the emperors themselves. A portion of a law conferring supreme power on Vespasian in AD 70 backdated his accession to his rebellion against the reigning emperor in AD 69, and listed only three previous emperors as having had powers comparable to those conferred on him. These were Augustus, Tiberius (AD 14–37) and Claudius, the grand-nephew of Augustus (AD 41–54). The state's official record thus effectively airbrushed from history five men who had previously occupied the same post as that now held by Vespasian – and had been listed as such by Suetonius – while Julius Caesar wasn't even deemed part of the group.

A fundamental tension

What, then, became of these five missing leaders? The answer lies in Roman attitudes to power and the appropriate behaviour of an individual. The Roman ruling classes were supposed to set positive examples for their fellow citizens through their exercise of *virtus*. If they succumbed to the unbridled passions of the *domus*, they were not fit exemplars for others, and could therefore be struck off the list of 'approved' emperors. The emperor did not rule through divine right, but by virtue of a legal process that entitled him to wield power over other members of the governing class. For all his imperial pomp, he still remained a representative of that class – a first among equals, so to speak. This fact is echoed in his title of *princeps*, or 'leading man'.

Tacitus expressed this point lucidly when comparing the task of the historian in Republican Rome to his role in the imperial age. Whereas historians were formerly required to be well versed in all the diverse aspects of public life, 'now, with public affairs transformed so that there is no salvation for the state unless one man rules', their sole subject of study was this sole ruler and his dealings with those around him. This sea-change in the mode of governance came about as a result of the political crises that shook the Roman state to its very core in the century before Augustus. The advent of one-person rule must be seen in the context of a wider process of change affecting the nature of government in the Roman world.

The fundamental tension between the individual ruler and the system that Tacitus identified would remain central to the history of Rome from the first century BC to the point at which the system failed to provide for the needs of society at the end of the fifth century AD. In the light of this, the conventional view of the Caesars as a succession of more or less colourful autocrats needs to be revised. First and foremost, they were representatives of the needs of the Roman people.

ONE

Great Caesar's Ghost

A Succession of Strong Men: Rome from Gaius Marius to Caesar

(107–44 BC)

Rome's transition from a republic into an empire took place in the period of social turmoil that followed the infamous assassination of Julius Caesar by his former political confederates. Yet while all ancient historians see Caesar as a pivotal figure in this transformation, they disagree over his precise historical position. While some regard him as the last of the triumvirate of strong men who dominated the political landscape of the Roman Republic in the first half of the first century, others prefer to see him as the progenitor of a dynasty of emperors that endured until AD 68 and included some of the most illustrious and notorious holders of the office.

Ancient writers' views of Caesar's assassination depend very much upon their attitude to the imperial system. Suetonius (AD 69–130), who hoped that his accounts of the lives of the emperors would provide examples for future rulers, was in no doubt that it was fully justified: Caesar, he claimed, had abrogated his leadership responsibilities by failing to pay due respect either to fellow members of Rome's élite or to the institutions of the Republic. By contrast, the Greek biographer Plutarch (*c.* AD 46–120, in his *Parallel Lives*) described Julius Caesar's death as a catastrophe that upset the natural order of the world. As for Caesar himself, he is reported to have said, with characteristic acuity and foresight, that if he were assassinated the result would be chaos. But what were Caesar's origins and how had both his own life and that of Rome in general proceeded up to his untimely death in 44 BC?

The Julii Caesares

Gaius Julius Caesar was born into the patrician class – the hereditary aristocratic ruling élite of Rome – in 100 BC. His family claimed descent from extraordinarily exalted ancestors, in the shape of both of the legendary founders of Rome – Aeneas and Romulus. Furthermore, through these mortal forebears they were also connected to two deities: Aeneas was thought to have been born to the goddess Venus and a man named Anchises, while Romulus was the offspring of a woman of noble background, Rhea Silvia, who gave birth to him and his twin brother Remus after being raped by the god Mars. The legend goes on to relate how the twins were set adrift on the River Tiber but were saved by divine intervention and went on to found the city of Rome.

With two gods in the family tree, most of the early Julii Caesares lacked any real incentive to enhance the earthly status of their family. For most of their history they pursued a languid aristocratic lifestyle that left almost no mark on the annals of Rome. It was only with the election of Julius Caesar's uncle as a consul and the later accession of his father to the office of praetor that the family attained any kind of prominence. However, the most significant of all Caesar's immediate forebears was not a male relative at all but rather his aunt Julia (*c.*130–69 BC), who in *c.*110 BC raised the profile of her family at a stroke through her marriage to Gaius Marius, the most renowned Roman of the age.

The career of Gaius Marius (157–86 BC) was as glorious as it was unexpected. He was not born a patrician and so could not call upon a long lineage of illustrious ancestors to advance his political career. A further handicap was that he came not from Rome but from the town of Arpinum, some 60 miles (100 kilometres) distant. Rather, Marius' rise to power was based on sheer personal ability combined with a talent for ruthlessly eliminating anyone who stood in his path. In the 20 years before Caesar's birth, Marius carved out a niche for himself as an expert on military affairs, at a time when the governing élite was experiencing a dearth of talented military tacticians and commanders from among its own ranks. Exploiting the political scandals sparked by a series of military fiascos, including a disastrous war in North Africa and several badly botched campaigns in southern France, Marius succeeded in getting himself elected consul in the face of determined opposition from the patrician establishment. In his new role, he swiftly brought the war in Africa to a successful conclusion. As if to underline Marius' skill and his opponents' ineptitude, just as he was ending his campaign, two Roman generals in southern France saw their armies wiped out by invading German tribesmen on the same day; this disaster arose from their pigheaded refusal to cooperate with each other.

Marius was elected consul for a second time in 105 BC (and would be re-elected every year thereafter until 100 BC

– his final tally of seven consulships was hitherto unparalleled in Roman history). That same year, he took command of the demoralized armies in southern France and northern Italy. In developing his career through his military prowess, Marius moulded himself into the first *princeps*, a military strong man who used his army power base to exert political control. Marius' example would prove a potent model for his as yet unborn nephew.

By 100, Marius had defeated the German invaders and shortly thereafter retired from public life, since he was by then in his sixties. Yet the situation in Rome continued to worsen, for which Marius himself may have been partly to blame. The major reforms he instituted in the Roman army had forged a strong bond between himself and his men that far outstripped the loyalty they felt towards the government of the Republic. The principal reason for their disaffection had to do with money. The average period of service for a Roman soldier had grown considerably over time; moreover, many men spent much of their tour of duty in provincial garrisons and no coherent plan existed for their retirement. Whether soldiers ultimately received any recompense for their years of service depended entirely upon how well connected their commanding officers were in political circles. A general with influence would secure special terms – usually land grants – for his men when they retired from the army. Marius had been one such commander, and his generosity had even extended to granting non-Romans citizenship in recognition of their loyal service.

Land and citizenship

The issue of who was entitled to be a Roman citizen was fast becoming the burning question of the day. In 100 BC, most inhabitants of Italy were not actually citizens of Rome. The towns where they lived were nominally allied to the Roman state through treaties imposed on them during Rome's victorious wars of expansion in the fourth and third centuries BC. Since then, they had reluctantly taken the role of Roman vassal states. But in 133 BC this uneasy peace had been shattered by the agitation of a plebeian tribune named Tiberius Gracchus (163–133 BC).

Concerned at the decline he perceived in Roman *virtus* (the quality of manly courage and steadfastness), Gracchus concluded that this was the upshot of many Romans abandoning traditional life on the family farm. His suggested remedy was a law redistributing land that Rome had originally seized from the cities of Italy, but which had since been left largely under their control. Gracchus' legislation infuriated not only the inhabitants of the vassal cities but also many Roman senators, who disapproved of what they regarded as his wilful disruption of the status quo. Although the divisive law was passed, its chief architect promptly paid with his life, murdered by political enemies.

Ten years later, Gracchus' younger brother Gaius (154–121 BC) introduced a series of laws designed to further reorganize the state. One of his proposed reforms was that all Italians should be made citizens of Rome. Conservative senators calling themselves 'the Nobles' (*nobiles*), who had opposed

Tiberius, were just as outraged by Gaius' proposals, and, when he failed to win re-election for a third term, they summoned troops into Rome to massacre him and his supporters.

Over the next two decades, the related issues of land distribution and Roman citizenship arose time and again, but were never resolved. The basic problem was that, while many poor Romans were attracted by the prospect of receiving free land from the state, they were not prepared in return to share the advantages of Roman citizenship with other cities of Italy. Conversely, the Italians would not stand for massive land redistribution unless they were given a stake in governing the country. Marius was thrown headlong into this long-running controversy in 100 BC, when he deployed his troops to crush the supporters of yet another tribune who was agitating in favour of radical agrarian reforms.

The rise of Sulla

The spectre of land distribution and citizenship reared its head once more in 91 BC. When the tribune who was sponsoring the new reform bill suddenly turned out to be dead, the Italians, incensed by years of foot-dragging and abortive attempts at legislation, rose in revolt. Gaius Marius came out of retirement to command one of the armies that Rome put into the field to face them. At the head of another army was Lucius Cornelius Sulla (*c.* 138–78 BC), formerly a lieutenant of Marius, but now opposed to his former commander. In the course of this so-called Social War – named after the *Socii*, the Latin term for Rome's erstwhile Italian allies – Sulla soon proved to be an outstanding general in his own right.

Two momentous events marked the year 89 BC. First, the Roman state split the Italian resistance by passing a bill offering citizenship to the inhabitants of any city that lay down its arms. Many accepted the offer, and the war turned decisively against those who chose to fight on. At the same time, King Mithridates VI (132–63 BC) of Pontus (a state on the Black Sea coast of modern Turkey) launched an attack on Roman lands in the eastern Mediterranean. The senate voted that command in this war, which promised to be a far more profitable and glorious venture than the ongoing mopping-up operations in Italy, should go to one of the consuls for the following year. Sulla was duly elected and put in charge of the campaign against Mithridates.

Sulla did not hold on to his prize for long. A tribune introduced a group of bills which, in addition to offering Roman citizenship to the Italians on far more favourable terms than before, also transferred command of the Mithridatic War to Marius. Sulla, outraged at what he regarded as an illegal act by the tribune, turned to his army for support. He was easily able to exploit the troops' anger at being deprived of a chance to share in the spoils that would flow from reconquering the eastern provinces. And so Sulla and his legions marched on Rome to force the senate to rescind its decision. Encountering only minimal resistance, he occupied the city and sentenced his political opponents to death before marching east once more. Meanwhile Marius, who barely escaped with his life, fled to North Africa.

Before resuming command of the Mithridatic War, Sulla had tried to secure his position in Rome by getting his supporters elected to the two consulships for 87 BC. Yet he failed in this and was forced to witness the election of his sworn enemy Lucius Cornelius Cinna (d. 84 BC) to one of the posts. Sulla had the military might to remove Cinna, but instead let him remain in office provided he swore to uphold the legislation that Sulla had introduced. Cinna lied; shortly after the start of his consulship, he broke his oath and led his own army against Rome. Marius returned from North Africa to join the armies that were now fighting their way into the city, massacring all of Sulla's supporters who did not flee or go into hiding. At the end of the year, Marius was elected consul for the seventh time, but died soon after taking office.

Over the following years Sulla succeeded in defeating Mithridates. The spoils of victory were great; not only did he loot vast treasures from the eastern provinces, but his coffers were also swelled by money from Mithridates, whom he had permitted to remain as king of Pontus in return for huge reparations payments. These finances enabled Sulla to reinvade Italy. By the end of 82 BC he had defeated his main enemies and had himself installed as dictator for as long as he wished. Sulla's dictatorial rule provided an object lesson for later rulers of Rome.

The bloody regime of Sulla

Sulla immediately embarked on a reign of terror. During his advance on Rome, he had committed a string of atrocities, including massacring prisoners, executing opposing generals and destroying districts that held out against him. Once installed in the city, Sulla posted lists of men who were 'proscribed', namely condemned to death. Although the first targets of Sulla's proscriptions were his political opponents, soon anyone with property or wealth began to be included. Sulla personally presided over this bloodbath, encouraging bounty hunters to bring him the severed heads of proscribed men in return for a reward. The estates of the victims were confiscated by the state, and for the most part were sold off at knockdown prices to Sulla's supporters. Those districts of Italy that had supported Sulla's enemies were subject to massive confiscations of land, which were then divided up into sizeable farms for Sulla's retired veterans. In the dictator's savage reckoning, since he could never hope to reconcile his enemies to his newly purified Roman state, the only logical course of action was to kill them and eradicate their former power bases. Yet perversely the sheer brutality of Sulla's campaign actually succeeded in hardening opposition against him. And so, even though the civil war ended on the main Italian front in 81 BC, desperate men fought on for nearly a decade in more remote Roman outposts such as North Africa, southern France and especially Spain. Further sporadic revolts even occurred in Italy itself. The last and most famous of these was the great rural uprising led by the gladiator Spartacus (*c.* 100–70 BC); while many of the rebels who took part in it were slaves, it was notable that Spartacus also managed to attract many dispossessed former soldiers to his ranks.

Sulla lived until 78 BC, resigning his dictatorship a few months before his death, which was probably hastened by his excessive fondness for drink. In a cynical comment on absolute power, Julius Caesar later claimed that Sulla's decision to retire simply proved that he didn't know what he was doing. In fact, Caesar was extremely fortunate to have survived Sulla's reign of terror. According to a story that Caesar himself later put about, he had been on the list of people that Sulla wanted killed. He was only saved by the intervention of friends and the Vestal Virgins. In pardoning him, Sulla is alleged to have remarked that there were 'many Mariuses' in the young man. More probably the fact that Caesar's mother was related to some of Sulla's most important supporters was the key to his salvation. Still, Rome was not a good place for him to be, and Caesar found it prudent to complete his higher education in Greece until the situation in Rome calmed down.

The irresistible rise of Caesar

Caesar's defining character trait was his great ambition. He won renown as a junior officer in the eastern Mediterranean – Mithridates never gave up his desire to conquer Rome's eastern holdings, and launched another attack there in 76 BC. Having proved his *virtus* in war, Caesar returned to Rome and began to rally support among opponents of the political establishment by cultivating a personal style that marked him as a radical. He wore clothes that were generally regarded as too modish and became known as something of a ladies' man. He also ran up huge debts, and was forced to borrow heavily from one of Sulla's former generals, Marcus Licinius Crassus (*c.* 115–53 BC), who had been responsible for suppressing Spartacus' revolt. Crassus had amassed a vast personal fortune through trading in slaves, mining interests and property speculation. Yet he was an intemperate personality who made many enemies, even falling out with his former ally Sulla. In particular, Crassus was almost pathologically jealous of Gnaeus Pompeius Magnus, better known as Pompey (106–48 BC). Though still only in his twenties, Pompey had displayed great military skill in Sulla's service – earning himself the nickname *adulescentulus carnifex* ('the teenage butcher') – and carved out a reputation as Rome's coming man, despite never having held political office.

Unfazed by the envy of Crassus, with whom he shared the consulship in 70 BC, Pompey spent most of the 60s commanding Roman armies abroad. When pirates raided the coast of Italy and kidnapped two Roman magistrates, Pompey was charged with the task of sweeping them from the Mediterranean. Within a year, he was claiming outright victory and had engineered his own appointment as commander-in-chief of the Mithridatic War. Pompey brought this conflict to a successful end three years later.

Caesar, meanwhile, continued to groom his political career. Elected aedile in 65 BC, he restored the trophies of Marius' victories against the Germans – destroyed by Sulla – to their former place of honour. In the same year he held a lavish public funeral for his aunt, Marius' widow, and laid claim to the political mantle of Marius himself. During his lifetime, Marius had been anything but a radical, but he now became a rallying point for enemies of the post-Sullan regime. Caesar made sure that he was identified closely with the myth he spun around his uncle.

In 63 BC Caesar was elected as praetor, setting up a run for the consulship three years later (the interval between the two offices had become statutory for everyone except

Pompey, who had never held any office other than consul), and as *pontifex maximus*, the high priest of Rome. This latter office was more political than religious. The Roman state religion was overseen by several collective priesthoods, of which the most influential were the pontiffs, whose leader Caesar now became. Their main function was to oversee other groups of priests. The office of *pontifex maximus* also brought with it several perks, chief among which was occupancy of the Regia in the heart of the Roman Forum. Residing here put Caesar quite literally in the centre of the city's political life. Yet the two election campaigns also left him deep in debt.

Manoeuvring for power

By the end of 62 BC Caesar's financial problems were so serious that Suetonius recounts that he was obliged to slip out of town in the dead of night to avoid being seized by his creditors. Like many Romans of his day, Caesar saw the opportunity to govern a province – a privilege accorded to praetors either during or after their year in office – as a chance to recoup the enormous sums he had spent while running for office. Political campaigns, then as now, were extremely expensive undertakings, and Caesar had earned a reputation for extravagant spending. In 65 he had purchased so many gladiators for the shows which his post of aedile obliged him to stage that his enemies in the senate passed a law restricting the number of performers any one person could engage. Caesar's successful contest of the two elections in 63 would have entailed even more lavish outlay. According to Roman law, a man standing for election was permitted to offer a cash gift to every member of his tribe. In Roman eyes, this did not constitute a bribe. Rather, it was regarded simply as 'munificence', and displays of such generosity guaranteed a person popular acclaim in Rome. By contrast, what Romans found truly distasteful was excessive private luxury, and so Caesar was careful to make it clear that the vast sums of money he borrowed were for the benefit of the Roman people rather than his own pleasure.

Aside from Caesar's fondness for fancy clothes and his vanity (by this stage he was trying to conceal his incipient baldness with a combed-over hairstyle) he was notably abstemious in his private life. One enemy even remarked that he was the only sober man who ever tried to ruin the Republic. Caesar's studied frugality stood in marked contrast to the profligacy of the old regime. Many of Sulla's friends had become as self-indulgent as their former general, erecting enormous villas and throwing extravagant private banquets. Caesar also appears to have treated his slaves humanely and was popular with his gladiators, perhaps owing to his unwillingness to expose them to fights to the death. Where his personal life was open to criticism was in the bedroom, and it was this Achilles' heel that his enemies targeted. They declared his public displays of *virtus* through generosity a sham, pointing instead to his immodest conduct in the very heart of the *domus*.

Personal indiscretions

On one occasion Caesar even arranged for a love letter from the sister of one of his fiercest political opponents, Marcus

Portius Cato the Younger (95–46 BC), to be ostentatiously delivered to him while the senate was in session. Thinking that Caesar had just received a secret message that would implicate him in a conspiracy against the state, Cato demanded that he read it aloud, only to be humiliated by the public airing of its contents.

Caesar's enemies claimed to have proof that, while serving as an ambassador at the court of Nicomedes IV of Bithynia in 80 BC (a kingdom bordering the former lands of Mithridates in northern Turkey), he had allowed himself to be sodomized by the king. Their objection was not so much that Caesar had had sex with another man, but that he had taken the passive role. He was not, therefore, a 'real man', but a *cinadeus* – a man who played the 'female part' during lovemaking. One enemy even quipped that he was 'every woman's husband and every man's wife'. Caesar was furious, and remained intensely defensive on the subject for the rest of his life. Yet he failed to prevent the rumour from spreading, and even his soldiers, who seem genuinely to have admired him, later sang lewd ballads about Caesar as the 'Queen of Bithynia'. This scurrilous story was all the more hilarious to Caesar's contemporaries since it was totally at odds with his carefully groomed public persona of the virtuous, clean-living man.

Caesar managed to weather both his financial problems and the slanders of his opponents. His one-year term as governor of Spain netted him enough money to enable him to discharge his debts and stand for the consulship of 59 BC. He easily won the election and began to consolidate his position. In this he was aided by the ineptitude of his enemies, who had managed simultaneously to alienate both Crassus and Pompey. Crassus had tried to establish a power base in Rome by representing the interests of the equestrian corporations. However, these bodies were soon embroiled in a financial scandal concerning taxation in the province of Asia (western Turkey). The senate refused to remit the money they owed the state, threatening them with bankruptcy. For his part, Pompey found himself at loggerheads with the senate when it refused to authorize retirement payments to his soldiers and blocked his administrative reforms in the eastern provinces. Spotting an opportunity for an advantageous alliance, Caesar first arranged for his only child, Julia, to marry Pompey, and then made political overtures to both Pompey and Crassus. Exploiting his position as consul (in which capacity he was allowed to put bills before the people without prior approval from the senate), he promised to introduce legislation to help the two men overcome their present difficulties if they, in return, would give their backing to a bill granting Caesar a five-year command in the province of his choice.

This naked political skulduggery provoked scenes of uproar in the senate, during which Caesar's consular colleague and leader of the faction opposing his legislative programme was doused with the contents of a chamber pot. It seems likely that Caesar himself engineered this furore as a diversionary tactic, testifying to the fact that he was already well versed in the black arts of politics. In any event, the manoeuvre achieved its aim, with Pompey and Crassus getting what they wanted and Caesar securing not one but three provinces. At the start of 58 BC he left Rome to govern the provinces of Transalpine Gaul (southern France), Cisalpine Gaul (northern Italy, also known as Gallia Togata, or 'Toga-wearing Gaul') and Illyricum (present-day Croatia).

Caesar the general

This period – from 58 to 50 BC – laid the foundation of Caesar's reputation as the greatest general in Roman history. His enemies hoped that his lack of experience as a military commander would prove his undoing and that he would fall victim to one of the many fierce tribes in the badlands beyond Rome's borders. Yet Caesar soon confounded them, showing himself adept at transferring to the battlefield the skills that had brought him political success. Behind the often deceptively simple accounts that he wrote of his campaigns – ultimately collected together in his work *The Gallic Wars* (*De Bello Gallico*) – lay a boundless capacity for forward planning, a keen understanding of the psychology of his opponents, an impressive flexibility when confronted with new problems and a profound confidence in his own ability.

Time and again in Caesar's narrative, an apparently throw-away remark reveals that supplies were being prudently laid up in advance, detailed intelligence gathered and strategic plans altered to exploit changing circumstances or to respond to unforeseen challenges. Above all, Caesar knew that absolutely no faith should be placed in intelligence offered by people who stood to gain from supplying information, that wars are won not on the battlefield so much as at the conference table and that the enemy was watching and reacting to his every move. For this reason, he never employed the same tactics twice in battle. He also spent a great deal of time before and after the campaigning season winning hearts and minds among those Gauls who saw that their own interests were best served by supporting him.

Yet despite his overall record of success, there were also setbacks, which proved that even Caesar had human failings. For example, he was sometimes too quick to assume that his solutions were acceptable to everyone. In the winter of 54–53 BC he divided his legions into several camps to avoid any single Gallic tribe having to shoulder the burden of tens of thousands of Roman legionaries billeted on its territory and exhausting its food and fodder supplies after the bad harvest that year. He may well have thought that this concession went far enough, since no tribe would surely be foolish enough to stage a revolt on its own. This was a fatal miscalculation: a force of up to 8000 men was wiped out when their commander was tricked into abandoning his camp. Caesar had plainly not devised any contingency plan for his officers to follow in case of trouble. Similarly, he is quick to blame a Roman defeat during the siege of a Gallic city in 52 BC on his men panicking. But an aside by Caesar on this incident paints a different picture: he concedes that the terrain made it hard for commanders to adapt his orders to events as they unfolded on the ground. Caesar spent a great deal of time trying to communicate his strategic and tactical vision to his subordinates, but seems to have felt, at times, that people ought to read his mind. In the long run, this style of leadership would prove fatal to Caesar when he applied it to the running of the Roman state.

While Caesar was away campaigning in Gaul, several

events had conspired to change the political landscape in Rome dramatically. For a start, one of Rome's triumvirate of strong men was dead, killed ignominiously in battle in a far-off land. Jealous of both Caesar and Pompey, Crassus had embarked on a military adventure of his own by launching an illegal invasion of the Parthian empire. This realm, which included modern Iraq and Iran, was the only remaining major power on Rome's borders. Crassus was dismissive of enemies whom Rome had never fought and made no effort to grasp their strategy or tactics. Predictably, his ill-advised campaign ended in a crushing defeat, as his large army was routed outside the city of Carrhae, the present-day Harran in Turkey, in 53 BC. Crassus himself was cut down in this bloody fiasco. The only consolation for Rome was that the Parthians, excellent though they were at holding their own ground, as yet lacked the organization to pose any real threat to its eastern provinces.

While Crassus' death removed a major rival to the ambitions of Caesar and Pompey, it crucially also meant that there was now no longer any figure of comparable stature who could act as a mediator between them. In any event, even before Crassus' demise, the bond between Caesar and Pompey had already been dealt a fatal blow by the death of Julia, Caesar's daughter and Pompey's wife, in 54 BC. Increasingly alarmed at Caesar's inexorable rise, Pompey formally severed all links with him in 52 BC and began to prepare for the possibility of war.

Crossing the Rubicon

By the summer of 50 BC Caesar had united all of what is now modern France, along with parts of Germany and Belgium, under his rule. Proud of his achievements, the illustrious general felt that he was entitled to dictate the terms on which he would return to the Roman political arena. In particular, Caesar's demand that he be allowed to stand for the consulship while remaining in Gaul put him on a direct collision course with the senate. This was a crucial sticking point; to prevent any recurrence of the kind of dictatorship imposed by Sulla, Roman law had long since required army commanders to relinquish control of their legions before entering the city – a prerequisite to running for political office there. But if Caesar obeyed, so divesting himself of his military muscle, he knew that his enemies would waste no time in arraigning him on charges of abuse of power during his first consulship. Although, as the returning hero, he was fully confident of winning an election, a trial would instantly annul his candidacy.

Caesar resolved this dilemma by confronting his enemies in Rome head-on with an invasion of Italy. On 11 January, 49 BC, he crossed the Rubicon River, which marked the southern boundary between his province of Cisalpine Gaul and Rome's Italian provinces. His famous reported comment on his action was 'The die is cast' (*acta alea est*). As Caesar advanced, Pompey staged a tactical withdrawal to the port of Brundisium (modern Brindisi, on the 'heel' of Italy). From there, he planned to embark the force of more than 20,000 men that he had mustered to Greece to join other armies he was assembling in the eastern provinces. However, Pompey's authority was beginning to crumble by this stage. One of his subordinates ignored several urgent messages from his commander and was cut off and forced to surrender 10,000 men at Corfinium in central Italy.

This proved to be the defining moment of the war. When the garrison at Corfinium – which included many leaders of the political opposition – surrendered, Caesar took the soldiers into his service and released the rest. This act of clemency, unheard of in previous civil wars, was a propaganda coup that rallied many people to Caesar's cause. The war lasted until August 48 BC, when Pompey's army was routed at the Battle of Pharsalus in northern Greece. This decisive showdown had a swift and brutal outcome, and the action reveals to us the way that the two great masters of warfare in the Roman world understood their craft. Both commanders were in no doubt that Caesar's veteran infantry, although outnumbered, would have little trouble in overcoming Pompey's inexperienced footsoldiers. Pompey gambled that he could win the battle by deploying his more numerous cavalry on his left flank to swiftly neutralize Caesar's cavalry before attacking the rest of his army from the rear. It was not a bad plan, but unfortunately for Pompey Caesar also knew that this was the only way that Pompey could win and so took steps to counteract his tactic. Thus it was that he forwent the customary three-line formation of his infantry in favour of a fourth line, which he used to attack Pompey's cavalry head-on as soon as it had, as expected, overrun his own cavalry. When Pompey saw his cavalry turn in flight, he realized that defeat was inevitable and fled the battlefield as Caesar's troops completed their rout of his forces. Behind him, Pompey left 6000 of his men dead, while a further 24,000 were taken prisoner. This ability to see things through his enemies' eyes was perhaps Caesar's greatest advantage as a general.

On the political front, even as the war raged, Caesar began to shape a new regime that would remain very much a work in progress for the rest of his life. The problem was how to reconcile his dominance with the structures of the state. The dictatorship seemed to Caesar the key to his dilemma. He briefly took the office in late 49 BC (when he also secured the consulship for a second time) and again, for a longer spell, after Pharsalus.

The Deaths of Pompey and Caesar

Meanwhile, Pompey fled to Egypt, where agents of King Ptolemy XIII, knowing that Caesar was already on his way there, assassinated him. Arriving in Egypt, Caesar soon became embroiled in a dynastic power struggle between Ptolemy XIII and his sister, Cleopatra. Siding with Cleopatra (whom he lost no time in making his mistress), he quickly defeated Ptolemy and installed his lover and her brother on the throne. This affair scandalized Rome, since it suggested Caesar had an unhealthy interest in royal power. However, by May of 47 BC he was on the move once more, this time to Asia Minor to quell a revolt in Pontus led by Pharnaces, a son of Mithridates (the occasion of Caesar's famous boast *veni, vidi, vici*: 'I came, I saw, I conquered').

The civil war dragged on after Pompey's death; his supporters raised an army in North Africa, which was only defeated in 46 BC. That same year saw further outbreaks of trouble, as Pompey's sole surviving son Sextus rallied support in Spain. Yet while Caesar's military skills showed little sign of waning, his political acumen now began to desert him. During a brief stay in Rome in 46 BC, he took a new approach to the dictatorship, accepting the office for ten years and then, two years later, in perpetuity. He was also made consul continuously from 46 BC. All the while, his autocratic attitude to power was alienating fellow members of the ruling class.

Having put down all the major insurrections, Caesar finally returned to Rome in August 45 BC. The senate voted him divine honours and the month of his birth was renamed July. He pointedly refused the title of *rex* ('king') but ruled henceforth as the king of Rome in all but name.

Caesar planned to leave Rome again on 18 March, 44 BC, to campaign against the Parthians. Just prior to his departure came the Ides of March, the 15th day of the month, which a soothsayer had warned him to beware of. Spurning her advice, he attended a meeting of the senate, where he was approached by a group of men apparently presenting a petition. As they surrounded him, they drew their daggers and stabbed him to death. More than 60 senators were involved in the conspiracy against Caesar – including men he had spared and some of his own officers. Like Suetonius after them, these men were adamant that Caesar had effectively signed his own death warrant by riding roughshod over the cherished traditions of the state. It now remained to be seen how many in the Roman world shared their view.

A Time of Turmoil: Octavian and Antony

(44–30 BC)

Thirteen years separate Caesar's murder from the Battle of Actium, the naval engagement off the coast of Greece that ushered in the final demise of the Republic and the accession of Rome's first emperor. Many later Roman writers recognized the key significance of this battle; for example, the historian Cassius Dio (*c.* AD 155–after 229) asserted that it marked the point when the Roman monarchy began.

The tale of these intervening years is dominated by two men whose fortunes changed radically as a result of the events of 15 March, 44 BC. The first was Mark Antony (Marcus Antonius; *c.* 83–30 BC), the scion of a distinguished family, many of whose members had entered public life. For instance, Mark Antony's father had held the post of consul 19 years before the death of Caesar. The second was born Gaius Octavius (63 BC–AD 14). His father, an equestrian, was the first member of the family to become a senator. But far more significantly, his mother was a niece of Julius Caesar.

Contenders for power

Antony had long been a protégé of Caesar and in 44 BC followed in his own father's footsteps by being chosen as

Caesar's partner for his fifth consulship. That same year, the 18-year-old Octavius was awaiting his great-uncle's arrival in Greece to join him on his Parthian campaign. When Caesar was assassinated, Antony automatically became the head of the Roman state for the duration of the year he was consul, while Octavius was made Caesar's son and heir through an adoption noted in the dictator's will. He duly assumed the name Gaius Julius Caesar. Roman tradition suggests that he might also have had the *cognomen* Octavian to indicate his biological family. Political enemies continued to refer to him by this name throughout his life, by way of emphasizing his humble beginnings, while he refused absolutely to use it.

The evolving relationship between Antony and Octavian splits roughly into three phases. The first, in which Antony was the dominant partner, spans the period from the assassination to around 37 BC. In the second phase, lasting for the next three years, the two men held equal power, while in the years immediately leading up to Actium – the final phase – Octavian's star was in the ascendant. In many ways, the men were polar opposites, and their diametrically opposed characters played a major role in determining their career trajectories. So, while Antony was capable of displaying great *virtus* on the battlefield, his reputation was undermined by scandalous conduct in his private life. Octavian, by contrast, was pusillanimous in battle (tending to fall violently ill whenever danger threatened) but proved himself extremely adept in the political arena, especially in cultivating a popular public persona. The one trait that the two did share was utter ruthlessness.

The seven years that followed the assassination of Julius Caesar saw a continuation of the internecine strife that Caesar had sparked with his civil war against Pompey. What was at stake was not a restoration of the Republic – even Caesar's assassins, who may well have taken their drastic action with this aim in mind, seem rapidly to have realized that it was an impossible dream – but rather which faction should succeed Caesar, and what precise form this succession should take. Both sides soon abandoned the notion of one-man rule in favour of a limited collective style of leadership that was less offensive to Roman tradition. When, during his funeral oration for Caesar, Mark Antony openly condemned Caesar's death as murder by conspiracy, public opinion turned against the party of the assassins, and its leading members Brutus and Cassius were driven into exile. After initial power struggles among the leading members of the Caesarian faction, including a mutiny inspired by Octavian (who had turned 19 on September 23), which robbed Antony of the troops he was planning to use for the occupation of Rome, a bitterly fought civil war took place in the first half of 43. During this time Octavian was appointed praetor to serve with the two Caesarian generals who had been elected for that year. When the consuls died in two (successful) engagements against Antony's forces outside Mutina (Modena) in northern Italy, Octavian emerged as the leader of the army against Antony, who was in full retreat for Gaul. Reinforced by allies in Gaul, including Marcus Aemilius Lepidus (d. 13 BC), the former deputy of Julius Caesar in the dictatorship of 44 BC, Antony invaded Italy; but his men refused to fight Octavian's while the assassins were still at large.

Compelled by their men to make peace, Octavian, Antony and Lepidus settled their differences and promptly assumed control of the state through a triumvirate (often called the Second Triumvirate to distinguish it from that of Caesar, Pompey and Crassus). In this group Lepidus played the role of Crassus before him, as a counterbalance to the competing ambitions of his colleagues. At the end of 43 BC they made their position legally unassailable by passing a law proclaiming them *triumviri rei publicae constituendae*, or 'board of three for putting the Republic back in order' – a piece of political 'spin' of breathtaking temerity in any age. While claiming to be acting in the best interests of the Republic, they were in fact writing its obituary. Through this legislation the three men had, in effect, appointed themselves dictators.

The triumvirate tightens its grip

It was not long before the triumvirate faced its first crisis. Each man commanded his own army, making a total of some 100,000 men under arms. This was almost half as large a force as that later deployed by Rome's first emperor to control his entire empire, and there was simply not enough money to pay the troops. The solution of the *triumviri* was, in the manner of Sulla, to spread a climate of fear by reinstating the dreaded proscriptions. History, subsequently manipulated by the victorious Octavian, apportions blame for this new spasm of bloodshed to Antony. Even so, the accusation may well be grounded in fact. Not only was Antony the senior partner in the triumvirate at this stage, but his immoral private life was also closely modelled on that of

Sulla. Like him, Antony drank to excess and enjoyed the company of dissolute actors. He also followed his dictator predecessor in regarding the eastern part of the Roman world as his natural power base.

The Second Triumvirate's proscriptions were responsible for one of the most brutal periods in the entire history of Rome. More than 3000 members of the upper classes were summarily executed, including one of the most notable Romans of all time, Marcus Tullius Cicero (106–43 BC). Cicero was the greatest orator of his age, a relatively principled and conservative politician and the most vociferous opponent of Antony in the confused months after Caesar's death. His violent death and its gruesome sequel testified to the savagery that was meted out daily during this new reign of terror.

Meanwhile, Brutus and Cassius were rallying support in the east – sometimes using violent coercion – to mount a challenge to the rule of the triumvirate. The core of the army they assembled comprised legions that Pompey had once raised for the war with Caesar, and that Caesar had left in the east, hoping to win their loyalty in his forthcoming Parthian campaign. But the memory of Pompey had remained strong among these troops, making them willing recruits to the assassins' cause.

In the late summer of 42 BC, Octavian and Antony defeated the party of the assassins in two battles near Philippi in northern Greece. During these engagements, Antony covered himself in glory, while Octavian disgraced himself by taking to his tent with an 'illness' shortly after the first action commenced, and only just making good his escape when Brutus' soldiers overran the camp. Following his victory, Antony absorbed the army of the assassins into his forces and set about founding an Antonian empire in the east. Meanwhile, other Pompeians now emerged in the west. Pompey's only surviving son, Sextus, joined together various fleets that had been assembled over time to fight the Caesarians and began a war off the coast of Italy that would last until the summer of 36 BC.

Key events in the period 42–36 BC included a civil war in Italy; two meetings of the *triumviri* in 40 and 37 BC to reconfirm their authority; and an ongoing see-saw struggle with Sextus Pompey. For Octavian, the greatest of these challenges was the civil war of 41 BC, which erupted when he tried to settle veterans from the Philippi campaign on land that had been confiscated from Italian towns. The rebellion was fomented and led by Antony's younger brother Lucius, who was consul for that year, and Antony's wife Fulvia. Victory for Octavian was only assured when armies led by allies of the elder Antony failed to pledge their support to his brother. The conflict ended with a siege of the city of Perusia (modern Perugia), which was eventually starved into submission. Lucius was exiled to Spain, and Fulvia to Greece, where she died.

An uneasy peace

When Antony returned in September 40 BC the two men patched up their differences. Antony sealed the reconciliation with Octavian by marrying his sister, Octavia, before returning east. In 37 BC, following military setbacks for both

Octavian (fighting Sextus Pompey) and Antony (against the Parthians), they renewed the triumvirate once more. Antony's invasion of the Parthian empire, which collapsed because of his own carelessness and lack of suitable logistical provision, was officially intended to avenge Crassus' disaster and the Parthian invasion of Roman territory after Caesar's assassination. It also, from Antony's point of view, would have contrasted nicely with Octavian's war against other Romans (or, as he put it, runaway slaves and pirates). In the end, it was Octavian who emerged as the stronger partner when he finally managed to defeat Sextus the following year, and summarily stripped the vacillating Lepidus of his authority as a *triumvir* without consulting Antony. Lepidus was banished to an undistinguished retirement within Italy.

Now the power struggle was free to develop unimpeded between the two main players. Antony's problems continued to grow after 36 BC. Although he and Octavia had two daughters, their relationship was strained. Even before he married Octavia, Antony had become besotted with Queen Cleopatra of Egypt. Cleopatra encouraged this infatuation, and in the years that followed, Antony's passion for her, and for life in her capital of Alexandria, became a scandal, just as it had once been for Julius Caesar. Antony dressed and partied as a Greek, and martial, virile Rome had always regarded Greece as the home of lewdness and effeminacy. Not even the most lurid propaganda that Octavian spread about Antony's conduct came close to conveying the real state of affairs. A contemporary dedication to 'Antony the Great' from a local drinking club that archaeologists found carved on a stone at Alexandria provides eloquent proof of his debauchery.

Antony's overindulgence had long been infamous; one of Cicero's most memorable attacks on his character includes a description of the hung-over Antony vomiting while attempting to attend to public business in the Forum.

Even more damagingly, Antony's opponents now began to accuse him of infecting other Romans with his vices. Stories spread of wild parties, including one at which a senior officer stripped naked, painted himself blue, and flopped around on the floor wearing a fish tail in imitation of a sea god. Antony even tried to respond in a self-justifying essay, *On his Own Drunkenness*, sadly now lost. But his conduct only fuelled Roman distrust of the licentious East and gave credence to Octavian's image of him as a wilful despot who would, given the chance, rule Rome like a foreign potentate.

Octavian, in the meantime, managed to bring a semblance of order to the government of Italy. He stopped settling veterans on confiscated land and made sure that the people had enough to eat. In one particularly striking display of public service, Marcus Agrippa (*c.* 64–12 BC), Octavian's chief lieutenant and the architect of the victory over Sextus, accepted a reduction in rank – having already been consul – to serve as an aedile. During his term of office, Agrippa made great improvements to the city's water and sewerage systems, including rebuilding the main drain, the Cloaca Maxima. Octavian now tried to project an image of himself that was in accord with the traditional Roman ideals of frugality and self-reliance. Although it is hard to imagine that anyone seriously believed his claim to have given up sex in his late teens for the good of his health, or his contradictory claim that he had only indulged in adulterous relationships with the wives of his enemies to learn their secrets, he had settled into a stable marriage with a woman of impeccable aristocratic heritage named Livia. They had become a model couple, and Romans favourably compared their life of uncomplicated domesticity to the licentious behaviour of Antony and Cleopatra.

Octavian makes his move

The legal authority of the *triumviri* was due to expire on December 31, 33 BC. When several Italian towns pledged their allegiance to him in 32 BC and urgently petitioned him to lead a campaign against Antony and Cleopatra, Octavian made a decisive move to seize power. In February of 32 BC, after one of the consuls attempted to read a letter from Antony to the senate, he entered Rome at the head of an armed guard, marched into the senate house, seated himself between the consuls and proclaimed his continuing authority as head of state. Shortly thereafter he produced what he claimed to be a copy of Antony's will, in which Antony made clear his intention to move the capital to Alexandria. The consuls fled to Egypt, and Octavian took advantage of the crisis that he had engineered to obtain a further grant of supreme authority in the war that he now declared against Antony.

Antony anticipated Octavian's actions and in the late summer of 31 BC assembled a huge force with the intention of invading Italy. Cleopatra joined him on this campaign. Octavian now showed consummate skill in directing his commanders' response. They cut Antony's supply lines and blockaded his force in the Bay of Actium on the east coast of Greece. Octavian's army, led by Statilius Taurus, won an initial skirmish, while his fleet, under Marcus Agrippa, dominated the sea-lanes. As food ran out and disease became rife, on 2 September, 31 BC, Antony made a desperate bid to break out. Although historical accounts of Actium are sketchy and confused, with some hinting that the outcome was something of a foregone conclusion, while others speak of a fierce fight, there exists one compelling piece of evidence suggesting that a full-scale naval engagement did indeed take place. Shortly after his triumph, Octavian founded the settlement of Nicopolis (literally 'Victory City') on a peninsula jutting into the Ionian Sea (in what is now Greece). Here, a monument commemorating the victory was discovered by archaeologists. It was decorated with the prows of ships taken in the battle, indicating that Antony's losses were heavy. Combining this information with some from our written accounts, it appears Antony tried to break through the centre of his opponents, and that, as he did so, Cleopatra's squadron hoisted its sails and fled. Antony first followed in his own massive flagship, which he later abandoned for a faster vessel. The remainder of his fleet that survived the battle retreated into the bay, where it later surrendered. As was the case with his Parthian adventure, Antony was undone by his love of grandiose plans unsupported by basic logistics.

Augustus' victory was sealed a year later when his armies entered Alexandria as Antony committed suicide in Cleopatra's arms. The queen also later took her own life by clutching a venomous snake to her breast.

Foundations of the Empire: The House of Augustus

(29 BC–AD 14)

Octavian came back to Rome in 28 BC; many in the city feared that his return would herald a consolidation of his position as dictator, backed as he was by a huge army. However, on the Ides of January, 27 BC, he convened a meeting of the senate at which he renounced the extraordinary dictatorial powers granted him to command the armies of Rome in the war against Antony. But at this same session, the senate, alarmed that he was about to relinquish his wise guardianship of the state, urged him to carry on as consul. As an additional honour for his service to Rome, the grateful senators bestowed on him the name Augustus, or 'revered personage'.

In naming him Augustus, the senate completed a process of transformation in Octavian that had begun several years before; in 42 BC, when Julius Caesar had been declared a god, his adopted son Octavian had taken the names 'Gaius Julius, son of the divinity Caesar'. Six years later he had changed his first name, or *praenomen*, from Gaius to *imperator*, or 'victorious general', in celebration of his victory over Sextus Pompey. Now his new name, Caesar Augustus, while acknowledging a debt to the older Caesar, also proclaimed to the entire world that Octavian was a new man whose *virtus* outstripped that of any other mortal. Unlike his adoptive father, however, he was not divine. He kept his feet very firmly planted in the world of mortals, despite the fact that people throughout the Roman world now offered sacrifices to him in gratitude for his defeat of Mark Antony. He attended dinner parties with his friends, was scrupulous in consulting the senate and was generally accessible to the average Roman. His unofficial title of *princeps* ('first citizen') had been bestowed on prominent citizens before him (such as Pompey), and he made it clear that he could wish for no higher accolade. In accordance with this, he also modestly referred to the various duties that the senate delegated to him, and the people confirmed, as his *statio*, or allotted station in life.

The making of Augustus

Yet, by any measure, Augustus' accomplishments in the years after Actium had been truly impressive. Not the least of these was to bring the long period of civil war to a definitive close. This was a signal success, and may have stemmed from the fact that Augustus had not followed the pattern of Sulla and Caesar. They had imposed their authority on Rome only after first having established their power base in the provinces, and in so doing had never really been able to impose their will throughout the empire. Augustus, on the other hand, had made Rome his constituency from the outset. The fact that he defeated Antony as the legitimate head of a functioning government enabled him to integrate the former supporters of his rival into the state.

At the same time, his difficult early years had taught him a valuable lesson about the thorny problem of disbanding and resettling a large force of armed men. First, he was careful to ensure that those demobilized soldiers who still retained connections to the Italian homeland were resettled at his own expense, and not by confiscating land from Italian towns. In addition, since many of the soldiers, especially those who had served under Antony, had no real roots in Italy any more, Augustus met little resistance in resettling them in far-flung military colonies abroad. In this way, hundreds of thousands of men were successfully discharged, thereby reducing the army by more than half its strength to a permanent force of 28 legions – roughly 150,000 men. The remainder of Rome's armed forces were made up of supporting 'auxiliary' units recruited from the provinces, whose numbers were roughly equal to the legionary force.

When the senate conferred his new station on Augustus, they also endowed him with a variety of different powers as he sought a framework within which he could run the state without resorting to assuming a position evocative of Caesar's dictatorship (the office had been formally abolished shortly after the Ides of March, 44 BC). The two most important of these were his *imperium* as one of the two consuls every year (a reversion to Marius' way of doing things at the end of the second century BC), and *tribunicia potestas*, the powers of a tribune of the plebs. These latter powers included the right to summon assemblies of the people to vote on laws, and the right of intercession or the right to veto any action taken by another magistrate. They also rendered him sacrosanct, so that anyone who dared to raise a hand against him would be committing a crime against the gods (though, given that more than a few tribunes from Tiberius Gracchus onwards had been murdered, the protection this offered was more symbolic than real). Finally, the senate made him titular governor of several provinces, including Spain, Gaul, Syria and Egypt. Since these provinces were also the ones that had garrisons, the upshot was that Augustus now commanded 26 legions, the vast bulk of the Roman army.

Augustus consolidates his rule

The legal powers vested in him in 27 BC effectively made Augustus the head of state, but he did not dare govern the empire on his own. In the course of the civil wars he had come to depend heavily upon two close friends, Agrippa and Maecenas (70–8 BC), to help him. These two men were a study in opposites. Maecenas, who never held public office, was a wealthy patron of the arts and something of a party animal. Agrippa, a masterful soldier, had been consul in 37 BC and shared the consulship with Augustus when the structure of government was reformed in 28 and 27 BC. It was common knowledge that Agrippa and Maecenas disliked each other, but the very fact that the emergent Augustan regime could accommodate two such contrasting figures attested to its collective nature, further dispelling fears that Augustus was imposing monarchical rule.

In addition to Maecenas and Agrippa, there were a number of other men who retained very powerful positions within the senate. These included Asinius Pollio (76 BC–AD 5), who had secured Augustus' friendship by refusing to support the younger Antony in 41; Messalla Corvinus (64 BC–AD 8), who had served both Cassius and Antony before declaring his undying support for Augustus in the early 30s; Statilius Taurus (*c.* 60 BC–*c.* AD 10) who had commanded the land army in the Battle of Actium; and Munatius Plancus (87 BC–AD 15), the man who had once humiliated himself by performing the drunken fish dance for Antony but had judiciously switched sides just before Actium. Augustus' pardoning of men such as Munatius Plancus was reminiscent of Caesar's clemency, but unlike Caesar, he ensured that those he spared would stay loyal by giving them prestigious and useful roles within Roman society.

Augustus was also keen to avoid Caesar's mistake of micromanaging and antagonizing his trusted lieutenants in Rome, and so decided to absent himself from Rome for a while on campaign. Ever prudent, he wanted to avoid taking on a truly dangerous enemy (which for the present ruled out Rome's nemesis, the dreaded Parthians) but nevertheless wanted to find a suitably worthy opponent to justify the major logistics of raising and moving an army. And so he fixed his gaze on Spain. Spain had been the springboard from which Hannibal had launched his invasion of Italy at the end of the third century BC. After finally ousting their Carthaginian foe, the Romans established two provinces in the country, but had continued to meet significant resistance from the Spaniards. In particular, ever since Pompey had campaigned there in the 70s BC, it had become a hotbed of Pompeian sympathies. With their long history of turbulence and disloyalty to the Caesarian cause, the independent tribes of Spain therefore provided Augustus with a tempting target.

With much public fanfare, he duly declared war on them in 27 BC; they proved a tougher nut to crack than he had anticipated, but his generals gained enough ground by 25 BC for Augustus to claim that he had solved a problem that was more than a century and a half old. Even so, it took a further 15 years, and the intervention of such high-profile generals as Agrippa, to bring Spain firmly to heel and integrate it fully within the provincial system.

Essential reforms

By 23 BC, it was becoming clear to Augustus that he needed to effect changes in his mode of governance. Some voices of discontent began to be raised about his tenure of the consulship for every year since 31 BC. He had mooted the idea of replacement ('suffect') consuls stepping in during the course of the year, but this did not satisfy the ambitions of aristocrats who still yearned for consular office and the kudos it brought. Augustus' protracted occupancy of the consulship also placed a major question mark over his claim to have 'restored' Republican government in 28 BC.

Following a serious illness, therefore, Augustus surrendered the consulship halfway through the year. Yet this by no means signalled that he was relinquishing his hold on true power. The senate now voted him further honours, including a grant of *imperium* in Italy, and the *imperium maius* or 'superior power' to that of any provincial governor, as well as confirmation of the *tribunicia potestas* for life. The subtle interplay between these two roles testifies to Augustus' political sleight of hand and his keen appreciation of the tenor of public opinion in Rome. While *imperium maius* handed him effective control over the provinces, the *tribunicia potestas* equipped him with all the legal authority he needed to administer Rome itself. Playing down the grant of special *imperium* within Italy, the *tribunicia potestas* became the symbol of Augustus' civil authority. Indeed, his reign later came to be dated from when he was first granted this particular power. This underlines the extraordinary nature of the position that Augustus had fashioned for himself: an office originally created to protect the Roman people from the wilful acts of a magistrate had become the defining power of the emperor.

Moreover, in terms of public relations, the title *tribunicia potestas* was infinitely more palatable to Roman sensibilities than that of dictator, as Sulla and Caesar had styled themselves. As if to underscore this point, Augustus refused the dictatorship at the end of 23 BC when the senate offered it to him to help solve a threatened grain shortage. He was concerned to maintain the illusion that his authority was dependent on the will of the people. This may all have been political theatre, but it was an extremely convincing performance.

Securing the succession

Political theatre of another kind was played out the following year, when a group of senators plotted to kill Augustus. Several of the conspirators were extremely prominent citizens – one was even Maecenas' brother-in-law – a fact that sent shock waves through the establishment. By this stage,

Augustus was 41. Agrippa was possibly a year older and the life expectancy of most Romans did not extend far beyond 50. As bungled as the conspiracy of 22 BC turned out to be, it was a timely reminder to Augustus that he had still not truly ensured the long-term security of his rule or made provisions for a successor. It was clear that he urgently needed to start looking for younger heirs to carry on his legacy.

The system of succession that took shape over the next few years was based on the familiar Roman principle of collegiality. Augustus' eldest nephew Marcellus (born 42 BC), recently married to his only daughter Julia, had died suddenly in 23 BC. During his own life-threatening illness that same year, Augustus had indicated that Agrippa should succeed him, and now arranged that he should marry Julia, while also promoting the careers of the two sons of Livia by her first marriage. Her elder son, Tiberius (42 BC–AD 37) was earmarked for prominent military responsibilities during the campaign that Augustus was planning to mount in the east.

Rome's arch-enemy Parthia had recently been torn apart by a dynastic power struggle, and in the course of these upheavals the pretender to the throne had decamped to Roman territory with two sons of the ruling incumbent as hostages. This presented Rome with a golden opportunity to put pressure on Parthia. Augustus and Agrippa headed east, and, after tough diplomatic wrangling, the Parthian king made a number of important concessions in return for his sons' release. These included officially recognizing the River Euphrates (in present-day Syria and Iraq) as the border between the two empires, granting Rome the power to appoint the king of Armenia – whose realm occupied much of what is now eastern Turkey – and returning military standards captured from Crassus and Antony. The return of the legionary standards was an easy gesture for the Parthians to make, but was of huge symbolic significance to the Romans, who still regarded their loss by the previous generation as a source of profound national shame. Augustus proclaimed the peace that he concluded with Parthia as a great victory, and not without some justification, since it removed at a stroke any potential grounds for Rome having to wage war on its old enemy. No Roman army could possibly have occupied Iraq and Iran, or even a significant portion of that territory, without getting bogged down in endless warfare. There were simply not enough soldiers to control an area that was culturally and politically too complex for the Romans to manage.

Indeed, Augustus avoided imposing direct Roman administration upon many Semitic borderlands of the empire where traditions of Graeco-Roman government, based upon city-states, were wholly alien and liable to stir up local resistance. If Augustus felt that Palestine was better off with Rome's client king Herod (I) the Great (74–5 BC), then it was obvious that he would not even entertain the thought of sending Roman governors to Iraq.

Back to basics

Returning to Rome in 19 BC, Augustus embarked on a new phase of his reign. Even so, he would still spend most of the next decade away from the capital. Rather than pursue military glory for himself, he was now intent on focusing all his efforts on the moral regeneration of the Roman state by reviving the customs and traditions of the past. At the same time, he cemented his legacy by giving his stepsons free rein to display *virtus* in war, a vital quality if they were to be presented as worthy successors. Over the next decade, armies under the command of Tiberius and Drusus (38–9 BC), the younger of his stepsons, occupied Switzerland and southern Germany.

Meanwhile, in Rome, Augustus initiated his campaign to clean up both public and private life. In 19 and 18 BC respectively, he introduced legislation to expel 'unworthy' men from the senate and to regulate the marital and reproductive habits of the city's upper classes. New laws were introduced governing marriage, and draconian measures were brought in to curb sexual offences. One law was specifically geared towards encouraging the élite to produce more children: men whose wives bore three or more children were given preferment in public office. By contrast, those who refused to marry were penalized, including being cut off from their inheritance. Another piece of legislation made adultery a crime for both sexes. The penalties it imposed were harsh: any man who refused to divorce a wife who was having an affair could be charged as a pimp. Many Romans resented this intrusion of the state into the realm of the *domus*, but these measures were important symbols of an imperial commitment to a more orderly society, and thus helped consolidate the new regime.

Around the same time, in 17 BC, Rome celebrated the 800th

anniversary of its founding. The lyric poet Horace – one of several writers who flourished in a period of extraordinary literary achievement, the Latin Golden Age, which began in the late Republic and ended with Augustus' death – wrote a poem marking the occasion. This festival was the culmination of many years of work restoring temples and other public buildings that had fallen into disrepair. The years of civil war were decried as a period in which immorality had been allowed to run rampant, the cults of the gods had been ignored and personal expenditure on private luxury had replaced the pursuit of the common good. Augustus also staged a number of extraordinary spectacles for the Roman people and funded extensive construction of new venues for shows. For example, a huge new theatre was built and named after his deceased nephew Marcellus; the Circus Maximus, where the hugely popular chariot races were held, was improved and the first permanent amphitheatre for gladiatorial shows was constructed by Statilius Taurus. Taurus' magnanimity was part of a trend whereby prominent citizens commissioned lavish public works. This had begun in 39 BC, with Asinius Pollio's patronage of the first public library in Rome, while Agrippa later built a gleaming new portico in which he encouraged members of the Roman élite to display their art collections. Augustus pointedly refrained from having his own name associated with new buildings because he wanted to emphasize that this investment in the welfare of the Roman people was a communal enterprise. Likewise, in financing the restoration of temples he made sure that he did not efface the record of the original builders – further demonstration of his interest in and reverence for the Roman past.

In 12 BC, Augustus assumed the role of *pontifex maximus*, celebrating this new honour by erecting a massive new Altar of Peace by the banks of the Tiber, near to the spot where he had already built his own mausoleum. Rome was now a very different place, bearing out Augustus' proud boast that he had found a city of brick and transformed it into one of marble. The many new public buildings had transformed the cityscape, while Roman possessions overseas had been enlarged by conquests in the Alps and Germany. Yet this new civic and imperial pride came at a price: Augustus now presided over a state where nonconformity was viewed with increasing suspicion.

The reluctant heir

As Rome changed, so too did the regime. Agrippa died in March, 12 BC, leaving the new generation as heirs apparent. Agrippa's widow Julia was remarried to Tiberius, who was forced to divorce Agrippa's daughter, whom he seems genuinely to have loved. The new marriage was not a success; the grim Tiberius was ill-matched to a younger woman who was notorious for her sexual promiscuity. In 9 BC, Drusus died when he fell from his horse while on campaign, and Augustus began to invest his hopes for the succession in two of the sons (Gaius and Lucius) that Julia had borne during her marriage to Agrippa. Tiberius, to whom the burden of military command of new campaigns in the Balkans now fell, became increasingly restive. In 7 BC, thoroughly disaffected, he announced that he was withdrawing from public life and retiring to Rhodes. His departure marked the start of a difficult decade.

With advancing years, Augustus seems to have become very hard to live with. Even when he and his wife Livia were both present in Rome, he continued to communicate with her by letter. A man of ostentatiously simple tastes, he delighted in dice games that the serious and academically minded Tiberius scorned. He was also shameless in his favouritism, doting on his grandsons but spurning Drusus' son Claudius (10 BC–AD 54), who stammered and had a club foot and whom Augustus banned from showing his face in public. He was also adamant that a woman's place was at home behind the spinning wheel, and his attempts to impose his abstemious lifestyle on those around him led to a serious rift with his daughter Julia. In 2 BC, just after her sons had been dispatched on campaign, Julia was found to have engaged in dubious activities with several members of the aristocracy. One of her misdemeanours was an orgy in the Forum, while there was also some suspicion of her involvement in a nascent plot to kill her father. She was banished into exile on an island.

Further crises rocked the state with the sudden deaths on campaign of Julia's two sons, and Augustus' preferred heirs, in AD 2 and 4. The reluctant Tiberius was recalled to Rome and installed on the Palatine Hill. Two years later he re-emerged as the heir apparent, was shipped off to fight in Germany, and then to command a major military operation in the Balkans (Illyricum), where recently conquered tribes had risen in revolt. In AD 8 the palace was shaken by another conspiracy, this time involving the daughter of Julia and Agrippa, also named Julia, and her brother, known as Agrippa Postumus since he was born after his father's death. Agrippa Postumus had already been sent into internal exile for allegedly deranged behaviour (open criticism of his grandfather seems to have been part of it), and was now dispatched to an island. Julia was found to be pregnant by someone other than her husband. Augustus saw to it that the child was killed and that she was exiled.

At the same time, Augustus lashed out at Rome's most brilliant living poet, Ovid (Publius Ovidius Naso; 43 BC–AD 17), whose works included a poem on the art of love, which had been in circulation for some seven years but which Augustus now suddenly denounced as offensive. To be sure, Ovid's poem celebrated extramarital love and also contained some wonderfully witty send-ups of Augustan propaganda – suggesting, for example that imperial processions provided excellent opportunities to meet lovers. But that was not enough, in and of itself, to cause the poet's downfall – he refers also to an error that angered the emperor. We don't know what that error was, but we do know the result: Ovid finished his life in Tomis, a city on the Black Sea coast of what is now Romania.

A military catastrophe

In AD 6, Augustus introduced his last, but arguably one of his most important, reforms when he set up a new treasury to guarantee retirement bonuses to soldiers who had completed 20 years of service. Funded initially by a large gift from Augustus' private fortune, and thereafter by taxation (including an inheritance tax that was deeply unpopular with senators), this measure was the final step in creating a professional career structure for private soldiers and ensuring the army's loyalty to the imperial house. In Tiberius, the army also now had a skilled commander, supported by a cadre of competent senior officers who all owed their positions to the regime. However, this period is chiefly known for one of the most devastating defeats in Roman military history, a disaster attributed to the strategic incompetence and naivety of the commanding officer. In AD 7, Quinctilius Varus, who was related to Augustus by marriage, was sent to govern the province of Germania, a region between the Rhine and Elbe rivers that Drusus had recently fought hard to subdue. In AD 9 Varus was deceived into believing intelligence supplied by a supposedly loyal Germanic chieftain named Arminius, who commanded an auxiliary unit. Varus was lured into leaving his camp and withdrawing his three legions to the Rhine to avoid being cut off for the winter by a rebellion among the tribes. Arminius then sprang his trap, ambushing and destroying the entire Roman force in the Teutoburg Forest.

Written accounts of the catastrophe give quite different versions of what happened, and what was happening in Germany at the time. We are fortunate, then, that in recent years archaeology has provided new evidence that has helped clarify the record. At the site of Waldgirmes in the modern German state of Hesse north of the Rhine, where the Roman-style city in the process of development at this time was abandoned within a few years, we see both how serious the Romans were about establishing a province north of the Rhine and how Varus' disaster did actually cause a major change in Roman policy. On a more specific level, part of the battlefield, long lost to history – where Varus' legions (the Seventeenth, Eighteenth, and Nineteenth) were slaughtered in AD 9 – was found north of the German city of Osnabrück in the early 1990s. Its discovery has helped historians gain a more accurate impression of how the engagement unfolded, and puts into context the various sketchy Roman accounts of the battle. Traces of German fieldworks have been identified on the Kalkriese, a hill bordering on the road that the Romans were taking south when they were ambushed. Arminius and his tribes launched repeated attacks on the Romans from this vantage point in the course of a three-day running battle. The Roman infantry was badly hampered by being forced to fight on swampy, heavily wooded terrain poorly suited to their tactics; the Romans' fighting units could not manoeuvre successfully, and were split up and picked off by the Germans.

The disaster in Germany hit the regime hard. Augustus is reported to have wandered the palace banging his head against the walls and crying 'Quinctilius Varus, give me back my legions!' He seldom appeared in public after the catastrophe and his health was plainly beginning to fail. Tiberius recovered the situation to some extent, reinforcing the frontier on the Rhine before handing over command to his nephew Germanicus, who was tasked with retrieving the standards that had been lost with Varus. The three legions, however, were never replaced. Augustus and Tiberius seem to have agreed that the period of expansion was over and that the empire should remain within boundaries marked by the Rhine and Danube rivers in Europe, the Euphrates in the east, and the Sahara in North Africa.

Five years later, Augustus left Rome to travel to Naples. He fell desperately ill, and died on August 19, AD 14. Tiberius, who the year before had been accorded equal authority to Augustus everywhere throughout the empire but Rome, now succeeded him.

Eccentric Stability: Emperors from Tiberius to Nero

(AD 14–68)

Augustus put the imperial system on such a firm footing that even the dysfunctional behaviour of his four successors could not overturn his achievement. The pillars of the new regime were the army's loyalty to the *princeps*, concern for the welfare of the population of Rome and the emperor's patronage of loyal members of the ruling class. The overarching ideological principle that informed all the regime's policies was domestic propriety. Romans recalled that the years before Actium were haunted by violence and uncertainty, and the ideals of the Republic became inextricably linked with civil war.

Augustus' very success in promoting his mode of governance as the only effective antidote to anarchy resulted in widespread fear that civil war would erupt as soon as he died. This fear was not even allayed by the fact that Tiberius already held a firm grip on power, and persistent rumours of impending turmoil continued to circulate. Some people wondered if Agrippa Postumus might break free from his island prison to challenge the new regime (the rumours were not even scotched when Postumus was executed by his guards, an act of gratuitous brutality for which Tiberius denied all responsibility). Others speculated whether Tiberius' popular nephew Germanicus (15 BC–AD 19), now commanding the powerful army on the Rhine, might choose not to bide his time and wait to succeed Tiberius but instead make an immediate bid for power.

Tiberius and Germanicus

In the event, matters came to a head when four Roman legions stationed on the Rhine and three on the Danube (the province of Pannonia) staged mutinies at the news of Augustus' death. The immediate catalyst of the mutinies was anger over harsh conditions of service: men were being forced to serve beyond their due retirement date, while also suffering brutality at the hands of their centurion officers and receiving derisory pay. Yet the underlying cause that made the troops' simmering grievances boil over into open insurrection was their uncertainty about the future. The Danubian mutiny was swiftly and decisively put down by Tiberius' son Drusus (13 BC–AD 23) and Aelius Sejanus (20 BC–AD 31), the newly promoted commander of the praetorian guard, who were dispatched to deal with the crisis in the Balkans, around the time of Augustus' funeral in September. However, the mutiny in Germany was a far more serious affair; Germanicus' men murdered several brutal centurions and there were mutterings in the ranks that he should seize the throne. Yet although Germanicus refused to accede to their demands, the histrionics he displayed in quelling the unrest in his ranks called his judgement and leadership into question. At one point, the general drew his sword and threatened to commit suicide unless the men returned to their proper loyalty; one soldier was so unimpressed by this display that he offered his own sword, saying that it was sharper. Eventually, through some persuasive last-ditch rhetoric, and concessions to the troops on pay and conditions, Germanicus calmed the situation.

Despite some shortcomings as a commander, Germanicus ultimately turned out to play a key role in the dynastic succession of the Julio- Claudian family. His wife, Julia Agrippina, was exceptionally fecund and gave birth to nine children, no fewer than six of whom survived infancy. Two of these offspring of their union ensured the continuation of the imperial house – one as the emperor Caligula, the other as the mother of Nero. Germanicus himself disappeared from the historical stage in October, AD 19, when he suddenly fell ill and died in Antioch, Syria.

Meanwhile, Romans were becoming ever more alarmed at the tyrannical turn Tiberius' rule was taking. In particular, he increasingly resorted to invoking the *lex maiestatis*, the law governing actions that might 'diminish the majesty of the Roman people' (that is, high treason), to silence his enemies, real or perceived. There was widespread abuse in the application of this capital offence, since anyone who accused a person subsequently found guilty stood to gain a share of the convicted man's estate. Tiberius' overuse of this extreme sanction was just another manifestation of his aloofness and disdain for the finer arts of political persuasion. In public relations terms, Tiberius completely lacked his predecessor Augustus' personal touch in the exercise of authority and his flair for winning friends and influencing people. As a result, he maintained extremely poor relations with the senate, whom, according to the testimony of the later Roman historian Tacitus, he derided as 'men fit to be slaves'.

The news that the people's champion and heir apparent was dead sent ripples of shock through the empire. Tiberius was reviled, and his likely successor Drusus was far less popular than Germanicus. The finger of suspicion for Germanicus' death pointed at the governor of Syria, Gnaeus Calpurnius Piso (*c.* 44 BC–AD 20). There was a long-running enmity between the two men, and just before the onset of Germanicus' fatal illness, he had forced Piso to resign his post. Worse still, there was some circumstantial evidence to suggest that Piso had poisoned his rival on the secret instruction of Tiberius. No one dared say this openly, but suspicions mounted when the former governor returned to Rome to defend himself on a charge of *maiestas* arising both from the assassination rumours and his subsequent efforts to retake the province from Germanicus' officers by force of arms. Piso's defence was that he was Tiberius' man on the spot and his fulsome protestations of unswerving loyalty may only have served to convince the emperor that his placeman was actually about to make incriminating revelations. Conveniently, following a visit by Sejanus, Piso was discovered to have committed 'suicide' by slitting his own throat.

The rise and fall of Sejanus

Drusus did not long survive Germanicus, dying in AD 23. A plot almost certainly lay behind his sudden demise, though unlike Germanicus' death, no rumours circulated at the time.

However, after Sejanus fell from favour and was killed eight years later, clear evidence of a conspiracy emerged. From as early as AD 19, Sejanus had been conducting an affair with Drusus' wife Livilla. His political ambitions were also on the rise and he began to entertain hopes that, if he made himself indispensable to Tiberius, the emperor might begin to regard him in the same light as Augustus had viewed Agrippa and appoint him as his successor. Sejanus realized that it would immeasurably strengthen his hand if Drusus were to die and he marry his widow. Drusus duly fell victim to a mystery illness, but the second part of Sejanus' plan was thwarted when Tiberius refused him permission to marry Livilla. Even so, from this point Tiberius seems to have placed ever greater trust in the leadership powers of his lieutenant, and had statues of Sejanus erected throughout Rome. At this stage, the obvious heirs to the throne were the two teenage sons of Germanicus, Nero and Drusus, but they and their mother Agrippina antagonized Tiberius by continuing to hold him responsible for Germanicus' death. Thoroughly sick of the business of governing, Tiberius retired to his villa on Capri in AD 28, leaving the day-to-day running of the state in Sejanus' hands. The following year, his patience with Agrippina and her sons finally ran out and he had all three banished to the same island where Augustus had once exiled his daughter Julia.

The succession now looked as if it must fall to Agrippina's third son Gaius Caligula or the young son of Drusus, Tiberius Gemellus (AD 19–38), who were both favoured by Tiberius and who lived with him on Capri. Faced with these new obstacles, in AD 31 Sejanus appears to have decided to seize power for himself and hatched a plot to kill Tiberius and the surviving male members of the imperial house. The conspiracy was unmasked by Germanicus' mother, who sent a slave girl named Caenis along with one of her trusted freed male slaves to warn the emperor. Tiberius' response was swift and brutal: Sejanus was condemned by the senate, strangled, and his body thrown to the Roman mob who had always hated and feared him in equal measure and who now delighted in tearing his corpse to pieces.

Tiberius spent the final years of his reign as an embittered recluse. His tendency to brooding introspection – a contemporary once characterized him as *tristissimus hominum* ('the gloomiest of men') – now assumed paranoid proportions. Members of the senate lived in fear they might be suddenly charged with treason, and some long-serving provincial governors lapsed into incompetence. One of these men was Pontius Pilate, the governor of Judea, who was finally dismissed in AD 36, a few months after he had executed a teacher from Galilee at the behest of the religious authorities in Jerusalem. It was one of the few times that he seems to have been willing to go along with what they wanted, but Jesus of Nazareth was the sort of independent religious leader who had caused him trouble at various points during his years in office. His brutal response to the actions of another holy man in the course of the year would finally convince the governor of Syria that he had to go.

As for the emperor, surrounding himself on Capri with a coterie of academics and astrologers, he disengaged himself from all practical concerns, including the crucial question of his succession, as he began to have serious doubts about the fitness of his nephew Gaius Caligula to assume the mantle of emperor. These doubts gave way to study of the stars, which only confirmed his tendency towards helpless inertia, since it indicated to him that Caligula's accession was inevitable. In March of AD 37, aged 79, Tiberius fell ill and died of natural causes, though stories spread suggesting that he was actually smothered by Sejanus' successor as praetorian prefect, a man named Macro (21 BC–AD 38).

Caligula the monster

Tiberius' death provoked unbridled celebration among both the senate and the people of Rome. Yet the fact remained that when he came to power, he had been eminently well qualified to succeed Augustus; no one had commanded more armies and provinces than Tiberius, nor been consul so many times. Moreover, despite his deep unpopularity, his reign had left the empire in a far stronger position. He had not embarked on damaging military adventures but had consolidated existing boundaries, and as a result the treasury was in a very healthy state on his death. He had therefore been, for all his growing eccentricity, a symbol of stability from the outset. The same could not be said for his successor. Caligula had held just one junior office, and had no official position when Tiberius died. So, whereas Tiberius had simply inherited the role of *princeps* from Augustus, to formalize this new accession the senate and people now took it upon themselves to define the legal position of the emperor by passing a bill to confer that position on Caligula. To those who did not know him, the young Caligula, the son of a popular father, seemed the perfect antidote to his great-uncle. Caligula instantly won great acclaim by abolishing treason trials. However, it soon became apparent that Rome's euphoric celebration of her new emperor was badly misplaced. Caligula had never had to demonstrate *virtus* in a collective environment.

The formative period of his life had been spent at Tiberius' villa on Capri, and there his chief companions were the sons of eastern client-kings whose attitudes towards power were very different from those of the average Roman. Caligula had fully imbibed their imperious attitude. His closest friends were his sisters, and it was rumoured that he had incestuous relations with at least one of them, possibly all three. In response, Caligula's propagandists now sought to deflect public attention by disseminating lurid stories about how Tiberius had spent his waning years. He was alleged to have developed a taste for watching young people have sex; in the public mind, the image of the dour, academic ex-general was supplanted by that of the septuagenarian paedophile. This salacious smear campaign could not, however, mask the essential truth. The intelligence offered to Tiberius by his stargazing had been accurate: Caligula lacked experience of collective decision making and was wholly unsuited to wielding absolute power.

Rome now witnessed a series of unsettling events. Macro was executed on a charge of treason within a year of Caligula taking power. Those who were tired of the overbearing influence of the praetorian guard's commander may have been glad to see him go, but there was now no voice to control the emperor. Caligula began to suggest that he was a god, and began to indulge his whims (including sexual assaults upon female guests at his parties). It took less than a year before the first conspiracy against him came to light, and its aftermath revealed another unsavoury characteristic of the new ruler: he liked to watch people be tortured. Shortly thereafter, Caligula left Rome to campaign in the north. This escapade was meant to prove that the emperor really was a man of substance, but instead turned into a fiasco; a planned invasion of Britain was aborted and Caligula's troops were ordered to collect seashells to carry back to Rome as tokens of the emperor's glorious victory over the sea-god Neptune. Caligula announced his intention of making his favourite pampered horse, Incitatus, a member of the senate. Anger mounted, and a number of senators and military men plotted to assassinate the emperor.

On January 24, AD 41, while Caligula was watching a theatrical show, a tribune of the imperial bodyguard stabbed him to death. Never before had this loyal body of men shown itself willing to betray the emperor, but Caligula had made the mistake of alienating their officers, especially an experienced man named Cassius Chaerea, who masterminded the assassination in the *cryptoporticus*, or underground tunnel, that linked the palaces on the Palatine hill. The plot against Caligula taught future conspirators an important lesson: first ensure the complicity of the praetorian guard, and secondly, restrict the plot to a very small circle of people with direct access to the emperor's person.

An unlikely successor

Shortly after the assassination, the senate convened a meeting at which several of its members proposed a return to Republican government. This was clearly not going to be acceptable to the praetorian guard, who owed their privileges to the imperial system. Interestingly, despite the recent dashing of their hopes in Caligula and their long, painful experience of Tiberius' rule, the Roman people apparently had no wish to see the Republic restored either, assembling in the Forum and loudly proclaiming that they would not stand for a return to senatorial rule.

Popular myth recounts that the praetorian guard discovered Caligula's uncle Claudius hiding behind a curtain and, on a whim, declared him the new emperor. The truth may be more prosaic: the officers of the guard knew that they were going to need an alternative to Caligula, and the obvious choice was Caligula's uncle, Claudius. In fact, he may well have willingly joined the praetorians in their camp as soon as he learned that Caligula was dead, suggesting that he had foreknowledge of the plot and colluded in his nephew's demise. After a day of intense negotiation between the various parties, the senate welcomed the appointment of the new emperor.

Claudius is an intriguing figure. He is most familiar to contemporary readers through the historical novels *I Claudius* (1934) and *Claudius the God* (1935) by the British writer Robert Graves, which cover the reign of the first four emperors; drawing on Tacitus, Plutarch and Suetonius,

Graves presents a man who learns to play up his disabilities, especially his supposed simple-mindedness, so as to avoid appearing a threat to his peers, and so survive. This portrait is probably well grounded in historical fact. Born with a club foot, and possibly also suffering from cerebral palsy, Claudius had been kept in the background throughout the reign of Tiberius. Caligula had deigned to share the consulship with him in AD 37, but thereafter had rarely missed an opportunity to humiliate him. The two men were fundamentally different characters. Claudius had spent his formative years in the palace reading widely, and writing. History was his particular love, and he seems to have developed a genuine affection for Roman antiquity. But, like Caligula, he had no real experience of political life, and reportedly found the company of senators difficult. Having no power base among the senatorial classes, he naturally turned for advice to the freed slaves who administered the increasingly complex affairs of the imperial household, which controlled vast territories throughout the empire. In modern terms, Claudius can be seen as a technocrat, valuing the company of other people who knew how to get things done. Conversely, his abiding weakness was his lack of political guile in not recognizing that many of those who served him did so not in order to further the public good but for their own ends.

Achievements and setbacks

Claudius was also keen to demonstrate to a sceptical Roman senate and people that he was a strong and decisive leader. So it was that in AD 43, two years after coming to power, he organized a highly efficient invasion of Britain, winning kudos for capturing a prize that had even eluded Julius Caesar, in whom Claudius seems to have been particularly interested. The operation itself was meticulously planned and executed by Claudius' skilled commander, Aulus Plautius. Four legions and several auxiliary units amounting to some 40,000 men took part in the assault. Plautius quickly succeeded in establishing a bridgehead on the island. The decisive battle took place at the River Medway in southeast England, where the Batavian auxiliaries, recruited from the area at the mouth of the Rhine, outflanked the Britons under King Caractacus after fording the river in full battle gear. After two days, the Britons were defeated and the Romans gained a firm foothold from which they began the long process of pacifying the island. That process would take nearly half a century because, despite Claudius' success in achieving his initial military and strategic objectives, the occupation – as always happens with military operations motivated by short-term political ambitions – turned out to be a costly and protracted affair with no thought-out endgame.

The ultimate costs and consequences of the invasion were not in view when Claudius hurried north to share in the glory of his forces as they completed their victory, and even gave his son the honorific 'Britannicus' (offered to Claudius himself by the senate, but refused) in commemoration of the triumph. Meanwhile, at Rome, the highly competent freedmen he appointed as secretaries of state also ensured that the administration of Rome and her empire ran smoothly. One of his most impressive public works projects was the construction of the vital new commercial port of Portus north of Ostia at the mouth of the River Tiber (another project initially conceived by Julius Caesar). Linked by canal to the Tiber, Portus could handle year-round shipments of the grain needed to make bread, the staple of the Roman diet.

It was only in the later 40s that Claudius' turbulent private life began seriously to compromise the achievements of his administration. Claudius gradually became estranged from Messalina, his third wife, who was much younger than him. He took slave mistresses, and she in turn took lovers of her own. Messalina's licentious conduct began to scandalize Rome; there were rumours that she spent an evening in a brothel seeing if she could make love to more men than an experienced prostitute. In AD 48, while Claudius was out of town, she even went through a mock wedding ceremony with one of her partners, Gaius Silius. It is possible that the pair were plotting to usurp the emperor's power, or that they were simply set on defying the conventions of popular morality. In any event, the incident galvanized Claudius into drastic action, and Messalina was summarily executed along with several of her lovers.

Heeding the advice of his freedmen, Claudius took a new bride straight away, and his choice fell on his niece Agrippina. The relationship was plainly incestuous, but Claudius had the law changed to accommodate his wishes. Agrippina moved into the palace with her son Nero (AD 37–68), who was three years older than Britannicus. A highly ambitious woman from impeccable stock (her grandfather by adoption was Augustus and her father Germanicus), Agrippina made sure that Nero was introduced to public life, and soon amassed enormous power for herself within Claudius' *domus*. She realized that Britannicus could not legally succeed Claudius until he had reached manhood at the age of 14 in February, AD 55. In late AD 54 she arranged for Claudius to be fed poisonous mushrooms at a banquet. Nero was proclaimed emperor at the tender age of 16, and Britannicus was poisoned a few months later. The people and especially the senate, many of whose members had been unable to penetrate the charmed circle of freedmen who enjoyed Claudius' confidence, greeted the news of Nero's accession with delight.

The last of the Julio-Claudians

It took some time for it to emerge that Nero's appointment as emperor was a disaster. Initially, he had little interest in governing and left effective control of the state in the hands of competent people handpicked for the task by his mother. This enabled him to devote himself to the pursuits he favoured – he fancied himself a poet and actor. The reins of power were held at this time by the famous Spanish-Roman philosopher and man of letters Seneca the Younger (4 BC–AD 65) who was Nero's former tutor, and the praetorian prefect Sextus Afranius Burrus (d. AD 62). A clear measure of their practical competence was their appointment of a seasoned and gifted soldier, Domitius Corbulo (AD 7–67), to take charge of a new conflict that had arisen with the Parthians over control of Armenia. Corbulo acquitted himself well in this role.

Nero fiercely resisted any attempts by others to regulate his private life. As part of his mother's succession project, he had been persuaded to marry Claudius' daughter Octavia, whom he found deeply uncongenial. As emperor he began to take concubines and play the field of senatorial women. Agrippina, who was well aware that such conduct had precipitated her brother Caligula's fall from grace with the Roman people, signalled her disapproval. Nero soon tired of his mother's interference, and communication between them broke down almost totally. It was at this point that Nero first met Poppaea Sabina, the granddaughter of one of Tiberius' generals, and a woman of powerful personality.

He planned to divorce Octavia and make Poppaea his wife. Agrippina and the senior advisers counselled against this; Octavia was a valuable symbol of stability and continuity. Nero's response was to seek other counsel and hatch a plot to kill his mother.

In AD 59 Nero arranged for Agrippina to take a trip across the Bay of Naples on a boat that had been sabotaged so that its stern, where she would be seated, would break off during the voyage and sink. Yet Nero had failed to take into account that his mother was a strong swimmer. Having made it safely back to shore, the empress was an object of pity to the crowd that assembled as she dragged herself on to the beach. Her son showed no mercy. Learning of her escape, he planted a dagger on her freedman and, concocting a story that she had in fact planned to kill him, sent a detachment of guards to detain Agrippina and put her to death.

The murder of Agrippina changed everything. Seneca's and Burrus' influence instantly began to wane, as Nero's megalomania took a firm hold. Seneca was fired in AD 60, while Burrus died a year later. Octavia was falsely accused of adultery, divorced and executed around the same time that Seneca was dismissed. Poppaea was installed as empress, and a man named Tigellinus (d. AD 69), previously a supplier of chariot horses for the circus, joined Nero's inner circle. Tigellinus would prove a loyal confederate in encouraging the worst of Nero's vices, and was rewarded in AD 62 by being made prefect of the praetorian guard.

Meanwhile, the foundations of the empire began to totter. In AD 60, a violent revolt broke out in Britain, led by Boudicca (d. AD 60/61), the queen of the Iceni tribe. Our chief source for information about Boudicca's revolt in AD 60–61, Tacitus, exonerates the senatorial governor of Britannia (who also happened to be employing Tacitus' future father-in-law on his staff at the time), blaming the incident instead on the arrogance and brutality of the province's equestrian bureaucracy. According to Tacitus, when King Prasutagus of the Iceni in East Anglia, Boudicca's husband, died, a dispute arose over what portion of his kingdom Rome was entitled to claim, since the king had made his two daughters and the emperor Nero co-beneficiaries of his will. In stepped the imperial procurator Decianus Catus while the governor, Suetonius Paulinus, was away on campaign in Wales, to enforce Rome's will in a heavy-handed manner. Boudicca was beaten, and her daughters were raped.

Boudicca's cruel treatment ignited the powder-keg of British resentment of the occupation. The founding of the settlement at Camulodunum (Colchester) incensed both the Trinovates, in whose territory the colony was forcibly implanted, and the Iceni, their neighbours to the north. Inspired by hatred of all that was Roman, Boudicca's forces attacked Camulodunum, Verulamium (St Albans) and Londinium (London). The sheer scale of the destruction at these sites that has been unearthed by archaeologists testifies to the Britons' desire to expunge the physical creations of Roman rule, and slaughter all those who supported it. Early in the revolt her forces also crushed a Roman force sent from Lincoln to relieve Colchester. She was less fortunate when she met Suetonius Paulinus' main force somewhere in the Midlands. Her army was destroyed, and Tacitus says that she committed suicide shortly thereafter.

Four years later disaster struck closer to home, when a fire destroyed most of Rome. The Roman version of disaster planning was sketchy, and relief efforts were not coordinated by Nero, who allegedly reacted very badly to news of the conflagration: it is said that he recited a poem on the fall of Troy even though his 'press office' claimed that he was instrumental in fighting the fire. Nero found a convenient scapegoat for the fire in the form of a minor religious sect – the Christians. Followers of this faith were subjected to hideous tortures for their alleged guilt, including being covered in animal skins and having dogs set upon them, crucifixion, and being burned alive.

Nero's regime lurched from crisis to crisis. A year after the fire, in a fit of rage, Nero kicked his wife Poppaea Sabina in the stomach while she was pregnant, causing her death. That same year, a conspiracy was uncovered among members of the senate and the guard to kill the emperor and install a new ruler. A round of executions followed, and Tigellinus and his confederates took advantage of the situation to settle old scores. Seneca was forced to commit suicide, and within the year other enemies were arraigned on trumped-up charges. In this orgy of bloodletting, Nero's advisers blundered by charging Corbulo, the all-conquering hero of the Parthian War, with treason and executing him. Yet Corbulo had many influential friends and admirers in Rome. In AD 67, when Nero left for Greece to demonstrate his skill as a charioteer in the Olympic Games (which were rescheduled to fit round his visit), a serious conspiracy arose among various generals and governors.

Nero's Greek trip was a great success, and he was crowned victor in all the events he entered. However, he was immediately summoned back to Rome by a letter from his freedmen warning him of the conspiracy. Nero arrived too late to change the course of events. In March, AD 68, the governor of one of the Gallic provinces proclaimed his loyalty to the Roman government rather than to Nero; the governor of Judea, who commanded a powerful army assembled to suppress the revolt that had broken out there in AD 66, suddenly suspended military operations, and Galba, the governor of a Spanish province, had himself proclaimed emperor. The commander of the major army in Germany switched sides to support Galba. Within Rome itself a fifth column was at work, which enjoyed the support of the praetorian guard. Its commanders may have grown weary of Nero and taken the pragmatic view that their troops were no match for a seasoned provincial army. On 9 June, AD 68, the guard declared for Galba and the senate deposed Nero, declaring him an enemy of the state. Nero fled the palace, making for the house of a freedman named Phaon, not knowing that Phaon had already betrayed him. As he heard his captors approach, Nero stabbed himself to death. Vain and deluded to the last, the emperor's reported last words were 'How great an artist dies with me!'

TWO

Caesars and Their Subjects

New Dynasties: From the Flavians to the Antonines

(AD 68–180)

Between the deaths of Nero (AD 68) and Marcus Aurelius (AD 180), the century or so of stability that the Roman empire brought to regions under its control remains an astonishing achievement. While peace and prosperity were by no means universal, most crises were, by the standards of earlier and later eras, relatively short. One major exception to the general *pax Romana* was the province of Judea, covering the territory of the modern state of Israel, plus parts of Jordan and Syria. There, two major revolts, in AD 66–73 and AD 132–135, caused terrible destruction and loss of life.

Sixteen centuries later, at the start of his magisterial six-volume work *Decline and Fall of the Roman Empire* (1776–88), the English historian Edward Gibbon famously summarized this era in the following terms:

> If a man were called to fix the period in the history of the world, during which the condition of the human race was most happy and prosperous, he would, without hesitation, name that which elapsed from the death of Domitian to the accession of Commodus. The vast extent of the Roman Empire was governed by absolute power, under the guidance of virtue and wisdom. The

> armies were restrained by the firm but gentle hand of four successive emperors, whose characters and authority commanded involuntary respect. The forms of the civil administration were carefully preserved by Nerva, Trajan, Hadrian and the Antonines, who delighted in the image of liberty, and were pleased with considering themselves as the accountable ministers of the laws. Such princes deserved the honour of restoring the republic had the Romans of their days been capable of enjoying a rational freedom.

Context is everything. First, Gibbon was writing at a time when the burgeoning British empire was facing insurrection in its American colonies; the didactic thrust of his work was that governance must always proceed from civic virtue – a lesson that later rulers of the Roman empire forgot at their peril as, by implication, would the ministers of his own time. Second, the Enlightenment, with its stress on reason and order, which informed Gibbon's approach to his subject, followed on the heels of more than two centuries of turmoil in Europe marked by a succession of wars of religion and dynastic succession. Gibbon's glowing appraisal of this period of Roman history was tempered by his awareness that even the best of empires emerge from conflict and secure happiness for the many at the cost of the few. It is against this background that the accomplishment of the second century AD needs to be set.

Three brief reigns

It is unlikely that anyone in Rome in AD 68–69 would have predicted a century of stability. After Nero's suicide, a vacuum had opened up at the heart of the empire. It was filled by civil war – the first Rome had seen since the bloody struggle between Octavian and Mark Antony in 32–30 BC – and a succession of military pretenders, each of whose reigns lasted months rather than years. So ephemeral was their hold on power that AD 69 is remembered as the 'Year of the Four Emperors'. Servius Sulpicius Galba (3 BC–AD 69), a former general and consul, was governor of the province of Hispania Tarraconensis in AD 68. His rise to power was not the result of a determined campaign, or indeed decisive action of any kind on his part. On the contrary, he vacillated when Julius Vindex, leader of the first major revolt against Nero in AD 68, announced that Galba was his chosen candidate to succeed Nero. It was only when he was certain that the praetorian prefect had declared in his favour that he marched to Rome. Galba had no outstanding leadership qualities or populist flair, and in his brief reign earned a reputation for being callous, mean and snobbish. One likely explanation for his succession was that ambitious men in the army and senate backed his appointment as a stop-gap measure, calculating that, aged 71 and with no children, he would be sure to die before long and leave the field open for more dynamic personalities. As it turned out, his demise actually came far sooner than anyone expected.

Galba was far along the path to self-destruction even

before he entered Rome in September AD 68. Despite the fact that his position depended entirely upon military backing, he set about alienating key elements of the army. During Nero's vain attempt to muster forces to crush the growing rebellion against his rule, he had raised a legion from marines serving in the fleet in the Bay of Naples, promising these irregular troops equal pay to that received by regular legionaries. Galba now refused to honour this pledge and executed those who protested. In his dogged concern to get state finances back on an even keel at all costs, he even countermanded loyalty payments due to the praetorians who had ensured his rise to power. At the same time, he lost the support of the army of southern Germany (Germania Superior) by removing its popular commander, Verginius Rufus (AD 14–97). Verginius had been responsible for putting down Vindex's revolt against Nero, whereupon the army offered him the throne. He refused and offered his services to Galba. Galba probably owed his life to this decision, but was less than gracious. The soldiery regarded the dismissal of Verginius and his replacement by a nonentity as a calculated insult.

Trouble on the horizon

Meanwhile, changes were also afoot in the army stationed in Rome's other German province (Germania Inferior). Unwisely, in late AD 68, Galba appointed the ambitious Aulus Vitellius (AD 15–69), whose father had been Claudius' closest associate, to reimpose discipline on this force after their previous commander was murdered. Vitellius immediately began to manoeuvre himself into a position to seize power.

Perceiving that Galba was weak, and that the army in Germany had been insufficiently rewarded for its break with Nero, he ingratiated himself with the general staff in Colonia Agrippina (Cologne). Moreover, even before leaving Rome he had taken a sword that had once belonged to Julius Caesar from the temple of the Divine Julius. The fact that he was allowed to remove such a powerful symbolic trophy was a sign that he had lost no time in organizing an efficient fifth column in the capital. On 1 January, AD 69 matters came to a head when the legions at Mainz in Germania Superior refused to swear loyalty to Galba and smashed his statues. The next day the armies of both German provinces proclaimed Vitellius their new emperor.

Typically, Galba's response was to dither and, equally characteristically, to make an enemy of another erstwhile ally, Marcus Salvius Otho (AD 32–69). This Etruscan nobleman, prominent among the libertines who surrounded Nero, had once been involved in a wife-swapping arrangement with Nero – he had married Poppaea Sabina on the understanding that Nero would sleep with her until he could get rid of Octavia – and allegedly instructed Nero in the art of foot perfuming. Then, it seems, Otho had fallen in love with Poppaea himself, with the result that Nero forced him to divorce her and sent him to govern Lusitania (modern Portugal). Accordingly, he had every reason to support Galba during the revolution, and joined him on his march to Rome. This loyalty, plus an astrological prediction that he would be the next emperor, encouraged him in the belief that Galba would name him his successor. However, his hopes were dashed when Galba adopted the young Lucius Calpurnius

Piso (d. AD 69) as his heir on January 10. Galba's decision was motivated by sheer snobbery; despite Otho's pedigree, Piso was the scion of an indisputably nobler house, counting Pompey, Crassus and Calpurnia, Julius Caesar's last wife, amongst his ancestors. The appointment galvanized Otho into high-speed plotting. On 15 January the praetorian guard and other troops stationed in Rome declared Otho emperor. Galba panicked and set off across the Forum to confront the rebels, but was instantly cut down by Otho's men. The unfortunate Piso was tracked to the temple of Vesta, where he had taken sanctuary, dragged out, and butchered.

While these dramatic events were unfolding, Vitellius' legions were on the march from Germany to Rome to install their man as emperor. In the meantime, Otho managed to muster a strong enough force from Nero's former troops, gladiators and the praetorian guard to mount a credible defence against a force that represented the cream of the Roman army. His wider strategy was to hold Vitellius' advance units long enough to enable him to call up reinforcements from the province of Illyricum in the Balkans. The holding action failed when Vitellius' army defeated Otho's men in a hard-fought engagement at the Battle of Bedriacum outside Cremona.When he learned of the defeat, Otho committed suicide on 16 April to spare Rome further mayhem. His reign had lasted barely three months.

Vitellius reached the capital at the start of June and began the process of establishing his own regime in the face of serious opposition. In particular, Vespasian (Titus Flavius Vespasianus; AD 9–79), a first-generation senator, he had displayed considerable ability as a soldier during Claudius' invasion of Britain and had been appointed commander of the force sent to pacify Judea during the Great Jewish Revolt, disputed Vitellius' appointment. He rapidly garnered support among the eastern garrisons. On 1 July, AD 69, Vespasian was proclaimed emperor by the Roman army occupying Egypt, and the armies in Judea and Syria swiftly followed suit. This was a powerful military coalition, and Vespasian's campaign soon gained momentum among other units closer to Rome. The Balkan legions in the provinces of Pannonia, Illyricum and Moesia, fearing retribution for their support of Otho, soon declared for Vespasian (moreover, in some cases, they were commanded by men with strong links to the eastern commanders, having served under Corbulo).

Faced with this growing rebellion, Vitellius tried to hedge his bets. He dispatched his main force to northern Italy to confront Vespasian, but at the same time kept potential sources of mediation in play by not arresting either Vespasian's brother Sabinus or his younger son, the future emperor Domitian. Even so, his position became increasingly untenable. Vespasian's army crushed his legions on almost exactly the same spot where Vitellius had earlier defeated the forces of Otho and then marched on Rome. During the fierce battle for the city, Domitian and Sabinus took refuge in the temple of Capitoline Jupiter, Rome's most sacred monument. Domitian managed to escape, but Sabinus was captured by Vitellius' troops and killed despite Vitellius' efforts to save his life. When Vespasian's men finally secured control of Rome, they were no more merciful, stabbing Vitellius to death and hurling his body into the Tiber. Vespasian was proclaimed emperor while he was still at Caesarea in Judea. It is a mark of how heavily Roman emperors had come to rely on the army as a power broker that Vespasian dated his rule not from when the Roman people voted to confirm his installation but from 1 July, AD 69, when his troops acclaimed him.

The Flavian dynasty

On the face of it, the start of Vespasian's reign was highly inauspicious. He lacked a noble lineage; neither his former wife, the daughter of an obscure Roman equestrian, nor the freedwoman lover who replaced her were well connected. This freedwoman, Caenis, was the same person who in AD 31 had warned Tiberius of Sejanus' plot and who, according to rumour, had also shielded Vespasian from Nero's wrath on several occasions (for instance, when he dared to doze off during one of Nero's recitals). Yet Roman high society still looked down on her as a former slave. Compounding Vespasian's problems, the destruction of the temple of Jupiter during the assault on Rome portended the ruination of the city in the eyes of its superstitious inhabitants.

Away from Rome, things also augured badly for Vespasian. Judea was still in flames, and a massive rebellion had broken out on the Rhine, as the Germanic auxiliaries turned on the legions that Vitellius had left behind. At the same time, the first of three fraudsters who tried to capitalize on whisperings that Nero was still alive appeared in the Aegean region, playing a lyre and claiming to be the emperor. Yet Vespasian was made of sterner stuff than Galba. Leaving his son Titus to deal with the revolt in Judea, he travelled from Judea to Rome to put things in order. Titus moved on Jerusalem in the summer of AD 70, subjecting the city to a close blockade – during which many of its inhabitants starved to death – before launching the final assaults that progressively occupied the city from July to September. Most of Jerusalem was ransacked and burned, including, most devastatingly for the Jewish people, the Second Temple. The day on which this desecration took place, August 29 – known as Tisha B'Av in the Jewish calendar – is often referred to as the 'saddest day in Jewish history'. The fall of Jerusalem marked the official end of the war, which was celebrated with a massive triumph at Rome in AD 71, even though fighting continued until the then governor, Flavius Silva, laid siege to Masada in AD 73–74, building an enormous rampart with Jewish slave labour that enabled the attackers to position a siege tower against the walls. When the defensive walls were breached, the defenders of Masada committed mass suicide rather than fall into Roman hands.

The tragic and dramatic events of these years have left powerful reminders to this day. At Rome itself, in AD 80, the emperor Domitian commemorated his deceased elder brother's sack of Jerusalem by erecting the Arch of Titus (the model for all subsequent such edifices, such as the Arc de Triomphe in Paris), which still stands on the Via Sacra south of the Forum in Rome. In Jerusalem, the Wailing Wall on the Temple Mount is all that survives of the Temple destroyed during the Roman assault, while at Masada the siege rampart can still be seen along with the outlines of Roman camps in the valley. Since the founding of the modern state of Israel in 1948, the defence of Masada has become a powerful symbol of national identity and absolute determination to resist invasion. Troops of the country's armed forces attend swearing-in ceremonies on the plateau, during which they take the vow that 'Masada Shall Never Fall Again'.

Much less memorable today, though more serious at the time, was the revolt along the Rhine. The situation became ever more threatening in the first half of AD 70 when the rebels compelled the surrender of two Roman legions, and a wave of religious fanaticism, ably exploited by leaders of the revolt, encouraged people to think that the empire's days were numbered. Vespasian, however, proved equal to the task, sending his nephew to suppress the revolt on the Rhine, which he accomplished successfully before the end of the year. Vespasian could then concentrate on forging a genuinely warm relationship with the people of the capital.

A safe pair of hands

Vespasian had an unusual profile for a Roman emperor: he had two grown sons, worked hard at the job, and lived in a stable relationship with a woman he clearly loved. A first-rate soldier, his reputation for *virtus* had been earned on the battlefield as a legionary commander in Claudius' invasion of Britain in AD 43, and was confirmed by his sure handling of the hitherto chaotic Roman response to the Jewish revolt. The new emperor's domestic lifestyle was austere by the standards of the Julio-Claudians after Augustus. Perhaps the most obvious sign of Vespasian's new approach was his decision to tear down the Golden House of Nero and build a vast amphitheatre in place of an artificial lake that Nero had constructed within his palace. Although the official name of this new building was the Flavian Amphitheatre, it would become known to later generations as the Colosseum. This massive structure, which takes its modern name from the colossal statue of the Sun God that once stood next to it, was conceived as a monument commemorating the suppression of the Jewish revolt, which had finally came to an end after Flavius Silva captured Masada in AD 74.

Vespasian consciously strove to present himself as a ruler in the tradition of Augustus. In particular, he eschewed government through a coterie of favourites among the palace staff, the style of rule that was favoured by his immediate predecessors in the post. Rather, in the manner of Augustus, his closest advisers were drawn from the senatorial and equestrian orders, and he was not afraid to promote people of genuine ability irrespective of their background. A good example of his egalitarian attitude was the promotion of Ulpius Traianus (*c.* AD 30–100), a Spaniard of Roman descent who had commanded a legion during the Jewish revolt, to supreme commander of the eastern provinces.

In AD 79, after ten years of energetic and generally successful rule, Vespasian died, just before completion of the Colosseum. It was Titus (AD 39–81), his eldest son and successor, who inaugurated the new amphitheatre in AD 80 with one hundred days of spectacular games. This is one of the defining moments of Titus' brief reign. The other took place barely two months after his accession, when Mount Vesuvius, which dominates the Bay of Naples, erupted. The disaster was monumental. By the first century AD, the fertility of the surrounding region had attracted many people to settle and farm there, and major towns like Pompeii (population *c.* 15,000) and Herculaneum (*c.* 5,000) had grown up around the mountain's lower slopes. On the afternoon of 24 August, AD 79, after four days of minor foreshocks, the volcano exploded. For 19 hours, Vesuvius rained lava, rubble and volcanic ash over the surrounding region, completely burying Pompeii and Herculaneum, the one in volcanic ash, the other in a fiery mudslide, while killing an unknown number of their inhabitants.

One of the most prominent victims of the disaster was the author and naval commander Pliny the Elder, who was then in command of the Roman fleet at nearby Misenum and who went to investigate the eruption at close hand. He was killed by what vulcanologists now call 'pyroclastic flow', a cloud of superheated, choking gas. His nephew, Pliny the Younger, provided a detailed account of his death:

> My uncle perished in a catastrophe which destroyed the loveliest regions of the earth, a fate shared by whole cities and their people. On 24 August, my mother drew his attention to a cloud of unusual size and appearance . . . He changed his plan and what he had begun in a spirit of enquiry he completed as a hero . . . the dense fumes choked his breathing by blocking his windpipe . . . When daylight returned on the 26th, his body was found intact and uninjured, still fully clothed and looking more like sleep than death.

Many of the citizens of the towns destroyed by the eruption – which were abandoned and never rebuilt – were found in the same state as Pliny the Elder when the settlements were rediscovered in the 1740s. The ash-fall deposits that covered Pompeii preserved the people, houses and artifacts in remarkable condition. The site has yielded a wealth of information to archaeologists and historians on how the Romans of the first century AD lived. Titus himself responded as a good ruler should, visiting the scene of the disaster twice, and reportedly spent large amounts of his personal wealth on relief for the victims. This and his similar efforts following a major fire in Rome the next year helped endear him to his subjects, who mourned his loss when he succumbed to a fever on 13 September, AD 81.

Domitian (AD 51–96), the younger brother of Titus, was a very different sort of person from his father and brother. Although he retained many of Vespasian's advisers, his relationship with the court and the senate was strained by his overweening sense of imperial grandeur mixed with an unappetizing tendency to prurient self-righteousness. The former trait was manifest in his insistence on being addressed as 'master and god', an extreme variation of the polite Roman form of address *dominus* ('master', or simply 'sir'). The latter came to the fore when he assumed the title of censor for life in AD 84 and used this position to conduct several high-profile investigations into sex scandals. One of his witch-hunts resulted in two Vestal Virgins being buried alive when it was found that they had not lived up to their vows of purity. Yet, like many self-appointed guardians of public morality, Domitian's own conduct was far from beyond reproach.

Despite his personal shortcomings, Domitian retained the loyalty of the military, both in Rome and the provinces, while his dependence upon men who had risen to prominence under Vespasian protected entrenched interests. The army soon found itself busy along the northern borders of the empire, as Domitian annexed fresh territory north of the Rhine and embarked on a series of wars against the powerful Dacian kingdom (occupying roughly the area of modern Romania) that dragged on for almost 20 years. By the end of the AD 80s, however, discontent with his reign was beginning to translate into practical action, including an unsuccessful assassination attempt and a major revolt by the governor of Lower Germany. The revolt was rapidly and brutally put down, but Domitian now grew ever more suspicious of people outside his immediate circle. These problems were compounded in AD 92 when two legions were routed by the Dacians, a crushing defeat that left the Danubian provinces open to invasion until a new expeditionary force restored order.

During this crisis, Domitian ordered the execution of several critics of his regime, both real and perceived. His high-handed actions outraged many in the senate who, along with palace functionaries, plotted his removal. On 18 September, AD 96, the chief of the palace domestic staff stabbed the emperor to death.

A sense of relief

The death of Domitian was greeted with unbridled joy by the senate, which immediately expunged his name from all the public monuments he had built. The praetorian guard was less than ecstatic, however, and it was only the intervention of its commanders and the senate's promise of a generous 'gift', or *donativum,* that ensured the troops' support for the accession of the next emperor, Marcus Cocceius Nerva (AD 30–98). An elderly and well-respected senator, Nerva was the senate's candidate for the position and seems, like Galba before him, to have mainly owed his elevation to emperor to his age and childless state. Yet unlike Galba, he was alive to the necessity of maintaining the goodwill of the military, and promptly acceded to the praetorians' demands when they took to the streets, calling for the execution of Domitian's murderers.

Nerva was also aware that he had to choose a successor who would be acceptable to the army, and so named as his heir the commander of the legions in Upper Germany, the son of Vespasian's old marshal, Ulpius Traianus. His adoption of the younger Traianus – or Trajan as he is commonly known in English – brought a measure of stability to the political scene for the remaining year of Nerva's life. In addition to making an intelligent choice of successor, he endeared himself to the upper classes by discouraging prosecutions for treason, which had become something of a political game under Domitian, and granted amnesties to opponents of his predecessor who had been exiled. He died of a fever on 27 January, AD 98; his restrained use of power retrospectively earned him the accolade of being regarded as the first of the 'Five Good Emperors' who ruled Rome from AD 96 to 180.

Trajan proved a spectacularly good choice. Like Vespasian, he had worked his way up through the ranks, beginning with the minor official tasks that senators were given at the start of their careers and then holding subordinate commands in the legions before taking up more senior posts in Rome, where he was appointed consul in AD 91. Trajan's well-earned and growing reputation for efficiency constantly recommended him for higher office. Finally he commanded legions and governed provinces. By the time he became emperor, the 44-year-old Trajan knew the business of government inside out.

At the time of Nerva's death, Trajan was in Lower Germany. News of his succession was brought to him by the future emperor Hadrian, then assigned to the army in Germany, but, ever the professional soldier, Trajan was in no hurry to return to Rome. In fact, he only arrived in the capital in AD 100, where he immediately set to work altering the cityscape. On land next to the Roman forum, a new forum began to take shape that would ultimately house a vast library and the ancient equivalent of a shopping mall. At the same time, Trajan also began an extensive reconstruction of the Circus Maximus, the great arena for chariot racing. Augustus had installed marble seating on the lower courses, and Trajan now extended this over the entire structure. In conjunction with the earlier Colosseum, these two new major public-works projects now effectively surrounded the traditional heart of Rome with buildings put up solely for the benefit of the Roman people – a physical sign of continuity with Vespasian's regime and of the emperor's devotion to the welfare of his subjects.

Within the *domus*, Trajan's conduct seems largely to have coincided with the civic virtue that marked his public persona. Although the third-century historian Dio Cassius reports that he was given to excessive drinking and enjoyed the sexual company of boys, he was hard-working and imbued his staff with a sense that the 'spirit of his age' – a phrase that appears several times in the letters he exchanged with a governor in northwestern Turkey – required his officials to exercise wise government. These officials were charged with ensuring that rivalries between local politicians did not get out of hand, that town councils did not waste money on useless projects and that the administration of justice was honest. One of his appointments was that of the eminent senator and historian Tacitus to govern Asia in AD 112–13. Trajan also seems to have allowed those he trusted most a great deal of latitude, recalling Vespasian's treatment of his own father, and Augustus' management of the empire as a collective enterprise.

Within the palace, Trajan balanced the interests of senior officers with those of his family, which were dictated by Pompeia Plotina, the most powerful empress since Livia. Plotina was the power behind the throne, cleverly forging close relationships with senior functionaries while maintaining the trust of her spouse. Like many other Roman imperial matriarchs before her, her principal aim was to secure dynastic preferment for a close relative. She ensured that Hadrian, Trajan's nephew and the husband of her niece, Sabina, gained enough experience in government that he would be fit to succeed as emperor if she failed to bear Trajan a son (which, given that she was already in her 40s when Trajan came to power, did indeed turn out to be the case).

Trajan's Dacian campaign

Trajan did not have an expansionist agenda at the outset, but found himself obliged to counter an immediate threat to the empire from north of the Danube. After Decebalus, king of the Dacians (reigned AD 87–106), attacked Roman territory in AD 101, he instantly found himself the target of a Roman punitive expedition. By the beginning of AD 103, his armies were so badly beaten that he reluctantly accepted peace terms making him a subject of Rome. But in AD 105 he broke the treaty, with devastating results both for himself and for his people. Within two years Dacia, essentially modern Romania, was made a province, and Decebalus committed suicide to avoid capture by a detachment of Roman cavalry. His severed head was later displayed in Rome on the steps leading up to the Capitol.

The most striking account of the Dacian Wars is not a written record but a visual one – Trajan's Column, a 30-metre (100-ft) high marble pillar erected in AD 113. The location of the column, as visitors to Rome can see, is the forum of Trajan, east of the Roman Forum (near the Quirinal Hill), which took shape, with great speed, in the years after the Dacian war. In its entirety it stands as a powerful symbolic expression of Trajan's values. The forum's design, by the Greek engineer and architect Apollodorus of Damascus, now consists of five main elements: the column celebrating the Dacian wars, two libraries (one Greek, the other Latin), the massive Basilica Ulpia and the Temple of the Divine Trajan, probably a later addition – it is not situated at the centre of the forum but behind the Basilica Ulpia. As a group, these diverse structures serve to emphasize the military virtues of Trajan, and his belief in Greco-Roman culture as the pinnacle of civilization. With its spiral relief carvings telling the story of the Dacian Wars, the column offers the most detailed surviving picture of the Roman army on campaign, and of the central role played by the emperor. Trajan is shown no fewer than 59 times, engaged in various activities: offering sacrifices, returning in triumph to Rome, addressing his army, rallying the troops in battle and rewarding them for their victories. Another notable feature of the column is the picture it paints of the Roman army as a civilizing force – building bridges, cities and forts during its pacification of Dacia. After Trajan's death in AD 117, the senate voted to have his ashes interred in an urn in the column's pedestal.

Even as the Dacian Wars were ending, the king of Arabia died and Trajan decided that it was time to absorb this long-standing Roman client state directly into the empire. Trajan's annexation of Arabia (roughly the area of modern Jordan) as a province in AD 106 completed a process begun by his father Marcus Ulpius Traianus, who had incorporated many of Rome's client states around Syria into the provincial structure of the empire under Vespasian. A century of contact with Roman administration in these regions had stimulated growing urbanization, which in turn made them more viable areas where direct Roman rule could be applied.

If Trajan's Dacian Wars were motivated by a concern to preserve the security of the empire, it is hard to interpret his massive invasion of the Parthian empire in AD 113 as anything other than military adventurism. Following a plan of campaign likely inherited from the last days of Julius Caesar's reign, Trajan set out from Armenia and headed south into Mesopotamia (Iraq), capturing the western Parthian capital of Ctesiphon (near modern Baghdad) in AD 115. This was a major triumph, but it was to be short-lived. To the rear of Trajan's invasion force, the Jewish population of Cyrenaica (the North African coast west of Egypt), Egypt, Palestine and other border regions suddenly rose up against their Roman overlords, apparently inspired by messianic visions of the world's end. In Mesopotamia itself, the eruption of fierce insurgencies a year after the Jewish revolt convinced Trajan that the best he could hope for was to install puppet governments in former satellite kingdoms of the Parthian empire, so that any regime filling the power vacuum in Ctesiphon after Roman withdrawal would be too weak to pose a threat to Rome. He then began a fighting retreat, crushing rebel forces wherever he encountered them, and sending large detachments west to smash the Jewish revolts, a task they carried out with extreme brutality.

A legitimate successor?

As Trajan returned to the west in AD 117 he suddenly fell ill on the southern coast of Turkey and died on 9 August. Hadrian (AD 76–138), then governor of Syria, succeeded to the throne. While he was the only possible heir from within the imperial household, it appears that Trajan may have toyed with the idea of appointing someone else as his successor. Significantly, perhaps, Hadrian may only have been adopted as Trajan's son – thus putting his claim beyond all dispute

– as Trajan lay dying. Or possibly not; there were whispers that Pompeia Plotina had slipped a servant into Trajan's deathbed to impersonate the emperor and planned to make the announcement after the real Trajan had passed away without naming a successor. The rumour reflects serious tensions that were on the verge of erupting between senior generals and the royal household. Within months, even before Hadrian returned to Rome, four of Trajan's leading generals who were suspected of conspiring against Hadrian had been executed.

The executions shocked the political establishment, but effectively drove home the message that the new emperor would not tolerate dissent in any shape or form. A man of powerful intellect, Hadrian viewed officials as lackeys rather than colleagues and dealt firmly with anything he perceived as insubordination. The palace staff received warning of his imperious attitude when he fired two senior officials, a praetorian prefect and the biographer Suetonius (*c.* AD 69–*c.* 130), then his chief secretary for correspondence in Latin, for excessive familiarity with his wife Vibia Sabina. Since these dismissals occurred in AD 122, while Hadrian was in Britain, it may be that he suspected his wife of trying to assume a similar role to that played by Plotina in Trajan's court. Sabina herself was publicly embarrassed by this event, when Hadrian declared that he would have divorced her if he had had the freedom permitted to private individuals. Similarly, when a poet recited some lines suggesting that he was thankful that he wasn't following the emperor on what he portrayed as lice-ridden journeys around the empire, Hadrian responded with a poem of his own lambasting the poet as a lazy wastrel.

Another sign of Hadrian's impatience with the political establishment was his desire to be absent from Rome as much as possible; more than half of his reign was spent outside Italy. Even when he was in Italy, he preferred to stay not in the capital but in the massive villa that he built for himself at Tivoli. His overt intellectualism and dislike of senatorial life are somewhat reminiscent of Tiberius, a parallel reinforced by his intense interest in astrology. Like Tiberius, he was also concerned to consolidate and develop the empire's existing holdings rather than wage new wars of conquest.

The great wall that Hadrian ordered built across northern Britain from AD 122 onwards was as much a sign to his own people that the province's borders were set, as it was to the Caledonian tribes north of the wall (the Picts and Scots) that he had no interest in forcibly bringing them under the aegis of Roman rule. The wall itself is one of the most dramatic surviving monuments of Roman rule, extending 73 miles (117 kilometres) from Wallsend on Britain's east coast to Bowness-on-Solway in the west. Many sections of it are still standing, and it is likely Hadrian himself surveyed the line of the wall during his visit to northern Britain as construction was being planned.

For a distance of 42 miles (67 kilometres), the eastern end of the wall was built in stone, ten feet thick and about thirteen and a half feet high; the western portion was made of turf, roughly nineteen and a half feet wide at the base and ten and a half feet high. Small castles were set in the wall at each Roman mile (hence their name, 'milecastles'), while watchtowers were erected every third of a mile. Three legions were involved in the construction of the wall, and the design of each milecastle varies according to which legion built it. Nineteen feet to the north of the wall was a forward defensive ditch, the *vallum*; in most places, this measured ten feet deep by twenty-six and a half feet wide. A further series of 12 full-sized forts – the number was later increased to 17 – was built south of the wall, as was a second, slightly less extensive, *vallum*. The total garrison of the wall and its supporting forts typically comprised some 9,000 men.

Other similar walls, made of wood and turf rather than stone, were also constructed along the frontiers of Rome's German provinces, and it was during Hadrian's reign that the familiar image of the empire as a fortress was first promulgated, protecting civilization from the barbarian hordes beyond its frontiers and symbolizing Hadrian's determination to set limits to Rome's age of expansion.

Judea erupts once more

During his extensive travels in the provinces, Hadrian became involved in the most intense personal relationship of his mature years, with a youth from Bithynia named Antinous. Historical sources do not say precisely when Hadrian met his young paramour, but he is estimated to have been around 13 or 14 years of age at their first encounter. In AD 130 the relationship came to a sudden and tragic end when Antinous drowned in the Nile. In his grief, Hadrian spared nothing in commemorating his beloved, including renaming the town closest to the place where he had died Antinopolis, and granting several cities permission to offer divine honours to his lover.

It is testament to Hadrian's firm grip on the empire that his authority was not impaired by what would have seemed a major domestic scandal in the case of a ruler who commanded less respect. His subjects' forbearance was doubtless also mingled with self-interest; Hadrian's willingness to promote outsiders to the imperial ruling class began to change the senate from a predominantly Italian and western body into one that more closely reflected the population of the empire as a whole. This was perhaps Hadrian's single greatest contribution to the continued success of the empire.

While generally humanist in his outlook and fair in his dealings with his subjects, Hadrian had a serious blind spot for the sensibilities of one particular group: the Jews. With no regard for their traditions, he may seriously have expected them to rejoice at the 'honour' he bestowed on Judea when he refounded Jerusalem as the Roman city of Aelia Capitolina. The outcome was quite the opposite. Inspired by the Rabbi Achiva, and led by Simeon ben Kosiba (who assumed the name Bar Kochba, or 'Son of the Star', in response to a prophecy by Achiva), the countryside of Judea took up arms against the Romans. Hatred of the Roman occupation was compounded when Hadrian toured his eastern provinces in AD 129–30 and proscribed the practice of circumcision. The Bar Kochba revolt lasted for three and a half years, from AD 132 to 135, and was quelled only by massive and merciless military intervention.

By the early AD 130s it was clear that Hadrian was not going to have a son. The obvious successor would have been Pedanius Fuscus, the son of Hadrian's uncle, the venerable Julius Severianus, but Hadrian, who appears to have had a very difficult relationship with Severianus, would have none of it. In AD 136 he ordered them both to commit suicide and adopted Lucius Ceionius Commodus, whose name was changed to Lucius Aelius Verus. Aelius was the stepson of one of the men whom Hadrian had executed after Trajan's death, and his sudden adoption may have been out of remorse for this earlier injustice. It also had the advantage of ensuring that the throne would fall to a mature man with children of his own; Aelius had a young son, and one of his daughters was betrothed to a youth, Marcus Annius Verus, whom Hadrian also favoured. Then disaster struck – Aelius died on 1 January, AD 138, within months of his adoption, and Hadrian cast about for an heir whom he could trust to look after the interests of Aelius' children. In February, AD 138, he adopted Aurelius Antoninus, the elderly uncle of Annius Verus, on condition that he would in turn adopt Verus and the son of Aelius. On 10 July of that year Hadrian died peacefully in a villa in the resort town of Baiae on the Bay of Naples.

Enter the Antonines

Aurelius Antoninus, who would become known to history as the emperor Antoninus Pius (AD 86–161), could not have been more different from his predecessor. He earned the name 'Pius' through his strict adherence to the wishes of Hadrian; indeed, his filial piety towards his adoptive father even extended to coercing an unwilling senate to proclaim Hadrian a god. However, in marked contrast to the much-travelled Hadrian, for the entire 23 years of his reign, Pius never left Italy. Instead, he remained in Rome and – as might have been expected of a man who had enjoyed an extremely successful senatorial career – was content to entrust the day-to-day business of government to experienced administrators. He also placed full confidence in provincial governors to suppress outbreaks of unrest during his reign, in Judea, Mauretania (North Africa) and Britain. Marcus Aurelius, as Marcus Annius Verus became known after his adoption, would later refer to Antoninus Pius as the model emperor: kind, diligent, polite to subordinates, unwilling to decide in haste and always putting the good of the community before anything else. Aside from Marcus Aurelius' personal recollections, little else is known of the man who ruled Rome at the height of its prosperity. During his reign – the longest since that of Augustus – there were no major wars, no scandals and no executions of prominent men, save one who had openly and unsuccessfully tried to incite a rebellion in Spain.

Long before Pius died, Marcus Aurelius had been marked out as the heir apparent, while the emperor permitted Lucius Aelius Verus' son Lucius to live in the palace only 'as a private citizen'. However, it had been Hadrian's express wish that Lucius and Marcus should eventually rule jointly, and, despite feeling no great affection for Hadrian, Marcus Aurelius felt honour-bound to obey his wishes. And so, when the senate met to vote him the few powers of an emperor that he did not already have, he refused to accept them unless the senate voted the same powers to Lucius. So began the joint reign of Marcus Aurelius (AD 121–180) and Lucius Verus (AD 130–169), an event unparalleled in Roman history.

Although the simultaneous election of two emperors

might seem a radical break with the past, it was actually the logical extension of a time-honoured practice stretching back as far as the early years of Augustus' reign. For nearly 20 years after Actium, Agrippa had been his co-emperor in all but name, while in the last years of Augustus' life so too had Tiberius. Likewise, Germanicus and Drusus had performed a similar role for Tiberius, and Titus had been virtual co-ruler with Vespasian, as had Trajan in the few months between his adoption by Nerva and the latter's death. It is also notable that, with the exception of Tiberius, all the emperors who had openly ruled in concert with one or more close confederates in their administration were regarded as very good rulers. Conversely, Domitian had alienated people by insisting on his sole prerogatives, and Hadrian's tight personal hold on the reins of power did not endear him to his subjects. Thus, while they had at times been forced to suffer the whims of autocratic rulers, Rome's governing classes far preferred regimes that were essentially collaborative. In any event, the mettle of the system of joint rule would soon be tested to its limits.

Vologaeses throws down the gauntlet

Even before Lucius Verus and Marcus Aurelius came to power, major changes were afoot on the empire's northern and eastern frontiers. Menacing new tribal groupings began to encroach on the areas adjoining Trajan's province of Dacia, which occupied an extremely exposed position north of the Danube. Meanwhile in Iraq, a new Parthian regime had come to power in the late AD 140s under King Vologaeses IV

(r. AD 147–191), who was determined to reverse the political effects of Trajan's victories. His timely withdrawal of Roman troops before they became bogged down fighting endless insurgencies had left Rome with considerable influence in the former Parthian client kingdom of Characene in southern Iraq. This region was especially important because it was a vital transshipment point midway along a major trade route to India and east Asia. Goods unloaded at the port of Mesene, near modern Basra, were carried up the River Tigris and across the desert to Syria by a network of traders based at the desert city of Palmyra, which was formally incorporated within the Roman provincial system. In AD 157, Vologaeses seized control of Characene and, even as Pius lay dying, prepared a massive invasion of the eastern Roman provinces. Pius' decision not to react militarily to the Parthian invasion of Characene was, with hindsight, probably correct; the region was no more amenable to Roman rule than it had been under Trajan, while Vologaeses would ultimately do himself more harm than good by launching an offensive into Roman territory.

However, at the time Rome's decision not to nip Vologaeses' aggression in the bud looked like a monumental error of judgement, as the Parthian king's forces swept inexorably westward. In AD 161 his armies defeated a badly led provincial garrison in Commagene, north of Syria, and moved into Syria itself. Marcus responded by dispatching a huge army and several highly competent generals to Syria, with Lucius in titular control of the operation. While Lucius remained at Antioch – lacking experience of direct command, his function must largely have been to chair meetings of people who knew what they were doing – the newly arrived forces drove the Parthians back into their own territory.

In AD 163, under the command of the gifted young general Avidius Cassius (*c.* AD 130–175), these armies began to retrace the expedition of Trajan, and two years later destroyed the city of Seleucia on the Tigris and sacked the Persian capital at Ctesiphon. Rome's forces advanced as far as Medea (modern Iran). At this point Vologaeses IV fled, and the Romans proceeded to consolidate their grip on the border regions by installing new, more loyal client rulers there. Stability was thus restored and, following one further Roman campaign in northern Iraq, the armies withdrew to the west in AD 166. Lucius Verus was awarded a triumph, but died of a stroke three years later.

The Antonine Plague

The Roman withdrawal took place against the backdrop of a sudden and devastating natural disaster. A pandemic illness took hold in Mesopotamia while the Romans were mopping up there. As they returned to their posts around the empire, the legions brought the disease with them.

The result was catastrophic, with some 10 per cent of the empire's population – as many as six or seven million people – falling victim to the illness, which subsequently became known as the Antonine Plague. Ancient medicine had no cure; the famous Greek physician Galen (*c.* AD 129–199) described its symptoms as diarrhoea, high fever, and the appearance of pustules on the skin after nine days. Galen's brief account has led later experts to speculate that the disease was most likely smallpox.

In keeping with the common practice of his age, Marcus turned to the gods. Apollo, speaking from his oracle at Claros in western Turkey, is said to have prescribed certain rites to dispel the demons that were held responsible for the outbreak. Marcus circulated the news throughout the empire. Nor was this the only oracle he consulted. In the reign of Antoninus, a Greek prophet named Alexander had set up a new oracle at Abonuteichos in northwestern Turkey. Alexander had a snake named Glycon, who answered questions posed by the faithful. Marcus duly asked Glycon's advice not only about the plague, but also about a new threat looming over the empire: the tribes north of the Danube were poised to overrun the frontier.

The early years of the Northern Wars, as the conflict against the Danubian tribes is known, were grim for Rome. Acting on the advice of Alexander's oracles, Marcus had tossed two lions into the Danube as a votive offering to the river gods to thwart the barbarians' crossing. This attempted sacrifice failed on all counts. The lions simply swam the river, and in AD 170 the tribes penetrated as far south as Aquileia in northern Italy, where Marcus himself came under siege, while at least one Roman army was routed in the central Balkans. Once again, Marcus invoked the gods' help, and claimed that this time they heard his prayers. In one case he is reported to have summoned a thunderbolt from heaven to destroy a siege engine; in another, the emperor's prayers (or the intervention of a favoured Egyptian magician) supposedly brought a thunderstorm to the aid of a hard-pressed legion.

Marcus' appeals to the gods for their aid in dealing with the problems that threatened his empire are one side of a complex personality, the other side of which appears in his most personal reminiscences. It appears that, to help him gain perspective on his imperial duties and responsibilities, he evolved an individual form of Stoic philosophy, jotting his thoughts down (in Greek) in a series of musings that have since become known as the *Meditations*. This personal diary, which he wrote while on campaign in the Northern Wars between AD 170 and 180 and never intended for publication, contains reflections on the meaning of life and the transient nature of all things on earth, including imperial power. Although the tone of the *Meditations* is often melancholic, Marcus Aurelius never renounces his belief in an organizing principle guiding the universe, or loses sight of the fact that, despite his enormous power, he was still but a mortal man.

His own mortality was certainly on his mind in AD 175 when Marcus declared his only surviving son, the 14-year-old Commodus (AD 161–192), his co-emperor and began to groom him as his heir, while at the same time relying on experienced generals for day-to-day control. Not all of them welcomed Commodus' promotion. As soon the news became known, Avidius Cassius, hero of the Parthian campaign and supreme commander of the eastern provinces, declared himself emperor. This was a rash act that garnered little support; Cassius was declared a public enemy by the senate and killed by one of his own men.

The final years of Marcus Aurelius' reign saw incessant fighting on the northern border. But by now Rome's forces were in the ascendant, and a series of treaties mentioned by the historian Cassius Dio indicate that Marcus had begun to re-establish a system of client states north of the border when he suddenly fell ill and died at Sirmium in Pannonia on 17 March, AD 180. Commodus succeeded to the throne, the first teenaged emperor since Nero. The new emperor lacked any experience of government, but was surrounded by advisers steeped in the principle of collaborative rule, and so the people of Rome expected continued stability. Their confidence turned out to be badly misplaced; it is not without good cause that Edward Gibbon began his tale of the decline and fall of the Roman empire with the accession of Commodus.

The contrast between the reign of the so-called 'Five Good Emperors' and that of Commodus may have been overplayed by later generations; certainly the tyro emperor's portrayal in the 2000 Hollywood movie *Gladiator* has more than a touch of Grand Guignol about it. Even Gibbon tacitly admitted that, since Rome's decline took 300 years to unfold, it would be unwise to place too much emphasis on Commodus' accession alone. But what he and later commentators were right to stress was that this event did mark the beginning of the terminal erosion of Rome's traditions of effective government.

Running the Empire: Emperors and Administrators

(AD 68–180)

Even Rome's most autocratic rulers had to rely upon a large and complex network of officials to conduct the business of empire. Military prowess was a key aptitude in ensuring a person's advancement, but a head for finance was also an invaluable skill. The transition from imperial Rome's turbulent early years to the long *pax Romana* of the second century AD was marked by a pronounced change in the style of governance.

Alongside the general dicta on humanity that Marcus Aurelius offers in his *Meditations*, he also makes a number of observations about people he knows and regularly encounters. These tell us a great deal about the circles in which a Roman emperor moved and the day-to-day considerations that motivated his actions. The people Marcus mentions fall broadly into two categories: members of the political élite and slaves in the imperial household. The ruler's daily concerns focus on life in the palace, and the best way to treat subordinates. For instance, Marcus notes that his station in life obliges him not to show anger, not to display signs of boredom and always to act fairly. Dealings with officials defined the parameters of Marcus Aurelius' existence and were central to his profound sense of duty; Cassius Dio says that he would routinely burn the midnight oil in order to finish his day's work. His responsibilities included hearing petitions from his subjects, reading reports from his officials, managing state finances, reviewing the dispositions of the army and appointing reliable people to run his empire. But who were these officials and what qualities did they need to perform their duties successfully?

The emperor's advisers

The officials who surrounded a Roman emperor at court were a microcosm of the government as a whole. There were members of the senate who had held various traditional magistracies, equestrians and freedmen. Each group had its particular sphere of influence. Generally speaking, senators were employed in areas relating to the command of armies and the government of provinces. Members of the equestrian order usually occupied posts that were connected with the finances of the state or in domains that were under the direct control of the emperor – notably, the extensive network of estates throughout Italy and the provinces that formed the *patrimonium* (the portfolio of property holdings bequeathed from one emperor to the next).

A favoured few equestrians obtained positions close to the emperor as secretaries, legal advisers or overseers of the grain supply of Rome. The importance of this latter post cannot be overstated: some 400,000 tonnes of grain were shipped into the city annually, and another 100,000 were required every year by the Roman army. Being appointed overseer of grain supplies was often a prerequisite for holding one of the city's two praetorian prefectures. Finally, freedmen tended to be entrusted with fiscal positions in the household and a variety of tasks connected with special matters of imperial concern such as the quality of entertainment in the palace, or public spectacles for the people of Rome. The common denominator of all three groups of officials was their proven aptitude in financial affairs. With the exception of a few senior imperial secretaries who were recruited directly into their positions on the basis of their rhetorical or juristic skills, all those who were elevated into the upper echelons of the imperial service had shown that they could be trusted with money. This fact alone meant that officials tended largely to be recruited from the landholding classes, where it was an integral part of a young man's education to learn from his parents how to manage estates and large households. However, men whose fiscal competence had helped them earn their freedom could also win promotion.

A less obvious, but equally important, quality shared by members of all three groups was their ability to work within a hierarchical structure. Almost all senators and equestrians who entered the imperial service were required to spend at least one or two years as middle-ranking army officers. During their military service, these men were transferred rapidly from unit to unit, the primary aim being for them to gain experience in dealing with subordinates rather than necessarily acquire expertise in military tactics or fighting skills.

Winning friends and influencing people

Good people skills and a head for finance may have been preconditions for getting ahead in the emperor's service, but they were not the sole factors that determined the success or failure of a person's career. Fewer than one-third of the men who embarked on a senatorial career ever reached its pinnacle – the consulship. A similar proportion of equestrians attained the highest-paid jobs at the top of the ladder.

How did a person climb the ladder? To answer this question we are fortunate to have the thoughts of a few men who made the climb, albeit to a variety of rungs, on their own. One of these men was Cornelius Tacitus, one of Ancient Rome's most important historians – and the source of much of our knowledge about the empire under the Julio-Claudians and the Flavians – and one of the biggest 'winners' in the system of imperial advancement. The son-in-law of a famous general, his ultimately distinguished senatorial career began in the final years of Vespasian's reign. Occupying various provincial administrative posts, he even flourished under Domitian; his renown as a public orator grew under Nerva and Trajan; and he was made consul in AD 97 and governor of Asia in AD 112–13.

Pliny the Younger (AD 63–*c.* 113) was an exact, though somewhat less distinguished, contemporary of Tacitus. The son of a landowner in Comum (modern Como in Italy), he went to Rome to complete his education, after the death of his father, when he was still quite young. He learned rhetoric, taking part in the trials of a number of provincial governors, and he too rose through a series of civil and military offices. Under Trajan, he was appointed governor of the combined provinces of Bithynia and Pontus (on the southern Black Sea coast) between AD 110 and 112, where he remained until his death. Despite the fact that he was never on the top rung of senatorial power, he amassed great wealth; it is estimated that his estates were worth some 20 million sesterces (a labourer's daily wage was four sesterces). Pliny's life, encompassing most of the main public offices open to a Roman citizen, is often taken as the quintessential model of a successful career under the imperial system. His *Letters*, written between AD 97 and 112, provide a unique record of Roman administration and everyday life.

A third person in this category is Cornelius Fronto (AD 95–166), who reached the consulship in AD 143 and was from Cirta in North Africa. His primary claim to fame was that he was a great orator. Later generations held that he was the best of his time, and a contemporary writes of him as if he were a virtual god on the cultural stage of the era. He is best known to us these days through his own collection of *Letters*, many of them to his prize pupil – the emperor Marcus Aurelius – as well as to Marcus' predecessor, Antoninus Pius. Finally there is Cassius Dio, whose father was in the senate before him, and whose history, especially as he attains his adult years after AD 190, is chock-full of highly informative stories about all sorts of people he knew. As a man who was consul twice, the second time as the colleague of the emperor Severus Alexander in AD 229, he too was one of the major winners in the system, despite the considerable twists and turns along the way.

What all these men have to tell is that – to quote an adage that still holds good even in more meritocratic modern societies – in imperial Rome it was not just what you knew but who you knew. A key to success was the ability to make and exploit useful connections. Clearly, a person's chances of advancement were boosted if any of his family members had the emperor's ear. Yet this could only propel one so far – a notable feature of the recommendations that have survived in the collections of Pliny the Younger and Fronto is that they are overwhelmingly aimed at people who are just setting foot on the first few rungs of the promotion ladder. What all of our sources tell us is that, to advance beyond the first stage of a career, a record of actual accomplishment and a proven ability to mix well in society were vital. When Pliny writes that a praetor named Larcius Macedo, forgetting that his own father was a freedman, treated his slaves harshly, his clear implication is that this man lacked the personal qualities expected of a senior official (elsewhere, Pliny makes it plain that he himself is deeply solicitous of his servants' welfare). Aside from this, Pliny seems also to have had a great gift for rhetoric. He made many appearances in the law courts, as did Tacitus, who was renowned as one of the finest orators of his age. Each legal case was a test not only of an orator's persuasive advocacy but also of their good judgement in picking the right person to defend or prosecute.

Likewise, the senate house was the venue for demonstrating political acumen. Here, aspiring statesmen vied to earn the respect of their peers: drawing out the business of the senate by arguing minor points merely irritated one's colleagues, whereas offering sensible suggestions on how to improve a proposal from the emperor helped establish a person's reputation for wisdom and independent thought. Great finesse was called for in political machinations; senators could only be arraigned by their peers, but if an individual began proceedings against a fellow senator who had behaved badly, in the hope of winning the emperor's favour, he was at risk of alienating his colleagues. The wise man knew how to balance the interests of his class against the interests of the emperor, showing independence without arrogance.

By the latter stages of his career a man would have chosen a path that suited his abilities. Some men displayed genuine leadership qualities, moving effortlessly from one senior position of command to the next in different armies. Such skills were especially sought after during Rome's long-running and arduous struggles against the Danubian tribes and the resurgent Parthians in the reign of Marcus Aurelius. During this period, martial ability was at such a premium that commanders who already had a proven track record of success were constantly on the lookout for others whose skills could support their own. For example, Claudius Pompeianus, Marcus' brother-in-law, championed the cause of one Publius Helvius Pertinax (AD 126–193), the son of a freedman, who showed exceptional talent in war, and defended him against critics who claimed that his lowly birth disqualified him for the highest offices. Marcus heeded Pompeianus' advice, and Pertinax gained both the consulship and the governorship of an important province. Later, he was to win the ultimate prize by becoming emperor, albeit only for three months.

Grace and favour

For their part, emperors had their own ways of deciding whom to trust. One tried and tested method was to invite a prospective appointee to dinner, or for the candidate to join the ruler for a few days to help him decide legal cases (Trajan did this, once, with Pliny). In a letter preserved by Suetonius, Augustus revealed to Tiberius that he had been dining and playing dice with a couple of senior generals. Augustus also maintained a council of senators that changed every six months so that he could get to know the men who served him. Nor were these occasions reserved for senators alone; letters from several emperors include reference to notable men of the equestrian orders who sat with them to deliberate on official business.

Many later rulers – notably the 'Five Good Emperors' – followed Augustus' example by revolving invitations to participate so that they could take the measure of as many members of the upper classes as possible. These sessions served a number of purposes, affording the emperor an opportunity to form his own impression of a person's judgement, giving potential appointees an insight into the emperor's approach to various issues, and (not least) performing 'public relations' function of allowing the ruler to demonstrate his decency. As the Younger Pliny put it after his audience with Trajan, 'What could be more pleasant than to witness the justice, wisdom and grace of the emperor in a quiet place where these qualities were easily revealed?' The extent to which Trajan relied on these meetings as training sessions is reflected in his later communication to Pliny as governor of Bithynia, reminding him that he knew 'very well that it is my fixed position that reverence for my name may never be sought from fear or terror or through charges of treason'. Trajan, who had himself spent many thankless years governing provinces under the notoriously nit-picking Domitian, set great store by giving governors free rein to exercise their own initiative. Instead of bombarding his subordinates with rules and regulations for every occasion, Trajan expected them to improvise in accordance with what they could reasonably intuit would be his wishes.

Changing imperial styles

Tacitus' writings chart the shift that took place in styles of governance between Augustus and Vespasian. In his *Annals*, Tacitus exonerates certain provincial governors from former times of the charge that their profligate lifestyles compromised their ability to do their job effectively. But the very fact that he feels it necessary to highlight their sybaritic excesses is eloquent testimony that things had changed by the time he was writing. All the men whom Tacitus cites advanced under Nero, an emperor who was a byword for self-indulgence, and for Tacitus their career histories are axiomatic of two general rules regarding the ruler and his officials: first, that the ambitious man must be able to read the mood of the emperor, and second that each emperor's habits are reflected in the behaviour of his subordinates. Certainly, Pliny, Tacitus and others who made their way in the second century AD seem to have been genuinely moderate in their personal habits. In this, they took their cue from the emperors of the day, especially Vespasian, Trajan and Marcus Aurelius. Even Hadrian, who had a penchant for all things Greek (often synonymous with decadence), shunned outright debauchery.

The conduct of the emperors from Vespasian to Marcus was a reaction against the inward-looking, *domus*-dominated administrative style of the Julio-Claudians. Imperial freedmen who occupied publicly prominent positions under Claudius and Nero were not so evident in the second century AD, but they had not vanished entirely. Vespasian, after all, lived with a freedwoman who had grown up in the palace, while the man who stabbed Domitian was Stephanus, the freedman in charge of intimate access to the emperor, or *cubicularius*. One of the cases that Pliny heard with Trajan concerned one Ulpius Eurythemus, an imperial freedman who held a procuratorship. He was charged with helping an equestrian procurator named Sempronius Senecio forge the will of a senator. Having laid the charge, the heirs then claimed they were afraid to appear, leading Trajan to exclaim that just as he was not Nero, neither was Eurythemus a Polyclitus. Even so, the case was still postponed and eventually dropped. The link between Senecio and Eurythemus reveals that influential freedmen socialized with equestrians, while the *cubicularius* was effectively on a level with the praetorian prefects, the most senior equestrian officials in the realm.

Where did such people come from? There is some evidence to suggest that 'imperial freedman' could be a voluntary career choice for people outside the élite. A papyrus letter from Egypt mentions a man who decided to go to Rome to become a freedman of Caesar, while a *cubicularius* of Hadrian named Aelius Alcibiades was honoured by his home city in western Turkey as a benefactor. At the end of the second century, the immensely powerful freedwoman Marcia, mistress of Marcus' son Commodus, and one of the effective heads of government in his last years, also gave substantial sums to her homeland. She had begun her career as a freedwoman of Marcus Aurelius' daughter. Strictly speaking, to become a freedman or freedwoman a person had first to be a slave, and thus should not have a 'home city' at all (being regarded merely as a chattel of their master). Yet the persistent suggestion from the time of Augustus onwards is that some freedmen and women had actually endured only very short periods of slavery, possibly facilitated by terms in the Roman law of slavery that permitted 'self-sale', and that, in some cases, they had willingly taken that condition upon themselves, as palace staff recruited servants with the necessary skills to participate in government. These aptitudes may have been sexual, cultural or fiscal. The key point was that freedmen brought to Roman government an indispensable range of experiences and skills quite different from those of senators or equestrians.

Even Pliny had to admit that it was right for Trajan to have influential freedmen so long as they shared the essential values of the governing class: a frugal lifestyle and a willingness to work hard. Yet behind this praise of hard work lies a veiled but potent threat. The emperor who shared the values of his subjects would live long and prosper. The emperor who did not would inevitably fall victim to those around him.

Civic Pride: Caesars and Their Cities

(AD 68–180)

'When were there so many cities on land or throughout the sea, and when have they been so adorned?' So asked Aelius Aristides (AD 117–181), a prominent Greek orator from western Turkey, in a eulogy on Rome delivered in the reign of Antoninus Pius. Aristides' praise of cities as markers of prosperity reflects not only his decidedly urban outlook, but also that of the Roman government. Another Greek writing at the same time, the historian Appian of Alexandria (*c.* AD 95–*c.* 165), obliquely made the same point when noting that the emperor was wont to refuse applications by barbarians to be taken under Roman rule on the grounds that they would not be viable to govern. By definition, barbarians were people who did not live in cities.

At first glance, this emphasis on cities might seem odd in an empire in which more than three-quarters of the population lived on the land. Yet almost all the land farmed by these people – if not owned by the emperor or the *res publica* – was attached to cities. From an administrative point of view, then, a Roman province was a collection of civic territories interspersed with tracts of imperial or public land.

Cities and civilization

The cities in a province fell, broadly speaking, into two categories: stipendiary and free. Stipendiary cities were liable to tribute, while free cities had an independent relationship with the Roman state. The precise nature of this relationship varied according to the history of the region; some free cities had stood by Rome during a past crisis and been rewarded with a special treaty, while others had been settled by Roman citizens. As *coloniae* of Rome, these latter cities were exempt from tribute payments. The vast majority of such colonies had arisen through the resettlement of veterans from the civil wars of the first century BC. The intention was that they would serve as centres of Latin culture and as sources of manpower when it was necessary to recall former soldiers to active service in times of emergency. In Rome's western provinces there also existed many urban centres known as *municipia*; these were places that had been granted civic constitutions from Rome, and whose typical inhabitants, though of provincial descent, enjoyed partial Roman citizenship. Moreover, if elected to a civic magistracy, provincial people were granted full rights of citizenship. Though inferior in status to the *coloniae*, the *municipia* demonstrated the Roman state's interest in rewarding provincials who abandoned 'barbarism' for the ideals of Roman civilization. In the eastern holdings of the empire, where the Romans were willing to accept that the values of Greek civic life were sufficiently like their own, there was no such deliberate attempt to transplant Latin culture. It remains one of the unique features of the Roman imperial system that the culture of a conquered people could be so thoroughly assimilated into that of the conqueror.

The job of the governor was to make annual tours of his province in order to settle legal disputes and ensure that the cities were being properly administered. Since it was usually impractical for him to visit every city, provinces were divided into judicial districts, or *conventus*, each containing a principal city where the governor conducted his business for a few weeks each year. There was considerable profit to be made from a governor's visit, with people coming from far and wide for an audience with him, and consequently cities vied fiercely with one another for the honour of being recognized as a provincial centre. This competition ordinarily took the form of expenditure on civic amenities such as theatres, market places, fountains and – in the western provinces – amphitheatres for staging gladiatorial combat. Prior to the reign of Hadrian, and only in the eastern provinces, a single city would be recognized as the metropolis – literally 'mother city' – of the province. After Hadrian, other cities were also granted the same status, thus generating further competition between the larger cities.

The imperial cult

Many further privileges accrued to a city once it had been given the status of metropolis. For example, such cities automatically became the site of the provincial assembly, an organ of local government that was independent of the governor. In this capacity, the metropolis was the place to which all the stipendiary cities of the province sent representatives to celebrate the annual festival of the emperor. Thus, to honour a city by designating it a metropolis was to make it the regional centre of the imperial cult. The imperial cult acted as the focal point for direct expressions of loyalty to the emperor. In the eastern provinces, the cult developed out of earlier votive traditions that became widespread around the time of the death of Alexander the Great in 323 BC. At first, these devotions were merely a way of expressing gratitude to individuals – not just rulers – who had rendered their city extraordinary services. However, over time, between the death of Alexander and the rise of Roman hegemony in the region, the use of divine honours became increasingly restricted to kings. Yet with the advent of Roman rule in the eastern Mediterranean and Asia Minor, the use of divine honours once more expanded to encompass private individuals, including a number of Roman governors.

Romans had a very ambivalent attitude towards ruler cult. Although, like the Greeks, they were quite at ease with rhetorical comparisons of mortals to gods, they strongly resisted the notion that any living Roman should be revered as a god by his peers. In philosophical terms, while most Romans believed that certain gods had once been mortal, they were adamant that they only assumed divine form after their deaths. This is why the divine honours that the senate voted Julius Caesar during his lifetime caused such grave offence, whereas the erection of a temple for the Divine Julius in the wake of the comet that appeared after his death was completely uncontroversial.

Augustus was largely instrumental in creating the cult of

the divine Julius, yet he understood clearly that, no matter how many temples were erected or festivals founded in his own honour in the provinces, no ruler cult would exist for him in Rome while he was still alive. But at the same time he realized that the ruler cult was a useful tool for provincial organization, and therefore agreed that the assembly of the three provinces of Gaul could offer sacrifices on his behalf (this observance was standard in all ruler cults, and distinguished the rites for rulers from those of the immortal gods, to whom the sacrifices were offered). Later, he permitted the culturally Greek cities of Asia Minor to set up temples to him.

When Augustus died, the symbolic ascent of his soul to the heavens was staged at his funeral. The decision to create a cult in his honour was widely regarded as an act of approbation, a popular way of passing favourable judgement on his reign. Thus, the imperial cult and power politics became inextricably intertwined; when Tiberius, for example, refused to allow a cult to be established for himself in Spain, Tacitus commented that this showed a lack of ambition on his part. Likewise, Hadrian's deification was not a foregone conclusion; the senate and the people evidently regarded it as a subject of legitimate political debate. Finally, Antoninus Pius forced the decision through. Romans took the view that the emperor should be aware that his posthumous reputation depended upon the goodwill of his subjects.

The understanding of the imperial cult at Rome was quite distinct from the way it operated in the provinces. In Rome, the formulae of deification were retrospective, whereas in the provinces they tended to be prospective. There, emperors received divine honours as soon as they ascended the throne, and every year without fail provincial assemblies would send a delegation to the emperor to inform him of the honours they had bestowed upon him. However, these delegations were far from being sycophantic acts of obeisance. Rather, the imperial cult provided a highly practical opportunity for provincials to engage with the distant power that controlled their lives. While in the capital, provincial delegates could forge useful political contacts, advance their careers and even air complaints against the governor.

The city and the countryside

The imperial cult bound the cities of the provinces together, and in turn bound the provinces to the emperor. As tangible proof of the positive effect of government and the cultural benefits of civilization, cities also played a vital role in conveying such values to the vast mass of people who lived in the countryside. Even in the most rural areas, peasants who did not live directly on estates owned by the emperor or aristocrats – and even many who did – congregated in villages that tried, to the best of their ability, to equip themselves with all the amenities of urban life. These villages put up public baths, assembly buildings, fountains and market places, in the hope that they might one day attain civic status. Settlements arose on the fringes of the Arabian desert, calling themselves 'mother villages' to distinguish themselves from lesser spots by imitating the titulature of cities.

In a number of settlements, some inhabitants attained a level of personal prosperity well above that of subsistence farmers – so great, in fact, that it could sometimes put their lives in danger. Some wealthy villagers only appear in the historical record because they were kidnapped and held to ransom. Their abductors were Roman soldiers working for imperial procurators who were seeking to feather their own nests by stealing from people whose oppression they reckoned the emperor would never notice. In many cases they may well have been right; but in other instances we know that the villagers were able to organize themselves, find a patron and persuade the emperor to address their grievances.

To his rural-dwelling subjects, the emperor was not a hated figure of oppression who was deemed responsible for imposing the rents or taxes that they had to pay, appointing the officials who tormented them or commanding the army whose soldiers terrorized them. On the contrary, he was an abstract symbol of justice who was commonly supposed to listen to even the most lowly plaintiff. Cassius Dio relates a famous incident in which Hadrian rebuffed an old woman who had come to him to complain of an injustice. To his claim that he did not have time to listen to her, she tartly responded, 'Then cease to be ruler.' Suitably chastened, the emperor reportedly stopped in his tracks and asked her to present her complaint. This story, which recurs in different forms throughout Classical Antiquity, is probably apocryphal, but it does eloquently bear out Plutarch's observation that 'nothing so befits a ruler as the work of justice'.

Other popular tales attest to how widespread the notion was of the emperor as a beneficent figure who could right all wrongs. For example, two Roman authors tell the story of a man who was magically transformed into an ass by a slave-girl with whom he was having an affair. When he is goaded and beaten, he cries out to Caesar to help him. Though clearly intended for comic effect, this story still reflects an attitude towards the imperial office that was widely held. And so, when a Jew named Paul of Tarsus – the future St Paul – who had been arrested in Jerusalem for preaching Christianity, protested that he should have his case heard by the emperor in person rather than by his representative in Judea, nobody found this at all preposterous, and he was duly packed off to Rome. The story of Paul as St Luke tells it in the Acts of the Apostles stresses the point that no matter was so insignificant that the emperor might not find out about it.

The crowd who gathered at the headquarters of the procurator of Judea in Jerusalem during the Passover season of AD 36 were voicing the same idea when they goaded Pontius Pilate into executing Jesus of Galilee on a charge of treason; the mob called out to Pilate that he would be no 'friend of Caesar' if he did not carry out the sentence. It evidently struck the author of the Gospel of St John as wholly plausible for a Roman magistrate to be swayed by the threat that a complaint of official misconduct involving a person of no significance whatsoever to the emperor – Jesus was not a Roman citizen – might lead to censure.

The imperial taxation system

The quaint notion that the emperor cared about every matter, however trivial, may well have its origins in the omnipresence of certain institutions of imperial rule. Foremost among these was the all-embracing Roman system of taxation, which made its presence felt in everyone's lives. All the inhabitants of the empire who were not Roman citizens were subject to a tax on their persons and a tax on their property, known as the tribute. On the other hand, citizenship made a person liable to certain taxes from which non-citizens were exempt, such as an inheritance tax that Augustus instituted in AD 6 to fund the resettlement of demobilized legionaries.

The imperial tax system was the single most obvious symbol of Roman control. The instrument that officials charged with tax collection used to assess how the tax burden should fall was the census. This exercise required every man to declare the number of people in his household, including the slaves he kept, and his riches. The most famous census in Roman history was that conducted by the Roman governor of Syria and Judea, Publius Sulpicius Quirinius, in AD 6, which the Gospel of St Luke in the New Testament associates with the birth of Christ ('. . . a decree went out from Caesar Augustus that all the world should be taxed'). New acquisitions of territory were always accompanied by a census, and the process was repeated on various schedules throughout the empire. In most of the empire these reassessments fell once a decade, in Syria once every 12 years, while in Egypt, they recurred every 14 years.

Once the assessment was complete, collection in the provinces was delegated to local officials – municipal councillors known as *curiales*. This cut the cost of administration even if it did not eliminate controversy. The registers of people's liabilities were not always regarded as fair, and disputes were frequent. To assist them in their collection duties, the *curiales* maintained gangs of enforcers, and if these thugs failed to persuade recalcitrant taxpayers to pay up, the officials were empowered to second troops from the governor. It was a system that depended on the threat of violence, a threat that loomed large over the great majority of the empire's population. Little wonder, then, that they were given to imagining that somewhere above it all there resided a beneficent emperor who could intervene to save them.

Ultimately, however, the Roman tax system was self-regulating; peasants who were too harshly treated would simply flee the land, thereby reducing the revenue stream to the empire. Moreover, local officials whose enforcement methods were excessively high-handed were precisely those who were likely to be embezzling potential income from the state. This is why it was so important for senior officials to develop an understanding of what went on at the local level, and to have first-hand knowledge of the conflicts that could, if unchecked, tear a community apart. The key role that they performed was to balance the interests of the local administrative class upon which they depended for day-to-day government and the interests of the governed.

The army

The central institution supported by the tax system (it required somewhere between half and three-quarters of all tax revenue) was the Roman army. Augustus had transformed the army from a force primarily based in Italy, whence had come most of the soldiers in the Republic and to which most aspired to return upon discharge, into a frontier force whose members were increasingly recruited from the provinces.

At the time of Augustus' death, the Roman military consisted of four types of soldier, whose professional status was marked by differences in legal status, equipment, training and salary. At the top were members of the new imperial guard, known as the Praetorian Guard, stationed only in Italy during Augustus' lifetime; Sejanus would later gather them into a single camp in Rome. They served sixteen years, were the best-paid, and were armed like regular legionaries but with extra training in urban warfare (they would be called upon to suppress riots in the city). Legionaries were next, serving for twenty years; they were supposedly all Roman citizens upon enlistment (in fact, citizenship was often conferred upon enlistment). Fighting as heavily armed infantrymen, their primary tactical purpose was to lure the main battle line of the enemy into hand-to-hand combat and destroy them. Auxiliaries came next, usually wearing less substantial armour than did legionaries; they would only receive citizenship if they gained an honorary discharge after twenty-five years' service. They were drawn from the various provinces and client kingdoms, and organized into cavalry 'wings' for horsemen, or cohorts with notional strengths of either 500 or 1000 men, usually all of infantry, though there were some special units that combined horse and foot. Finally there were sailors, who were essentially members of the *auxilia* who served at sea.

In AD 14, as a result of the decision not to replace the legions lost with Varus, there were twenty-five legions, each with a theoretical strength of 5,600 men, giving a total of 140,000 legionaries; the recently constituted praetorian guard numbered 10,000 men, and it is probable that there were around 170,000 soldiers serving with the *auxilia*. Assuming that there were roughly 20,000 men serving with the main battle fleets, which would henceforth be based at Ravenna and Misenum, the total military establishment of the Augustan age amounted to around 340,000. In the reign of Marcus Aurelius the number of legions had expanded to thirty, or roughly 168,000 legionaries and about 200,000 auxiliaries with, again, about 30,000 men serving in the guard and the fleets. The military establishment under Marcus, in terms of the empire's total population (which had increased by about 50 per cent in these years), was therefore smaller than it had been under Augustus, though it likely consumed about as much of the budget, since pay and benefits had been increased in the interim.

When not in the field, and for much of the period after Augustus, most of the army spent little time on campaign; soldiers could be found oppressing civilians or working on the empire's infrastructure. In their dealings with civilians, the army's record was often appalling. One Jewish text states that if a woman was kidnapped by soldiers one could assume she had been raped, not a fate that could be assumed if she had fallen in with brigands; elsewhere we find soldiers demanding bribes, kidnapping local worthies who they thought could pay a ransom, or compelling people to cart things around – the Biblical expression 'to go the second mile' derives from a Roman soldier's right to compel a civilian to carry kit for him.

When not making life hard for civilians, soldiers were typically employed in major public works projects such as the great transportation system that drew the empire together through new roads and bridges – still the marvel of Europe more than a thousand years after the Roman empire in the west came to an end, in the fifth century AD – or in elaborate training exercises. These often involved intricate drill, which created a strong esprit amongst serving soldiers, who were proud of what they were able to accomplish when they had officers who were committed to keeping them in top form (devotion to hard physical labour was by no means a universal attribute of Roman officers).

The problem with these exercises, though, was that they were often irrelevant to the specific areas where the soldiers were stationed, and based on increasingly archaic tactical doctrines. This much becomes clear when we look at two short books of the period that treat military matters, written by a historian and philosopher of Greek descent called Arrian of Nicomedia (*c.* AD 92–175). Arrian not only had a practical knowledge of contemporary warfare – as governor of the Roman province of Cappadocia from AD 130 to 138, he commanded an army that repelled an invasion by the Alan tribes from the steppes of central Asia – he was also a scholar of ancient history. In particular, he admired Alexander the Great, and his account of the campaigns of the Macedonian king remains the foundation for modern study of that era. Yet therein lay the problem; for all his undoubted accomplishments on the battlefield, when formulating tactics Arrian recommends infantry formations that are adaptations of the fourth-century BC phalanx used by his military hero. In writing on cavalry tactics, he is marginally more up to date, but even then he commends innovations borrowed from the Gallic and Spanish tribes of the first century BC.

That the fighting tactics outlined above were not Arrian's alone is made plain by another surviving text from the same period that comes from North Africa. It is in the form of an inscription recording a series of speeches that Arrian's patron Hadrian gave when visiting the area, praising the drills performed by various auxiliary units. Tellingly, one of these formations is precisely the same Spanish cavalry drill described by Arrian. The coincidence of this identical tactic being recommended in two different parts of the Roman world smacks of the dead hand of tradition. The troops that Hadrian was inspecting were the garrison that patrolled the northern boundaries of the Sahara, yet there is nothing in his speech to suggest that he took into account the very special requirements of desert warfare. Certainly, there was no centralized drill manual, and Roman armies had been known since the days of the republic for adopting the fighting and campaigning skills of their adversaries. The problem was that these days lay far in the past, and for a long time no new strategic or tactical thinking had been evolved to cope with changed circumstances.

Troubling as these aspects of Roman military doctrine might be from a long-term perspective, it was still the case in the first and second centuries that Rome's enemies had yet to catch up. The Roman army was still beyond question the most effective fighting force in Europe and the Middle East; and when not oppressing civilians, soldiers did have to work hard, and in so doing went some way towards justifying the image of soldiers as representatives of Roman civilization that figures, for instance, on Trajan's column. The other quality that we find on Trajan's column is devotion to the emperor: in these years the army was by and large extremely loyal to the imperial system, which is perhaps the single most important aspect of the Roman military in these years.

One reason why the army may have been so loyal to the imperial regime was that soldiers of the period viewed themselves as a privileged class apart from and above the civilians, whom they saw themselves as ruling – a distinction that, at least symbolically, was enhanced in the early third century by the fact that soldiers were not allowed to contract legal marriages before they left the service. But while they saw themselves as rulers, they also had to be ruled, often by officers whom they did not like very much. Even by the time of Augustus' death in AD 14, there was considerable hostility between enlisted men and their officers now that the rank of centurion (the commander of a century, usually comprising around 80 men) was becoming the first rung on the ladder for a normal equestrian career, which meant that centurions were usually drawn from the upper classes.

Because of the social gap between enlisted men and their officers, military administration came to consist of marginally intersecting spheres of interest. The average soldier seems to have viewed himself as a member of an élite group that ruled the area in which he served, while their officers, from the rank of centurion upwards (all of whom were allowed to marry), saw themselves as members of an imperial élite for whom military service ideally led to a move into the equestrian civil service or to a more significant social position altogether. Given such attitudes, there could be no specific military agenda; officers and men reacted to events in terms of what they understood to be their best interests – and the default setting for those interests was typically loyalty to the emperor. That may be the reason why events such as those of AD 69 were so very rare in the centuries after Actium. Indeed, it was the *unwillingness* of armies to march on Rome that set the imperial period apart from the era of Sulla and Caesar. The army's loyalty was thus the central pillar of the *pax Romana*.

All roads do not lead to Rome

Although it was the army that secured the empire, it was still the tax system that provided the basic forum of interaction between government and the governed, so it also helped shape the empire. In economic terms, the empire created a superstructure made up of a number of relatively autonomous zones, each of which centred either on a major city or on a large military garrison. In the west, these zones included the two main areas of military occupation along the Rhine and Danube rivers, each with a garrison of around 80,000 men, and Rome. In the east, the principal zones were the highly urbanized region of western Turkey (Asia Minor), which included Ephesus, Pergamon and Smyrna, as well as a host of smaller places, plus the area around Antioch in Syria. In all cases, the zones' hinterlands supplied the major cities or garrisons with revenue, goods and services. Rome, for instance, with a population of around one million people, required the excess agricultural resources of North Africa, Spain and Egypt to support its existence.

The fact that Rome needed food from abroad to survive

did not mean that the economic traffic was all in one direction. Continuing consumer demand in Rome directly benefited the regions that supplied it. For example, the infrastructure required to ship North Africa's agricultural surplus to Rome was directly responsible for regenerating Carthage as a major city. Similarly, in Egypt, the supply chain that led from the fertile Nile valley confirmed the status of Alexandria as a major city; in addition to handling large quantities of home-grown agricultural produce, the city was also a key entrepôt for the lucrative trade in luxury goods – chiefly spices – from Asia. On a smaller scale, the same process generated wealth throughout the empire. The garrisons on the Rhine were supported by the excess production of France, while the army on the Danube stimulated the growth of agriculture throughout the Balkans. In both areas, which had no significant urban settlement prior to the Roman conquest, a number of major cities grew up along or near rivers. In Germany, these cities included Bonn (Bonna), Trier (Augusta Treverorum), Mainz (Moguntiacum) and Cologne (Colonia Agrippina), with significant further development along the Rhône at Lyons (Lugdunum) and in the ancient city of Marseilles (Massilia). Along the Danube, large conurbations arose at Aquincum and Sirmium, as well as Siscia on the major east–west road to the south and Thessalonica. In Britain, London grew into a major trading city, while Córdoba (Corduba) in Spain emerged as the centre of the highly productive Guadalquivir valley.

By establishing a redistribution network for excess production, and creating a stable market for goods from far and wide, the Roman empire brought a hitherto unknown level of prosperity to the territories under its control. The system also enabled Roman emperors to alleviate periods of hardship in particular areas by diverting surpluses from regions that were thriving.

The striking feature of the imperial redistribution system is that all roads did not lead to Rome. While massive grain fleets did indeed sail there every year from North Africa and Alexandria, the rest of the trade flowed away from the capital. There were no ancient equivalents of the bullion fleets of early modern Spain sailing into the harbours of Italy, having despoiled the resources of the empire. Most of the tax revenue that was collected, either in agricultural produce (required for the land tax) or hard currency (deriving from the poll tax and various taxes on the transshipment of goods), was used to support the administration in the areas where it was collected, or in the areas serviced by the local redistribution network.

Fiscal flaws

The decentralization of the Roman system was its greatest strength, for it meant that if disaster struck in one area, the rest of the empire could remain relatively free of disruption. On the other hand, the fact that most tax revenue supported local needs also meant that emperors were often chronically short of cash. In response, over the course of the first two centuries, the emperors began gradually to reduce the quantity of pure silver in the basic silver coin, the *denarius*, to roughly 60 per cent, avoiding rampant inflation by tariffing the *denarius* against the basic gold coin, or *aureus*, at a rate of 25:1. The result was that inflation in the course of the two centuries after Augustus remained relatively stable, at around 0.25 per cent annually.

Although the emperors could control inflation by supporting the gold standard, and alleviate shortages by redirecting surpluses, their fiscal condition remained parlous. The tax system, based as it was on the relatively inelastic system of 10- to 14-year censuses, could not be counted on to generate massive new revenues when they were needed. Shortfalls in the budget had to be made up by the emperors who, from the time of Augustus onwards, diverted surpluses from their own income to the state treasury (*aerarium*). However, the transfer of imperial funds was not always enough. In the crisis of the Danubian Wars, Marcus Aurelius was actually forced to auction off palace furniture to meet his expenses. Nor was it just wartime that depleted the coffers; despite the fact that the empire enjoyed a long period of peace in the reign of Antoninus Pius, he still found it necessary to impose a luxury tax on the upper classes in the form of a 25–33 per cent surcharge on the sale of gladiators. By the time Marcus, in a magnanimous gesture celebrating his military victories, finally repealed the gladiator tax it had yielded between five and seven million *denarii* a year, the equivalent of about 7.5 per cent of the base cost of the entire Roman army.

The Imperial Melting Pot: Roman Culture

(AD 68–180)

The Roman empire embraced many different cultures, yet still managed to instil in the peoples under its protection a sense of being Roman. Not that this task was at all straightforward: ultimately, the authority of the Roman state depended upon the willing acquiescence of its subjects. If the terrible tale of the Jewish revolts of the first and second centuries reveal nothing else about Roman administration, it was that popular insurrection in just a small province had the capacity to stretch the resources of the empire to their limit. What, then, were the methods by which hearts and minds were won?

Rome's key policy of sharing power with local élites meant that it could not simply prescribe what it meant to be Roman and expect people to follow unquestioningly. Broadly speaking, the empire was divided between the Greek-speaking east and the Latin-speaking west, but this crude distinction conceals radical differences in the way that Latin or Greek culture was assimilated by the vast mass of people for whom neither language was indigenous. In Britain, Germany and Gaul, Latin was often a second language to either local Celtic or Germanic dialects.

E Pluribus Unum

Roman Africa – the province centred on Carthage – was a particularly interesting case. Though a Roman province since the end of the Third Punic War (146 BC), it retained a distinct linguistic and cultural identity. The first language of an African aristocrat might well be Punic (the dialect of ancient Carthage, which developed from the language of the Phoenician traders who founded the city) or some other local tongue. Even North Africans who attained high office in Roman service maintained a strong connection to their roots. For example, Lusius Quietus, one of the four leading generals executed by Hadrian at the start of his reign, was the son of a North African tribal chieftain, and probably spoke a Berber dialect. Likewise, the *Historia Augusta* (a late-Roman collection of biographies of emperors from AD 117 to 284) recounts that Septimius Severus (AD 146–211), the future emperor who entered the senate under Marcus, spoke Latin with such a heavy Punic accent that he pronounced his own name 'Sheptimiush Shervush'.

In Egypt, many local officials had a very poor command of Greek – we know of one village administrator there, Petaus the son of Petaus, who could barely spell his own name in Greek – because their first language was a form of Egyptian known as Demotic. In Syria, the dominant language was Aramaic, while in Asia Minor a hodgepodge of ancient languages continued to be spoken in preference to Greek; the Acts of the Apostles relate that when Paul of Tarsus performed a miracle in the city of Lystra in Asia Minor on his first missionary journey in AD 47, those who witnessed it cried out in Lycaonian. As late as the third century AD, the Roman jurist Ulpian (d. 223) noted that a governor had to be able to accommodate people speaking Phoenician and Aramaic, as well as Latin and Greek, in his court. Ulpian himself came from Tyre, a Roman *colonia* in the eastern Mediterranean that was an enclave of Latin culture in a district where otherwise Phoenician and Aramaic were far more common than Greek or Latin. One suspects that if Ulpian had been from Gaul, he would have included Celtic; it is certainly clear from the comments of two Christian commentators of the second century that the original languages of that region continued to be spoken, if not written, long after the start of the Roman occupation. Conversely, a Gaul named Favorinus (*c.* AD 80–150, whose other claim to fame was an undescended testicle) mastered the Greek language so perfectly that he became one of the foremost Greek orators in Rome during the reign of Hadrian.

A world of entertainment

Roman emperors promoted various practices that were designed to inculcate the values of Roman culture into the peoples of the wider empire. The incentive was that favours would be granted by Rome to those willing to assimilate. These initiatives included encouraging people to learn Greek and Latin well enough to be able to participate in government, to construct cities on a Greek or Latin model and to adopt Greek or Roman dress. Roman values were transmitted not only through the periodic appearances of senior magistrates, but also through various forms of public announcements – missives from the emperor were always read out in a public ceremony and then posted in a public place – or public spectacles.

Secular public spectacles came in three basic forms: theatrical events, athletic contests and public combats. Theatrical events might take the form of full productions of plays – usually, but not exclusively, works that were part of the standard canon of didactic works. However, they might also include solo performances of excerpts of 'greatest hits' from famous plays, sometimes set to musical accompaniment; poetic recitations, musical performances and choral acts; mimes (a generic term for 'low-brow' performances that ranged from situation comedies and clown routines to dancing displays); and pantomime, a form of tragedy involving a dancer, accompanied by a singer and percussion band, who performed a routine on a mythological theme. On some occasions, these events would be supplemented with performances illustrating an important event in the history of the empire – for instance, a papyrus has survived containing part of the script for a depiction of Trajan's ascent to the gods, which was staged in an Egyptian town after his death.

Athletic contests were based on the festivals of pre-Roman Greece, in which naked athletes competed in a series of races and track-and-field events such as the pentathlon. Another popular attraction was the triumvirate of combat sports: boxing, wrestling, and pancration, a brutal combination of the two. Athletic contests might also involve equestrian events. These included both horse races as we know them and races with chariots drawn by two- or four-horse teams.

Such chariot races were run on courses of varying dimensions, which could accommodate a large number of contestants – as many as 48 chariots at the hippodrome at Olympia in Greece.

By contrast, circus chariot races, which evolved in Rome's valley of the Circus Maximus, were run on a track of set dimensions. A maximum of 12 teams took part in such races, completing seven laps around a central barrier with tight turns at each end. These spectacles were fast and furious and extremely dangerous for the participants, with accidents a frequent occurrence. Another feature that distinguished chariot races within the circus from those elsewhere was that circus races were dominated by four professional factions – known from the colours worn by their drivers as the Blues, Greens, Reds and Whites. These factions had been responsible for organizing the circus races from as early as the fourth century BC.

Public combat had existed as a form of entertainment since Republican times, but was only expanded into a major spectacle throughout the empire after the Battle of Actium. It appeared in several guises, the most common of which were gladiatorial bouts between two or more men, variously armed. These gladiators might be free men or slaves (fighting as a gladiator could be financially rewarding) and were organized into *familiae*, or troupes, whose managers would sell or rent them to people who were going to provide games – which all civic magistrates were required to do each year. Given the very high cost to magistrates of gladiators, it was usually in the magistrates' best interests to make sure that all gladiators survived, so that they could be sold back to the manager of the troupe or so that they did not have to pay the death benefits that free men would negotiate in case of an unfortunate accident. Gladiatorial duels, which usually ended when one fighter was wounded, were seen as a quintessentially Roman event, summing up the martial virtues that had made the empire great and that could now be shared, at least vicariously, by all Rome's subjects.

Other types of public blood sports were a good deal bloodier. These included events in which professional hunters stalked and killed wild animals, and, most notoriously, the execution of criminals in combat. Such gruesome charades might involve the men being tortured in ways that recalled the mythological punishments of famous offenders against the gods. Alternatively, in a form of punishment known as 'exposure to the beasts', they were sent unprotected into the arena to be mauled to death by lions, tigers, bears or wolves. Another variant was to force condemned men to fight one another to the death in duels.

Unlike modern spectators, who avidly follow championship events that last for weeks or even months, the ancient audience required instant gratification. When people gathered to watch a sporting event, be it athletic, gladiatorial or equestrian, they expected to see close contests, thrilled to rapid changes of fortune and found it an added bonus if one or more of the contestants failed to make it out of the arena in one piece. In combat sports, for instance, all the contests would be crammed into a single day so that the spectators did not have to wait for the outcome. This meant that the eventual winner needed to record a gruelling series of decisive victories on the way to securing the championship, with almost no time between bouts. Since, in a sport like boxing, the victor had to win by an equivalent of a technical knockout each time, the final would be as much a test of stamina as it was of technical skill. Endurance, and the ability to withstand pain, were traits that were deeply admired by Romans.

The Roman psyche

But what did it mean, in essence, to be a Roman? Difficult though it is to divine the collective psyche of a former age – and a distant one at that – certain leitmotifs emerge clearly from looking at diverse aspects of Roman culture. One of these is a fascination with pain and suffering. For example, aside from their sheer entertainment value, gladiators struck such a resonant chord with the Roman public because they were powerful symbols of fortitude, putting life and limb at risk in bouts that almost invariably ended with some sort of injury.

This is not to say that the Roman attitude towards gladiators was unambiguous; on the one hand, they were reviled for being as low as slaves in the social hierarchy, but on the other they were greatly admired for their bravery, with some even being accorded celebrity status. A similar equivocal attitude attached to the question of suffering on the part of the fighters. A certain amount of bloodshed added to the spectacle, but mass deaths were neither inevitable (the fatality rate was only around 5 per cent in any given set of games) nor especially desirable. Gladiatorial contests were less about slaking a crowd's bloodlust than about providing a protracted display of fighting skill. It is for this reason, and not out of any solicitude for the gladiators' welfare, that fights to the death were banned everywhere except Rome after the Julio-Claudian period. Even there, they were rare occurrences, being staged only when the emperor was in attendance. Interestingly, by the time of Marcus Aurelius, combat with steel swords and tridents was often supplanted by the use of wooden weapons. This innovation was presumably designed to prolong the entertainment.

The motif of fortitude recurs in the epic tales that emerged as the one original literary genre of the imperial period. The heroes of these stories, such as Aeneas, were redoubtable wanderers who endured great hardship to achieve their ultimate goal of finding a home. Often they had to confront the threat or actuality of intense suffering during their journey. Both in the works of contemporaries like Virgil and Ovid and in those of the earlier Greek writers Homer and Sophocles, the Roman audience found itself captivated by lurid examples of suffering, such as that undergone by the character Philoctetes. The greatest archer to accompany the Greeks to the siege of Troy, Philoctetes was bitten by a serpent and, in intense pain from the suppurating wound that developed, was abandoned on the island of Lemnos by his companions when they could no longer bear to hear his cries of agony or smell the stench from his wound.

On stage, preferred themes also ran to the more extreme episodes from mythology: Medea, who murdered her children, was a great favourite with Romans – the young Augustus even wrote a play on the theme – as was the banquet at which Atreus fed his brother Thyestes the stewed bodies of his children, the madness of Hercules, or the bizarre sexual encounter between a Spartan woman, Leda, and the god Zeus, who had disguised himself as a swan.

The counterpoint to this fascination with pain was Romans' admiration for outward displays of intense calm. The ideal Roman man was a person who stoically kept his passions to himself, comporting himself in life with every bit as much serenity as the graceful stone statue that every prominent citizen aspired to have his native city erect in his honour. Yet behind this façade he might, like Marcus Aurelius, write letters to friends detailing the illnesses he suffered and the pain that he overcame. The orator Aelius Aristides, whose medical conditions strike modern readers as deeply psychosomatic, spent years seeking treatments from the priest of the god Asclepius and regarded his ailments almost as a religious devotion that brought him closer to the divine.

Religion and culture

Lacking the scientific and medical knowledge we now use to understand – and in some cases avert or alleviate – natural catastrophes, the Romans had only the gods to turn to when plague, earthquakes, storms or famine struck. Thus Marcus Aurelius consulted the mystic Alexander of Abonuteichos and his oracular snake Glycon when the barbarians threatened, and appealed to the god Apollo when the empire was blighted by the Antonine Plague. His conviction that the gods would speak through oracles and respond to his prayers derived from the Stoic philosophy that lay behind all his thoughts and actions. It was a basic tenet of Stoicism that the seamless nexus of events – Fate, in other words – was indistinguishable from the divine will of Zeus. This belief in a form of providential design entailed understanding the laws of Nature as the material presence of the divine in the universe. To exist in harmony with these laws was therefore Marcus' main aim:

> So far as concerns the gods, the messages sent from them, their aids and revelations, nothing prevents me from living according to Nature, even though I slip from this at times, through my own fault, by not observing the reminders and virtual instructions from the gods. (*Meditations* 1.17.6)

What distinguished Marcus' Stoic belief in fate and the gods (as well as that of other leading philosophical movements of the age such as Platonism and Pythagoreanism) was the idea that the many gods in the Roman pantheon all acted in accordance with the will of a single divine organizing principle. This was a highly sophisticated, intellectual viewpoint, however. For many others in the empire, the gods who were the focus of their devotions were considerably less well organized. The Roman empire was filled with shrines and temples to gods of all sizes and shapes, many of distinctly local origin, and people sought out the ones who could respond to their specific concerns. The highly undogmatic Roman approach to faith, which did not attempt to impose any official, authorized religion on diverse peoples, was one of the most significant stabilizing factors in the empire. Belief in the gods was hallowed by tradition, and was often backed up by extensive anecdotal evidence of divine intervention. For instance, temples dedicated to Asclepius, the god of healing, kept records of the ways in which he had cured the sick within their walls.

In addition, oracular shrines documented the responses that the gods had given there, while cities recorded moments when the gods had averted disaster or revealed new rites to them to heal rifts in their relationship. People were in no doubt that the gods existed, because they could see the results of their actions all around them. Moreover, they knew how to worship the gods because the gods themselves had instructed them how to do so. They were also aware that the gods gave different instructions to different people.

The most commonplace form of religious observance in the Roman empire was the act of sacrifice. People brought whatever offerings they could afford, either burning them on an altar if they were trying to reach a god thought to dwell in the heavens, or pouring them on the ground if they were trying to petition one of the deities that lived beneath the earth. The rich were expected to make greater sacrifices than the poor, for the order of worship ideally reflected the order of society. In the Roman mind, there was no separation of the political and religious spheres because the maintenance of the social order depended upon the happiness of the gods. Thus the Roman emperor was also a priest – from the time of Augustus onwards he held a variety of priestly offices in the state, chief among which was that of *pontifex maximus*. The leaders of communities throughout the empire would also usually hold some sort of priesthood in their lifetimes.

Oracles, charlatans and visionaries

The inseparability of politics and traditional cult was another manifestation of the key role that religion played as a force for social cohesion. For some, however, traditional devotions did not go far enough. Such was the importance of the gods that many sought more direct ways to appeal to them outside the established limits of cult, which they regarded as an essentially passive religious activity. One such mechanism used to establish a more immediate relationship with the gods was divination.

Modes of divination were immensely varied. One way was to pay a visit to oracles, where the gods were thought to speak through inspired prophets. In the main, at established shrines, the gods only spoke directly to people of a high enough social standing to merit direct communication. A more indirect method of approaching a god was to consult an oracle that worked by a system of lot. A classic form of this type of divination in Egypt involved putting two notes, each containing an identical query and an alternative response, into an urn and taking the one that was drawn out as the god's answer. Other methods involved rolling dice and matching the number rolled against a list of predetermined responses, or observing fish feeding in a sacred pool, the eating habits of sacred chickens, or the way that a cheese floated. At sacrifices the slaughtered beast would be inspected after it had been killed to see if some sign was evident in its entrails, the behaviour of the animal would be closely watched to make sure that it comported itself properly on the way to its death, and, in the Roman tradition, a close eye was kept upon the weather and the flight of birds.

Where these activities began to overstep the boundaries of acceptable behaviour was when people solicited the wisdom of the gods from clairvoyants, magicians or seers who claimed to possess sacred writing from the sages of the distant past. Worse still, they could be employed to cast a spell on enemies: another common form of ancient religious text that has been unearthed by archaeologists is the *defixio*, usually a lead tablet with a curse upon it that was buried in some place where it was hoped that a demonic spirit would be called forth. The second-century Greek satirist Lucian (AD 120–*c.* 180) lampooned such all-purpose charlatans in his essay *Alexander The Oracle-Monger* (an attack on the prophet consulted by Marcus Aurelius, Alexander of Abonuteichos) as 'those who advertise enchantments, miraculous incantations, charms for your love-affairs, visitations for your enemies, disclosures of buried treasure, and successions to estates'.

For all its tolerance of local religious practices, the Roman state took a very dim view of prophets who operated outside the parameters of the state, especially magicians who claimed to be able to invoke supernatural visitations. Such people were potentially very dangerous – visionary prophets were responsible for fomenting the Jewish revolt in the time of Trajan, and the German rebellion that raged after Vespasian ascended the throne was fuelled by the visions of a woman named Veleda. Every emperor from Augustus onwards issued edicts against all manner of unauthorized contact with the divine. People who dabbled in magic to jinx their neighbours, along with the magicians who advised them how to do so, were liable to be sentenced to death. Even so, people who felt driven to desperate measures could not be prevented from appealing to them, and even emperors were known to consult independent 'experts'. Hadrian, for example, showered gifts on an Egyptian magician named Pancrates, while Marcus let it be known that the miraculous downpour that saved his soldiers during the Northern Wars was the work of another Egyptian magician named Harnouphis. Hadrian also published the horoscope of one of the senators whom he executed as a way of proving that he had done the right thing: conveniently, it showed that the man was destined to be a traitor. The huge gulf between what the law demanded and popular practice in consulting such practitioners attests to the abiding Roman fascination with divine revelation.

One especially famous visionary of the Roman world was a long-lived man by the name of Apollonius of Tyana (*c.* AD 1–97). Credited with what seems to have been a preternaturally long life, Apollonius was also credited with having saved the city of Ephesus from a plague demon and with curing the sick through faith-healing. When he died, many people believed that he had ascended to heaven, and sacred objects that he was thought to have used to ward off demons were widespread throughout the Eastern empire centuries after his death.

Eastern cults

The Romans also had the sense that Graeco-Roman culture was relatively young compared with the ancient cultures of Egypt and Mesopotamia. Tourists – including the emperor

Hadrian – travelled to Egypt to marvel at ancient books of wisdom and sit at the feet of members of obscure cults. Egyptian temples were repositories of texts that dated back to the time of the Pharaohs, and Egyptians were more than happy to supply this tourist market with purported Greek 'translations' of books of ancient wisdom (usually the ideas were deeply Hellenized to suit the buyers' tastes and bore only a passing resemblance to the original text). Another powerful Eastern influence on Roman religious thought was the ancient Persian sage Zoroaster; again, however, as with the learning of Egypt, Romans' understanding of Zoroastrianism was not primarily based on scholarly study of the core texts, but rather on debased, mediated forms of the religion. This somewhat dilettantish interest in the wisdom of the East was part and parcel of educated Romans' unquenchable sense of cultural superiority.

Their fascination derived less from a desire to learn from other cultures than from a smug satisfaction that the world under Rome's control embraced the collected wisdom of sages from all eras and all places. The fascination with new religious understanding from outside the Graeco-Roman tradition lies behind the adoption of a number of Eastern cults in the first century AD, whose popularity continued to expand over following centuries. One of these was the cult of Isis and Serapis, originally invented, it seems, by the first Ptolemaic king of Egypt in the early fourth century BC. Supported by an extensive mythology and a large body of religious texts – especially hymns in praise of Isis – the cult took hold throughout the Roman empire. Another cult that gained a huge following was that of the Persian sun-god

Mithras, which came to prominence in the later first century AD. The Roman form of Mithraism came via a sect in the area of eastern Turkey known as Commagene, who adopted traditions of Persian worship that had existed there since the days of Alexander the Great.

Mithraism is an especially interesting cult both because of the complexity of its belief system and the speed with which it spread around the empire, having been devised, it seems, by a rather small group of initiates in the first century AD – the parallel with another religious movement that developed in Palestine at roughly the same period is striking, and speaks to a need on the part of people living in the empire for certainties that came from outside the bounds of traditional classical culture. Mithras' rites were based on a complex mixture of astrology and myth. Members of this all-male cult were arranged into a hierarchy of seven grades, with the highest grade usually reserved for the individual who had the highest social standing in the world at large. The seven grades, which corresponded to the seven planets known to ancient astronomy, were the Father (Saturn), Heliodromos or 'Sun Runner' (the Sun), Persian (Moon), Lion (Jupiter), Soldier (Mars), Nymphus (Venus) and the Raven (Mercury). Rituals of Mithraism included an initiation banquet commemorating the meal that Mithras took with the Sun after he had created the world by killing a cosmic bull. The flowing blood of the slain bull was supposedly the source of all life and vegetation on Earth. During this ceremony, the Father pointed a bow at a naked initiate, recalling Mithras' firing of an arrow at a stone, bringing forth water. Another rite, the procession of the Heliodromos, mimicked the journey of the sun through the equinoxes and symbolized the journey taken by the human soul.

Mithraism's appeal was enhanced by the stress that its powerful liturgy placed on secrecy; because Mithras had killed the cosmic bull in a cave, the cult's temples, or *Mithraea* (singular: *Mithraeum*), were all located under ground. There was also a great emphasis on loyalty and discipline, making Mithraism highly attractive to soldiers. *Mithraea* were especially common where legions were stationed – one such ritual chamber has been found under Hadrian's Wall, and another at Dura Europus, a garrison city on the empire's far-eastern edge, attesting to the way that new cults could become common intellectual currency throughout the empire.

The rise of Christianity

Aspects of both the cults of Isis and Mithras, which promised salvation in an afterlife to devoted acolytes, were reflected in yet another Eastern cult that emerged in the course of the first century AD. Unlike the other two, however, this cult was far less readily absorbed into the bounds of conventional society. True, the cult of Isis had on occasion been officially suppressed – even being outlawed altogether for a while in Rome during the reign of Tiberius after its priests facilitated a notorious sex scandal involving people of senatorial status – but it never fundamentally challenged the norms of Roman society. Still less the cult of Mithras, which could even be construed as being openly supportive of the status quo. The same could not be said, however, of the cult whose central tenet was that a Jewish prophet executed *c.* AD 36 by the

Roman governor of Judea was the son of God and the saviour of mankind.

The fervent belief of the first followers of Jesus in the corruption of the world around them, and the rejection by many of any deity other than the One God of Jewish scripture, set the new movement at odds with all its neighbours. Christianity, as it emerged from the teachings of the first generation of preachers after the execution of Jesus, appealed to people as a genuine alternative to current religious practices. To be sure, other religious groups – notably the Celtic Druids – had found themselves at variance with the Roman state, but none of these other movements had texts in a language – Greek – that was universally understood.

Christianity appealed especially to people seeking an alternative to conventional morality. Unlike the Isis or Mithras cults, it turned not on the marvellous actions of a god, but rather on the suffering of a human being who had dared to defy established authority. Within a couple of generations, Christians had begun to produce a literature unequalled in its complexity and modernity, addressing as it did not some mythic past, but the conditions of life in the here and now. Even though splinter groups produced their own books of revelation that made the message of Jesus far more arcane than its expression in the four gospels and the letters of the early teachers, they still adhered to a core narrative that was firmly established by the reign of Domitian.

People were drawn to the new faith both because it was wholly independent of the power structure of the state, and by its insistence on a strict moral code. The often brutal response of the Roman government only served to increase

Christianity's popular appeal and publicize its message. Nero blamed Christians for the great fire of Rome in AD 64, and later emperors came to regard the new faith as so subversive that it ought to be banned. But just as outlawing magic did not quell interest in it, neither did the proscription of Christianity, which was only enforced erratically. The rise of Christianity in the first two centuries AD was not unparalleled as a sociological phenomenon, but it was unique in providing an alternative model for approaching the divine in a world where divine action was profoundly important.

THREE

Reinventing Caesar

The Slippery Slope: The Beginnings of Rome's Decline

(AD 180–211)

One thing that emerges very clearly from the works of Tacitus is that he was no purblind admirer of every aspect of Roman culture or of Rome's military might per se. He knew that Roman armies often did not live up to the high standards of drill and discipline that were expected in the ideal world and that grave defeats could result from these shortcomings. He also recognized the tendency of Romans to rest on the cultural laurels of the distant past. Finally, he was all too keenly aware that, beyond the empire's northern frontiers, there dwelt many unconquered (and unconquerable) peoples who might, in time, be impossible to contain. Yet, despite his critical acumen, even Tacitus failed to pinpoint what we, with the benefit of hindsight, can identify as the empire's greatest weakness – the highly traditional nature of Roman thought.

Senior Roman officers were trained, first and foremost, in the arts of administration. And this, in a nutshell, was the Achilles' heel of the Roman army as the second century drew to a close and the third began. Rome had no war college, and Roman commanders' understanding of warfare seems primarily to have been based upon the analysis of examples of past success rather than a wider appreciation of the factors that underlay that success. The most renowned generals of history – Alexander, Hannibal and Caesar – had all had the ability to adjust rapidly to changing circumstances. The generals who served under Marcus, though perfectly competent, seem rather to have favoured tradition over experimentation, stressing micromanagement over broad strategic thought. This issue is well illustrated in a manual on generalship entitled *The Stratagems of War*, in which a Macedonian writer named Polyaenus gathered together the successful stratagems of famous commanders of the past. He dedicated his book to Marcus and Verus, who at the time (AD 162–165) were campaigning against the Parthians. The sweeping, anecdotal approach taken in Polyaenus' book to the art of war stood in a long and honourable tradition of learning from the past, but is rather short on the practical aspects of waging war against Rome's current enemies.

If he wanted a more technical treatment, an aspiring Roman general could consult, at the other end of the spectrum, a book like Apollodorus of Damascus' work on siege engines. Trajan's chief military engineer during the Dacian Wars, and the architectural genius behind his forum, Apollodorus begins promisingly enough by stating that an unnamed ruler had asked advice in attacking an enemy who held a fortified height in an unnamed place. He lists the devices that could be used against all manner of potential threats, all practical enough, until he goes on to propose the construction of all manner of eccentric devices that seem designed simply to show off his cleverness. Yet, for all their ostensible differences, both works focus on the minutiae of tactics and on displays of authorial learning in preference to analysing more fundamental strategic problems.

Ironically, in learning by rote the career details of their illustrious predecessors, the generals of the second and third centuries failed to take on board precisely those essential, spontaneous qualities – innovation and flexibility – that made them truly great. And so, notwithstanding its initial success, Marcus' invasion of Persia in AD 163 was based on a plan devised by Julius Caesar in 44 BC, while the Northern Wars fought during his reign dragged on interminably because the enemy steadfastly refused to offer battle under conditions that Roman commanders had been schooled to deal with.

The issues that Tacitus highlighted – cultural complacency and the vast expanse of the non-Roman world to the north – would come to dominate the 80 years following Marcus' death. Beginning with internal upheaval, the empire's problems were later compounded by the sudden emergence of a militarily competent Persian dynasty in the 220s. Persian successes would so weaken Rome's central government that its defences against the northern tribes crumbled. Consequently, for more than a decade after AD 260, the empire split into three parts. The catastrophes of the 250s and 260s ushered in an era of radical reform rivalling that which saw the emergence of the imperial office in the time of Augustus. By AD 337, the Roman emperor was a Christian and Rome had ceased to be the centre of imperial government.

Theatre of blood

Commodus became sole emperor with the death of his father on March 17, AD 180; his subsequent reign was hallmarked by moments of extraordinary theatricality and brutality. Throughout his 12 years in power, Commodus showed a marked aversion to hands-on governance. Instead, he devoted his time to pleasure, and, ultimately, to learning the arts of an amphitheatrical entertainer. Meanwhile, those of his lieutenants to whom he entrusted the reins of government did their best to upset the fragile balance achieved by the emperors of the previous century. In the end, the scales tipped over into civil war, heralding the rise of a new regime in which the tensions unleashed at the end of Commodus' reign would never be fully reconciled.

The basic problem with Commodus was simply that he wasn't very bright. Naturally inclined to sloth, he left the business of government to a series of favourites. They, in turn, alienated those who wished for a continuation of the Antonine style of collaborative rule, even though they were often unwilling to make the concessions necessary for that system to work. The first crisis of Commodus' reign, two years after his accession, arose from nothing more serious than his crass insensitivity to the feelings of his elder sister Lucilla, who felt that the emperor's wife was threatening the prerogatives due to her, as the widow of Lucius Verus. Her response to the slights that she perceived was to gather about her a group of discontented younger senators and hatch a plot to assassinate her brother. The conspiracy might even have succeeded, if the chosen assassin had not shouted, 'The senate sends you this' as he drew a dagger on the emperor, whereupon he was overpowered and disarmed.

What emerged from this bungled assassination was far from the conspirators' intentions. One of the praetorian prefects, a man named Tigidius Perennis, noticed the emperor's abject terror during the incident and decided to turn it to his advantage. Inveigling himself into a position of trust by exploiting Commodus' fears, Perennis dominated the government for the next five years. Perennis was the most powerful official since Sejanus, and just as brutal and efficient in eliminating his political rivals. He took control of organizing the security of the empire, a task in which he acquitted himself well. The generals that Perennis appointed successfully maintained order on the frontiers, and so the image of Commodus that was projected to the provinces was largely positive, in marked contrast to his appalling reputation in Rome.

Yet Perennis had made many powerful enemies in Rome, especially in Commodus' inner circle, and before long Commodus' chief *cubicularius*, Marcus Aurelius Cleander, conspired to remove him. When a delegation of soldiers from mutinous legions in Britain arrived in Rome to warn Commodus of an alleged plot against him by Perennis, Cleander corroborated their claims and secured the emperor's agreement in having the legionaries murder the praetorian prefect. Cleander, whose background as a former slave made it impossible for him to claim a position that was formally outside the palace bureaucracy, now managed the state under the title of *a pugione*, which may be translated as 'dagger bearer' or, perhaps more accurately, 'emperor's bodyguard'.

Cleander's influence remained unchecked for a number of years until AD 189, when the prefect of the grain supply, in collusion with other figures in the court – including Commodus' sister Fadilla and his mistress, Marcia – arranged for a riot to take place in the Circus Maximus. The plan was to discredit Cleander in the emperor's eyes, and it worked brilliantly. The trouble began when a gigantic mime actress entered the arena and told the crowd that Cleander was planning to starve them; when the mob took to the streets, Commodus ordered Cleander's immediate execution. Effective government now devolved to Marcia, Eclectus (the new *cubicularius*, with whom she had a longstanding romantic liaison) and the new praetorian prefect.

The biggest problem facing the new governing coalition was that Commodus was growing ever more difficult to control, especially in his megalomania and his affection for gladiators and for the god Hercules. In AD 190, he renamed Rome Colonia Commodiana in his own honour – the same year that he added the name Hercules to his own after displaying his skill as a beast hunter in the amphitheatre at Lanuvium, just outside Rome. Having trained extensively as a public combatant – he may even have moved into a gladiatorial dormitory for a spell – he decided to treat the Roman people to displays of his fighting prowess. At the *ludi Romani* in AD 192, Commodus appeared in the Colosseum as both a beast hunter and a gladiator, in a series of performances that were intended to evoke the 12 labours of Hercules. The events included Commodus fighting gladiators armed with wooden weapons. Among the wide range of other events were displays of archery – including, we are told, the decapitation of ostriches with specially designed arrows – and the massacre of physically disabled people who were dressed as mythological monsters to recall Hercules' role in the battle between the gods and the giants. At one point Cassius Dio says that Commodus even held up the head of an ostrich in front of where the senators sat, suggesting that he could do the same to them. This grotesque spectacle proved to be the final straw. On the last day of AD 192, Marcia fed Commodus some poisoned beef; when it appeared that he might recover, she ordered a professional wrestler, Narcissus, to finish the job by strangling the emperor.

Sold to the highest bidder

The plot to assassinate Commodus had been organized in such an impromptu and secretive manner that the conspirators had not even had time to arrange the succession in advance. So it was that in the middle of the night, the elderly Helvius Pertinax (AD 126–193), twice consul of Rome and one of Marcus' best generals, was approached by the assassins and offered the job. He duly became emperor on New Year's Day, AD 193. The appointment was a disaster, with Pertinax turning out to be a harsh and unpopular disciplinarian. In particular, the praetorian guard resented the fact that the palace staff had conspired to murder an emperor whose eccentricities had worked in its favour, and was instantly restive when presented with the fait accompli. In March, a group of 300 praetorians left their camp and stormed the palace. When Pertinax tried to face them down, he was killed. He had reigned for just 86 days.

The day and night after the death of Pertinax witnessed one of the most bizarre events in the long history of Rome. The praetorian guard was adamant that no man could be made emperor without its prior approval, but on this occasion had no candidate in mind. One of the praetorian prefects had gone to the camp to negotiate on his own behalf when there suddenly appeared outside the walls a wealthy senator named Didius Julianus (AD 133–193). Accompanied by a crowd of followers chanting slogans in favour of Commodus, he gained admission to the camp and, having promised to pay a much larger accession *donativum*, or gift, than his rival, won the guards' support. Accession gifts had a long history going back to the time of Tiberius, and the amount offered by Julianus was not much more than the sum Marcus Aurelius had paid when he became emperor. Yet the circumstances were far more nakedly corrupt when Julianus took office. In encouraging this public auction of the throne, Julianus colluded in the notion that the army held the whip hand in appointing a new emperor. This lesson was immediately taken to heart outside Rome.

Out of Africa

Long before AD 193, Tacitus had written in his account of the civil wars of AD 69 that the dread secret of empire was that it was possible to make an emperor elsewhere than in Rome. No sooner had the events surrounding Julianus' succession become known in the provinces than three provincial governors were immediately proclaimed emperor by their armies: Clodius Albinus (*c.* AD 145–197) in Britain, Pescennius Niger (*c.* AD 145–194) in Syria and Septimius Severus (AD 146–211) on the Danube. It is entirely likely that all three men, aware that Pertinax was in a weak position, had already planned some sort of intervention; his murder simply provided the excuse they needed.

Of the three new claimants to the throne, Severus was in the strongest position. The descendant of a wealthy North African family of Phoenician ancestry in the city of Leptis Magna, he had risen through the ranks of the senate to become commander of Roman forces in Pannonia by AD 191. The central European armies, totalling ten legions, were the most powerful in the empire. Moreover, Severus had taken care to forge an alliance with the other governors in the region – one of whom was his elder brother – and they were all at his disposal. And, last but not least, of all the pretenders to the throne, he was physically closest to Rome. Proclaimed emperor at Carnuntum (on the Danube, now in Lower Austria) on 9 April, Severus was in Rome by mid-June. As Severus approached the city, Julianus realized that resistance would be futile; he was soon dispatched by a member of the Praetorian Guard. His pathetic last words were reportedly 'But what evil have I done? Whom have I killed?' The betrayal of Julianus did the guard no good – Severus dismissed them and appointed members of his army in their place. He then departed to attack Niger and struck a deal with Albinus, trading the position of heir apparent, or Caesar, in return for his loyalty. This alliance was merely a temporary expedient.

Meanwhile, Pescennius Niger's actions in the east had already precipitated civil war. Heavily outnumbered, he knew that his only hope of success lay in quickly invading territory held by Severus and winning swift victories before his rival could concentrate his forces. For his part, Severus had needed few men to take Rome and so had lost no time in dispatching a large part of his army to face Niger. Before long, he had managed to displace the theatre of war eastwards through Turkey into Syria. Winning the final battle in May AD 194 at a place called Issus – previously famous as the site of a great victory by Alexander the Great – Severus spent the rest of the year hunting down supporters of Niger, rewarding those who had switched allegiance and launching an expedition against the western provinces of the Persian empire. The immediate pretext for this act of aggression was that the Persian king had aided Niger. Even before returning to Rome, Severus elevated Caracalla, the elder of his two sons, to the rank of Caesar. This amounted to a declaration of war on Albinus, who was crushed after fierce fighting in February, AD 197, at the Battle of Lugdunum (Lyons).

Rome's new dictator

Between his return to Rome in AD 195 and his departure to fight against Albinus, Severus took the remarkable step of retroactively having himself adopted into the family of Marcus Aurelius. This attempt to validate his claim to authority was backed by the specious assertion that Commodus was his brother. It could have been interpreted as a salute to the traditions of an earlier age, but Severus eschewed the merciful moderation of his new-found Antonine ancestors. Rather, his avowed role-model was the dictator Sulla, a fact he made plain in a thinly veiled threat to senators when they protested at his deification of Commodus. His large-scale executions of men who were suspected of sympathizing with his rivals certainly recalled Sulla's proscriptions.

Although Severus filled Rome with monuments to his regime, he clearly did not feel at ease in the capital. Immediately after defeating Albinus, he took off for a further campaign in the east, sacking the Persian capital Ctesiphon, and adding new provinces between the Euphrates and Tigris rivers in what is now southeastern Turkey. This was the first significant addition of new territory to the empire since the time of Trajan, and it soon proved to be a source of serious trouble. The new province, known as Mesopotamia, was a constant provocation and casus belli to later Persian kings, who saw Roman control of the region as a threat to their security.

In the years following his invasion of Persia, Severus continued to traverse the provinces, visiting first Egypt and then his North African homeland, where he rebuilt his home city of Leptis Magna to make it appear a suitable place of origin for an emperor. While he was engaged on his extensive travels, Severus turned over much of the day-to-day administration of the empire to his kinsman and fellow North African Gaius Fulvius Plautianus (d. AD 205). Plautianus had performed invaluable services for Severus in the perilous year AD 193 – including ensuring that his wife and children were spirited out of Rome before Julianus could do them harm – and was now sole praetorian prefect. He further strengthened his bond to the emperor by marrying off his daughter Fulvia Plautilla to Severus' son Caracalla. Plautianus enjoyed such favour at this time that statues of him were erected alongside those of close members of the imperial household. Cassius Dio claims that when unfounded rumours of Plautianus' demise swept the empire, civic officials tore down these statues and were subsequently executed for treason.

A troubled succession

In the course of AD 205 the relationship between Severus and Plautianus cooled dramatically. The agent of the change may have been Caracalla, who hated both his wife Fulvia Plautilla and his father-in-law. Accused of organizing a conspiracy, Plautianus was summoned to the palace and summarily executed. Effective control of the state now passed to a group of Severus' most trusted confederates, including Papinian (AD 142–212), the greatest jurist of the age. Another key member of the charmed circle was Severus' wife, Julia Domna (*c.* AD 170–217). Julia was related to the formerly royal house of the Syrian city of Emesa (Homs), whose members now held the priesthood of the sky god; Severus – like many emperors before him, spellbound by astrology – is reputed to have married her after he learned that her horoscope predicted she would marry a king. Their marriage was a happy one, and she bore Severus two sons in quick succession – Caracalla in AD 186 and Publius Septimius Geta in AD 189. The two boys were quarrelsome from the outset; tensions between them were not eased by the fact that their mother made it quite clear that Geta was her favourite. In his final years, their father made several fruitless attempts to reconcile his warring sons.

Ever ambivalent about Rome, Septimius Severus took

personal command of a campaign in northern Britain in AD 209 to push back tribes that had broken through the Antonine Wall. Operations went well, but the emperor fell severely ill and died at Eboracum (York) in February, AD 211. Prior to his death, Severus probably recognized that neither of his sons – both of whom accompanied him on his British campaign – was yet capable of ruling on his own. He therefore decreed that they should ascend the throne jointly; accordingly, in AD 211, Caracalla and Geta became co-emperors of Rome, an arrangement that had not been witnessed for 50 years since the joint rule of Marcus Aurelius and Lucius Verus. The sibling rivalry between Severus' two sons was driven by intense hatred and, before the year was through, their turbulent relationship was to end in bloodshed.

Inadequates and Misfits: Emperors of the Early Third Century

(AD 211–238)

Severus' reported deathbed advice to his sons was that they should 'live in harmony with one another, enrich the soldiers, and despise everyone else'. The second and final elements of this edict represent a radical break with the policies of the Antonine age. While careful to maintain good relations with the military, rulers from Tiberius onwards had always been wary of identifying too closely with it. It was a problematic new departure that the emperor's authority should now be seen to depend solely on the wishes of the army.

If Severus had hoped that his sons would learn to get along, he would have been seriously disappointed at the outcome. By the time they returned to Rome, the new joint rulers had ceased speaking to each other, and set about dividing the imperial palace between them, walling off direct access points between the two zones. The administration was hopelessly split between advisers such as Papinian, who were devoted to trying to make dual government work, and partisans of either side. In this power struggle, Geta was at a severe disadvantage. He was younger, possibly less ruthless, and certainly less well connected than his brother. By 25 December, AD 211, Caracalla felt that he had gained enough of an upper hand to summon Geta to a private meeting. It was a trap; centurions of the guard concealed in the room butchered him as he sought the protection of his mother, who had come to mediate the encounter. A wholesale massacre then ensued of anyone, including Papinian, who was deemed potentially disloyal to Caracalla. It is alleged that this round of bloodletting claimed up to 12,000 lives.

The unpopular populist

For all his calculated brutality, Caracalla seems to have craved popular acclaim. He spent a great deal of time at the circus, gave private exhibitions of his skill as a hunter and was a competent enough athlete to master driving a racing chariot, albeit not in public. In styling himself a man of the people, his intention may have been to let the populace of Rome know that he shared their pleasures, while expressly avoiding the excessive showmanship of Commodus. Early in AD 212, Caracalla also took the remarkable step of inviting the empire to share in his joy at having escaped unscathed the alleged plots of his brother by issuing an edict (the so-called *Constitutio Antoniniana*) that conferred citizenship upon all free-born inhabitants of the empire:

> Imperator Caesar Marcus Aurelius Augustus Antoninus Pius herewith decrees the following: After having received numerous requests and petitions enquiring above all how I propose to give thanks to the immortal gods for saving me by granting me victory over my enemies, I now deem it prudent to announce that I am minded to undertake in gratitude an act of great

magnanimity and piety, as befits the gods' great majesty . . . Accordingly, I am granting to all those non-citizens who dwell within the borders of the Empire the rights of Roman citizenship, including all those who live in cities of whatever kind but with the exception of the *dediticii* [prisoners of war settled in Roman territory]. It is meet and proper that the general populace should also henceforth share in the joy of my victory. This edict shall redound to the greater glory of the Roman people.

(from a papyrus found in Egypt in 1901 (includes editorial interpolations to make sense of the badly damaged Greek text))

Most of Rome's imperial subjects had not been citizens prior to the promulgation of this edict. However, even taking Caracalla's professed motivation for this decree at face value, the impact of the *Constitutio* was more symbolic than real; people were still attached to the empire through the mechanisms of local government, meaning that it mattered little whether they were formally designated citizens or not. More significantly, the age-old protections that Roman citizens had enjoyed from cruel and unusual punishments, such as exposure to the beasts and crucifixion, had long since been eroded, so that only people who were both citizens and locally important were now spared the horrors of those modes of execution. By the early third century, even high social status was not always adequate protection if the charge against a person was sufficiently serious.

Cassius Dio, for one, took a highly sceptical view of

Caracalla's supposed magnanimity when he claimed that the *Constitutio Antoniniana* was a cynical move aimed solely at increasing taxes raised in hard currency. One result of the edict was indeed that more people now became liable to inheritance taxes. The decree ultimately derived its name from Septimius Severus' forced attempt to cover his own dynasty in some of the reflected glory of the Antonines. However, the spirit of the age of these 'new' Antonines was very different from that of their illustrious second-century predecessors.

Caracalla plainly failed in his objective of winning over the Roman people, despite ordering lavish public works such as the extensive Baths of Caracalla in AD 212. Instead, he took off for the provinces, journeying from the Rhine to the Danube before proceeding further east. As he spent more and more time in the company of his troops, he followed the dying words of his father by shamelessly currying favour with the army. He increased soldiers' pay substantially (to 1250 *denarii* annually) and reportedly even marched on foot alongside the legionaries. The unashamed favouritism he displayed towards the military was only matched by his callous disregard towards civilian populations. In AD 215, Caracalla's response to insulting chants (regarding the death of his brother) from a hostile crowd that had assembled as he entered the city of Alexandria in Egypt was to unleash a wholesale massacre of his tormentors.

In the course of his travels Caracalla became fascinated with Alexander the Great, presenting himself as a new version of the great conqueror and even rearming some legions in the style of the ancient Macedonians. In AD 216, he resolved to undertake a serious military adventure, and emulate his hero Alexander by invading the Persian empire. By the end of that year, he stood on the plain of Gaugamela (near Mosul in northern Iraq), where Alexander had won one of his greatest victories, before withdrawing to overwinter with the army in Roman territory.

Caracalla had long fancied himself something of an antiquarian, with a particular interest in artifacts relating to the mythological past or to the gods. As he waited to launch his Parthian campaign, he decided to spend the first week of April, AD 217, viewing ancient ruins around Carrhae – modern Harran in southern Turkey – one of the oldest inhabited sites on earth. Venturing out from the city one day to visit a nearby temple dedicated to the moon goddess Luna, he dismounted from his horse to relieve himself. As he did so, a man who had been suborned by Marcus Opellius Macrinus (AD 165–218), one of the praetorian prefects, ran him through with his sword. This undignified end was not unfitting for a nefarious and obnoxious ruler.

A short interregnum

After several days of intense negotiation, the general staff agreed to make Macrinus emperor. Despite being implicated in the conspiracy against Caracalla, it was not a job that Macrinus sought with any great eagerness, as the situation confronting him was extremely dangerous. The king of Persia was advancing on Roman territory at the head of a substantial force, while discontent was rife among the rank and file of the Roman army. After an indecisive encounter with the

Persians, who agreed to make peace in return for an enormous indemnity payment, Macrinus withdrew the army to spend the winter in Syria. He would have been better advised to return to Rome.

Never popular with the army, Macrinus made the situation worse when he declared his intention of rescinding the additional pay granted by Caracalla to new recruits. Although existing soldiers kept their new pay packages, they felt threatened by the move. Another cloud was also looming on Macrinus' horizon: Caracalla's mother Julia Domna, who had accompanied her son to the east, died in the early months of his reign, but her sister Julia Maesa began to plot against the new emperor. Fearful that she would lose the prerogatives that went with being an imperial aunt, she withdrew to the family homeland of Emesa in Syria. There she encountered her teenaged nephew Varius Avitus Bassianus, who was the chief priest of the local sun-god Elagabal. Because he somewhat resembled Caracalla, she was able to convince soldiers of the legion stationed near the city that Bassianus was in fact his illegitimate son. The soldiers were already unhappy with Macrinus, and with the additional sweetener of a substantial bribe, promptly proclaimed the boy emperor when he was brought to their camp. Macrinus bungled an attempt to nip the revolt in the bud, but finally managed to muster a force to confront his rivals. The battle was evenly matched until Macrinus lost his nerve and fled the field. He got as far as Asia Minor before a centurion who had been sent in pursuit caught up with him and cut off his head.

The most eccentric emperor

Although his formal name as emperor was Marcus Aurelius Antoninus (reinforcing his spurious claim to be related to Caracalla), the young man from Emesa is generally known by a Latinized form of the name of his patron deity: Elagabalus (*c.* AD 203–222). His reign is one of the most controversial in Roman history, despite the best efforts of the effective palace staff that he inherited from Caracalla to rein in his excesses. The civil war that brought Elagabalus to the throne was essentially a struggle for control between members of the government who were closely associated with the palace and the more bureaucratic elements that had supported Macrinus. The ascendant palace group made genuine efforts to include members of the senate and senior equestrian bureaucracy in the regime.

Contemporary commentators such as Dio Cassius and Marius Maximus would later castigate the palace faction as a collection of worthless sexual deviants. This is probably a piece of retrospective self-justification, for both men were comfortably employed under this discredited regime. Marius continued to hold the prefecture of Rome that Macrinus had granted him, while Dio had a sinecure as overseer of financial affairs in his home province of Bithynia. The issue that would divide Dio and other decent provincial administrators from their patrons in Rome was the uncontrollably eccentric behaviour of the emperor.

Elagabalus believed passionately in the power of the sun-god and was intent on installing him as the principal deity in the Roman pantheon. Giving Elagabal the Latin honorific *Deus Sol Invictus* ('God the Undefeated Sun'), Elagabalus dressed in elaborate priestly robes and led dances around the god's altar. However, the emperor's exotic form of piety struck more conventional Romans as nothing short of a transvestite charade, and Roman senators had limited tolerance for such expressions of cultural difference. As if all this were not enough, the emperor then announced that the gods of the Roman pantheon were henceforth all subservient to Elagabal. The pinnacle of Elagabalus' scandalous behaviour was reached when he married the Vestal Virgin Aquilia Severa, a blatant violation of one of the most hallowed tenets of traditional Roman religious observance. The emperor claimed that 'godlike children' would result from their union.

While this religious controversy was raging, turmoil also reigned within the emperor's own *domus*. The imperial household was riven by factionalism, and relations between his mother Julia Soaemias and her sister Julia Mamaea were becoming increasingly strained. The matriarch of the clan, Julia Maesa, could do little to reconcile them. She may also have sensed that the emperor's very public eccentricities were becoming intolerable, that violent change was in the offing and that she should position herself so as to be able to exploit that change. In AD 221, she convinced Elagabalus to name his cousin, Severus Alexander (AD 208–235), as his heir. Too late, Elagabalus realized that by adopting a refreshingly conventional young man, he had effectively signed his own death warrant. At the beginning of AD 222 he went to the praetorian camp, and ordered them to murder Alexander. Although the precise details of what then occurred are confused, the praetorians (probably bribed by Maesa and Mamaea) ended up killing both Elagabalus and Julia Soaemias, dumping their bodies in the Tiber and proclaiming Severus Alexander emperor. The senate confirmed the decision of the guard and banished the cult of the alien god Elagabal to Emesa. This would not, however, be the last time that a Roman emperor decided to favour a religion based upon the worship of what was originally a Semitic mountain god.

The power behind the throne

Severus Alexander, who was probably aged about 11 when he ascended the throne, was no more capable of running the empire than his cousin. What he did have, though, was a much smarter mother than his predecessor. Julia Mamaea moved quickly to secure the loyalty of members of the traditional aristocracy. Men who might reasonably have thought that their careers were over – including Cassius Dio – were brought back into positions of prominence, and the court ceased to be dominated by members of the royal household. In many ways, the new regime looked like a vision of the age of Marcus Aurelius, when experienced statesmen advised a young emperor, who then acted according to this wise counsel. The problem was that appearances were deceptive in this case; Severus Alexander was in fact incapable of acting as a chief executive, and the government defaulted into a deeply conservative, reactive mentality. Under ordinary circumstances this might not have been fatal. But circumstances were far from ordinary. In AD 225, Ardashir, ruler of a southern Iranian principality, overthrew the king of Parthia and founded a new dynasty – the Sassanids – which became renowned for its religious fundamentalism and military prowess. The Sassanid dynasty was to rule Persia for over 400 years until Muslim armies conquered the region in AD 651. Once again, Rome found itself under threat from a familiar quarter.

Rome dithered as Ardashir consolidated his power. The emperor and his advisers had no coherent strategy and crucially failed to appreciate that the powerful driving force behind the Iranian revolution was a strict adherence to the principles of Zoroastrianism. Ardashir believed that he was doing the will of Ahura Mazda, the god of Light and Truth, by destroying the servants of Ahriman, the god of the Lie and Darkness. Instead, Rome continued to back the discredited old regime. It was only when Ardashir launched raids against the province of Mesopotamia, and the garrison there mutinied, that the central government decided to act. Alexander himself journeyed east with his mother to oversee the operations.

The only positive thing that can be said about the Roman invasion of Parthia in AD 231 is that, unlike previous such ventures, it at least tried to show originality by not slavishly following Caesar's superannuated battle plan. That said – given the complete lack of decent intelligence about Ardashir's dispositions – it would have fared far better if it had. Caesar had been a past-master at bringing pressure to bear at decisive points against his enemy; by contrast, Severus' generals did just the opposite. Splitting the army into three parts, they sent one into northwestern Iran, where forces hostile to Ardashir still held out in the kingdom of Media, another on the familiar route towards Ctesiphon from the north and a third down the River Euphrates in the direction of the kingdom of Mesene. These separate forces committed a cardinal military error by failing to advance in a coordinated fashion. No sooner had the southern column reached the vast marshlands that once extended north of the modern city of Basra than it was routed. The central column was stopped in its tracks, and only the northern expedition gained some measure of success.

These humiliations badly damaged Alexander's prestige, and he was desperate to try and recoup some success to offset the fiasco in Persia. Returning to Rome to celebrate a rather hollow triumph in AD 233, he departed the following year, again accompanied by his mother, for the German frontier. This effort to win back the loyalty of the army failed. In early March, AD 235, Alexander and Mamaea were murdered at Mainz in a mutiny led by a junior officer from Thrace called Julius Maximinus (*c.* AD 173–238).

Maximinus seized the throne for himself and immediately tried to secure his position by launching a series of attacks against the tribes north of the Rhine and Danube. He never set foot in Rome, and offended the populace by cutting back on subsidizing the grain supply. The traditional aristocracy plainly resented an upstart, and in February, AD 238, the senate lent its support to an elderly senator, Gordian (*c.* AD 159–238), who declared himself emperor in North Africa.

The year of the seven emperors

The initial phases of the revolt of AD 238 were deeply depressing. Gordian I and his son Gordian II (*c.* AD 192–238), who had also been declared emperor, were killed by soldiers under the command of the governor of the neighbouring province of Numidia, a loyal supporter of Maximinus. Realizing that Maximinus was unlikely to be a merciful victor, the senate then elected a board of 20 men to uphold the defence of the realm against the emperor, whom it declared an enemy of the state. This action of the senate was eloquent testimony to the great store it set by the principle of collegial government. In accordance with this, not one but two men, Pupienus (*c.* AD 178–238) and Balbinus (d. AD 238), were promptly declared co-emperors. When friends of the deceased Gordians instigated a riot among the Roman people because that family had been cut out of the succession, Pupienus and Balbinus agreed to include the nephew of the younger Gordian, a youth of 13, in their new imperial college as heir apparent. It is a sign of the deep and growing discontent with Maximinus that declarations of loyalty to this unlikely coalition began to arrive from many parts of the empire, even as the emperor led his battle-hardened army from the Balkans into Italy.

Even given this patent lack of enthusiasm for Maximinus, the events of the late winter and early spring of AD 238 must have astonished the contemporary world. When Maximinus entered Italy, his army came to a halt before the city of Aquileia, whose strong defences had once provided refuge for Marcus Aurelius in the early phase of his war against the northern tribes. Weeks passed while Maximinus tried unsuccessfully to capture the city. The army, which in all likelihood was not properly provisioned, grew restless, and, at the beginning of April, murdered its emperor.

Pupienus and Balbinus did not enjoy their remarkable triumph for long. The Praetorian Guard, which feared that it would be replaced in this highly volatile situation of shifting political allegiances, murdered the co-emperors and declared for Gordian III (AD 225–244). Since Maximinus had made his own son co-emperor when he invaded Italy, the young Gordian officially became the seventh person to hold the position of Augustus in the course of AD 238. His reign, which was dominated by members of the equestrian bureaucracy, would last for nearly six years before he fell victim to the new power that had arisen in the east.

Anarchy and Disorder: The Crisis of the Third Century

(AD 239–270)

Rome was so inherently unstable that it was AD 241 before the empire was able to mount a truly robust response to the challenge posed by the Sassanid empire. Gordian III made his father-in-law, an equestrian named Timesitheus, praetorian prefect. Timesitheus took a long time to muster Rome's forces and get them into position to attack. Yet when the assault finally took place, in AD 243, the Persians under Ardashir's son Shapur I (r. AD 241–272) were roundly defeated, being pushed back over the Euphrates and routed at the Battle of Resaena.

Timesitheus died suddenly, and his co-prefect, Julius Priscus, now the effective head of the government, elevated his own brother Marcus Julius Philippus (*c.* AD 204–249) to serve alongside him. They remained in office as the army, now with Gordian in titular command, launched an ill-advised invasion of Iraq in the winter of AD 244. As the Romans established a bridgehead on the Euphrates from which to advance on Ctesiphon, Shapur struck. The Roman army was defeated and Gordian was murdered in his camp. Philippus became emperor; he is known to history as Philip the Arab, since his family's origins lay in Syria.

A hands-on ruler

The reign of Philip marks an interesting turning point in the history of the third century AD. He was the first equestrian emperor to govern from Rome – neither Macrinus nor Maximinus had gone near the capital – and he took a decidedly proactive approach to the empire's more intractable problems. One of the major issues that he set out to tackle was imperial finance. The ignominious peace settlement he was forced to conclude with Persia after Gordian's defeat entailed large reparations payments (and was soon violated anyway). A further huge drain on the state's finances was the lavish celebrations held in AD 248 to mark the 1000th anniversary of the founding of Rome.

Despite his concern over the state of the imperial coffers, Philip would have viewed the outlay on the millennial games as vital for proclaiming his prestige. Another expensive but indispensable vanity project was the reconstruction of his native city of Shahba in modern Syria. As an outsider from a part of the empire that had not yet produced a ruler, Philip would doubtless have felt the need to burnish his Roman credentials by equipping his home town with magnificent edifices befitting the birthplace of an emperor. Philippopolis – as the new city 56 miles (90 kilometres) south of Damascus was called – is remarkable for its many fine buildings, including temples, a theatre and bath houses, all in the Roman architectural style.

To pay for all of this, Philip increased the number of people in each community who were responsible for making up any shortfall in annual tax payments from their own pockets. Regarding the overall administration of the empire, he realized that the Severan centralization of authority around the person of the emperor was deeply flawed. He counteracted this trend by appointing men to effectively serve as deputy emperors in various regions. His first two such appointments were family members – Julius Priscus in the east, and a relative named Severianus in the Balkans.

Yet if this decentralization was at root a good idea, another of Philip's money-saving measures – cutting subsidies to the tribes north of the Danube – turned out to be not such a prudent move. Since the chiefs who were loyal depended upon these payments to maintain their status, the effect of Philip's cuts was either to undermine loyalists or turn them against Rome. Trouble flared almost immediately after he took office, and, in the wake of the millennial games, more serious revolts broke out in the regions of Moesia and Pannonia. Gaius Messius Quintus Decius (*c.* AD 201–251), a senator who had once served Maximinus in the civil war of AD 238, was sent to suppress the trouble on the Danube. However, no sooner had he succeeded in his mission than his troops persuaded him to proclaim himself emperor. He marched on Rome and defeated and killed Philip at Verona.

Attempts to revive past glories

Few emperors have left such a strong impression on the historical sources as Decius, who was passionately attached to a vision of the traditions of the imperial past, while utterly lacking the ability to secure those traditions. One of his most notable acts, almost as soon as he had defeated Philip, was to promulgate an edict ordering all citizens of the empire to sacrifice for the welfare of the state. Another was to issue coins commemorating the 'good emperors' of the past, as part of what appears to have been a concerted attempt to rewrite the history of the early third century. A third was to take for himself the name of Trajan, thus associating himself with a past golden age of imperial rule.

Unfortunately for both Decius and the empire as a whole, he lacked the qualities of his namesake. None of his initiatives addressed the fundamental causes of unrest along the northern frontiers or in the eastern provinces, where rebellions had been smouldering since the later years of Philip's reign. Of the two threats, the one from the northern tribes – this time ancestors of the later Gothic peoples – was the more urgent. A large invading force of Goths swept across the Danube in AD 250, ambushing Decius and destroying a large part of his army before laying waste to the great city of Philippopolis (the settlement named after Philip of Macedon; now the city of Plovdiv in Bulgaria). Although Decius finally caught up with the raiders, his army was lured into swampy terrain and destroyed at the Battle of Abrittus in June AD 251. The emperor and his son both fell in this engagement. Trebonianus Gallus (*c.* AD 206–253), one of the governors of the Danubian provinces, succeeded to the throne.

Overwhelmed by enemies

In AD 252, Shapur I invaded the eastern provinces by moving up the Euphrates rather than across northern Mesopotamia, the expected route for a Persian attack. He crushed a Roman army at Barbalissos, before ravaging Syria and sacking Antioch. At the same time, a group of tribesmen from the Black Sea coast launched seaborne attacks, bursting through the Dardanelles into the Aegean and sacking many cities there, including Ephesus, the greatest city of western Turkey.

The years AD 251–252 rank as the worst in Roman imperial history: three major cities were sacked, two armies were destroyed and the emperor was seemingly powerless to prevent the carnage. When the Danubian army won a victory in AD 253, it proclaimed its own general, Aemilianus (*c.* AD 207–253), emperor. Aemilianus defeated Gallus in central Italy before falling prey to Valerian (AD 200–260), an ally of Gallus, who had arrived too late to help the former emperor.

For the next several years Valerian and his son Gallienus (*c.* AD 218–268), then a man of mature years, whom he appointed as his co-ruler – while elevating various sons of Gallienus to the rank of Caesar – had only intermittent success in reversing the downward trend in Roman power. Still, the joint rule of Valerian and Gallienus, with designated successors, presaged more successful similar arrangements later in the century, and demonstrated a recognition that the empire could no longer be governed by a single ruler if there were serious threats on multiple fronts.

For several years after the joint regime took effect, the Roman army was able to keep the tribes in check along the Rhine and Danube frontiers; and on the eastern frontier, a desperate action by the Roman garrison of Dura Europus, the fortress city on the banks of the Euphrates, prevented another major Persian invasion of Syria. Captured in AD 252, and retaken by the Romans shortly after that, the city's defences had been massively reinforced against a future siege. One result of those defensive arrangements was that a synagogue and the earliest-known Christian church, both located near the city wall, were buried as the walls were being reinforced against battering-rams. The splendid paintings of the synagogue, preserved in the dry environment of the desert, are now housed in the Damascus Museum, while the paintings from the Christian church are in the Yale Art Gallery in New Haven, where visitors may see the earliest Christian images of New Testament stories.

It was not only art that archaeologists found at Dura: they also discovered signs of a vast Persian camp set up outside the city walls in AD 256, suggesting that a major invasion had been set in motion, but the city held long enough to prevent a further advance. Amongst the signs of desperate struggle it appears that we also have the earliest direct evidence for chemical warfare, as the Persians used what was essentially poison gas to kill a group of Roman soldiers who entered a tunnel to try and prevent the enemy from undermining the walls. They died, but the Persian's mine failed to bring down the reinforced tower that was its target, and so the siege continued until finally the Persians poured into the town, slaughtering or enslaving the surviving defenders.

Valerian, who had plainly left the defenders of Dura to their fate, now took another tack in seeking to defend the existing frontiers. It appears that he now felt he could do this by eliminating those who did not subscribe to the cultural unity of the empire. It was he who, in AD 257, issued the first empire-wide edict ordering active persecution of the Christian Church, the seizure of Christians' property and the execution of Christians who did not recant their beliefs. This too presaged later developments, as Roman emperors sought to enforce greater ideological unity amongst their subjects than had been the case in the past. As with all such efforts to enforce conformity through persecution, it was a sign that the state was losing its ability to provide for its subjects' welfare in real terms.

An emperor in chains

In AD 259, after failing to defend western Turkey from yet another naval assault from the Black Sea, Valerian found himself threatened by a new Persian invasion. Shapur crossed into the Roman province of Mesopotamia in the spring of AD 260 to find a Roman army weakened by disease and on the verge of mutiny. When, after suffering a defeat south of Edessa, Valerian sued for peace, Shapur threw him in chains and sent him as a captive to Persia while his armies plundered the eastern provinces. He was the only Roman emperor ever to be taken prisoner. Later Roman tradition held that Shapur humiliated Valerian by using him as a human footstool when mounting his horse. Yet Persian sources claim that the ex-emperor ended his days in Bishapur, in south-central Iran, where he and some of his former troops were employed on engineering projects such as bridge-building.

The disgrace of Valerian's surrender precipitated a major crisis. In the east, as the Persian army overextended itself, the most senior official to survive the disaster, Fulvius

Macrianus (d. AD 261), rallied what was left of the army and drove the Persians back. In this campaign, he was given invaluable military assistance by Septimius Odaenathus (d. AD 268), prince of Palmyra. The Palmyrenes had every reason to fear the rise of the Sassanian kingdom, as the Persians began to threaten Palmyra's traditional dominance over key trade routes in the Middle East. Odaenathus had initially tried to counter the Persian threat through diplomacy, sending gifts to Shapur I. However, when his overtures were rebuffed, Odaenathus renounced Palmyra's neutral stance, raised a large mounted army and threw in his lot with Rome.

After repulsing Shapur, Macrianus had his sons declared emperors, and then invaded the Balkans, where two revolts had broken out at the news of Valerian's defeat. Gallienus defeated the uprisings and Macrianus' attempted invasion but, realizing that he could not restore order in the east without help, recognized Odaenathus as commander there. Palmyrene armies enjoyed considerable success against Shapur, and Odaenathus proclaimed himself 'King of Kings', governing and dressing in a style more evocative of a Persian king than a Roman official. Nevertheless, Odaenathus remained loyal to Gallienus, never challenging his authority to appoint his own officials to provincial commands. The fruitful symbiotic relationship that developed in Palmyra between local initiative and centralized control demonstrates the continuing effectiveness of the traditional Roman policy of allowing regional rulers a large measure of self-determination in their dealings with the central Roman administration.

In fact, Gallienus faced a far worse situation in the west

than in the east. Although he was able to deploy an army to regain control of the Balkans that had much greater battlefield mobility than traditional legionary forces, Gallienus could not reverse the effects of the revolt on the Rhine that had begun in AD 260. The leader of that uprising, Postumus, proclaimed the 'Empire of the Gauls' from his headquarters in Trier (Augusta Treverorum) and ruled the western provinces, including Spain and Britain, until his death in a military coup in the summer of AD 269. In AD 268, Gallienus, whose major effort to unseat Postumus had failed when he was wounded in battle during AD 265, fell victim to a plot by his own senior officers while trying to suppress yet another rebellion, staged this time by a senior commander in northern Italy.

A new model of governance

The eight years of Gallienus' sole reign presented a new model for governing the Roman empire that would, with refinements, re-emerge time and again over the next two centuries, before the western empire ceased to function altogether. This model conceived the empire not as a monolithic whole but as a series of self-contained units. The eastern provinces from Egypt to what is now Turkey formed a natural unit, as did the central European provinces along with Italy and – for the present, at least – North Africa, whose surplus grain was crucial for Rome's survival. The provinces north and west of the Alps could look after themselves. In the long run, the main issue would be whether central Europe should be joined to the eastern provinces or remain as a unit of empire in conjunction with Italy. While North Africa remained secure, Italy's importance remained unquestioned; the key question yet to be posed was what would happen to the empire if North Africa should ever be lost?

The death of Gallienus coincided with yet another crisis. The central European tribes launched a major attack in AD 268 by both land and sea. The emperor who succeeded Gallienus, a Balkan general named Marcus Aurelius Claudius (AD 213–270), comprehensively defeated his barbarian foes in two key battles later that summer, crushing the Goths at Naissus and the Alamanni, a new confederation of Germans that had emerged in the earlier part of the third century in southern Germany, at Lake Benacus. Emperor Claudius II's accession came as the regimes in both Gaul and Palmyra were undergoing radical changes; Odaenathus was killed by an assassin from within his own entourage at the spring festival of Elagabal at Emesa in AD 268, while the government of Gaul descended into temporary chaos after Postumus' murder. Yet Claudius completely mismanaged the opportunity that these changes presented. He was unable to turn the situation in Gaul to his advantage, and wrecked good relations between Rome and Palmyra by insisting that Odaenathus' position as general had died with him. After the defeat of a Roman expeditionary force in western Turkey, Palmyrene armies took over direct control of Arabia and Egypt. The driving force behind the operation was Odaenathus' young widow, Zenobia.

Claudius did not survive long enough to deal with the situation in the east. He died of disease while on campaign in the Balkans in the early part of AD 270, and was remembered ever afterwards as a great hero for his victories in AD 268. After a brief period of conflict, power passed to another of Gallienus' former marshals, again a man from the Balkans. This man would become the emperor Aurelian.

Steadying the Ship of State: Restoration of the Imperial Office

(AD 270–305)

Aurelian faced daunting challenges when he came to power. The events of AD 268–269 had upset the equilibrium between the three parts of the empire, and the northern tribes were once more on the move. Between AD 270 and 271, Aurelian was forced into a desperate defence of Italy. Despite losing at least one major battle and having to put down a revolt in Rome, he finally swept the enemy from his part of the empire. Aurelian then went on to cement good relations with the Roman people, constructing a massive new ring of defensive ramparts around the capital. At the same time, he took the bold step of renouncing Roman control over Trajan's Dacian provinces.

After achieving stability at home and commencing the withdrawal from Dacia, Aurelian's next step was to launch a two-pronged invasion of Syria through Egypt and Asia Minor with the aim of crushing the armies of Zenobia and capturing Palmyra. He rapidly achieved his objective, but sought reconciliation over revenge; Zenobia was taken to Rome, where she remarried. Her descendants were serving in the senate more than a century later. Back in Syria, many Palmyrene officials were allowed to remain in their posts, possibly as a reward for abandoning their erstwhile masters when Aurelian invaded. It appears that Aurelian tried to make the transition back to direct Roman control as painless as possible. Yet however well-intentioned his policies, they did not work; no sooner had he embarked on his homeward journey than an anti-Roman faction in Palmyra seized control of the city and defended it to the death. This time Aurelian showed no mercy. Palmyra's long history as one of the great trading posts of antiquity came to an abrupt end when his forces sacked the city in AD 273. The remainder of the trade that it had once controlled now shifted northwards to the cities of Mesopotamia.

The rehabilitation of Elagabal

Victory in the east had one other momentous outcome. One of the decisive battles against the Palmyrenes took place near Emesa (Homs), and when victory was assured, Aurelian suddenly announced that he had received aid from none other than the local sun god, Elagabal, who had been restored to his home under Alexander Severus some 50 years before. In homage, Aurelian ordered that the god's cult be reintroduced to Rome. In contrast to Elagabalus' theatrical observances, the deity was now worshipped in more sober fashion as the 'Invincible Sun', with none of the exotic trappings of the earlier cult. No one in Rome seems to have objected to the revamped cult, and Aurelian's action set an important precedent for the close identification of an emperor with a non-Roman divinity. The rationale for this new cult – a divine vision experienced by an emperor – would be invoked several decades later when Constantine introduced a heavily Romanized form of Christianity to the capital.

In reintroducing the cult of Elagabal, the new emperor dramatically reversed the avowedly chauvinistic, Romano-centric attitude to religion taken by Decius and Valerian. Aurelian's approach was far more in tune with the spirit of the age; he and his successors all came from the provinces, and as a result had a better feel for what would play well to an empire-wide audience. In tune with this trend, the concept of *virtus* that had for so long been the lynchpin of the personality cult of the emperor also began subtly to change. *Virtus* ceased to be identified with the moral code of ancient Rome, and instead became part of a more homogenized form of imperial propaganda with wider appeal.

Aurelian next turned his attention to the breakaway Gallic empire. Tetricus I (reigned AD 271–273), the most recent incumbent of the Gallic throne, realized that his days as ruler were numbered. Accordingly, he signalled his willingness through diplomatic channels to relinquish his throne and, in a face-saving exercise, arranged with Aurelian to desert to the Roman camp when the two armies met in battle at Châlons-en-Champagne. As a reward for his compliance, Tetricus was allowed to go into retirement with a sinecure administrative post in southern Italy. Within four years, then, Aurelian had achieved the seemingly impossible task of restoring the unity of the Roman empire. Success was, however, fleeting. There were many parts of the empire that had become freshly militarized in the years of chaos and that were still not fully reintegrated within the imperial system, including parts of Gaul, Syria, Egypt and southern Turkey. Aurelian did not command the loyalty of all of his military commanders, and he further compounded the problems of the empire by issuing a 'reformed' coinage that destroyed the existing tariff relationship between gold and silver, causing rampant inflation that was not cured for generations.

Confusion reigns supreme

In the late summer of AD 275, as he prepared for another campaign, Aurelian was murdered in Thrace (European Turkey) by members of his staff. Although his record as an administrator would for ever be marred by his monetary reform, his other achievements had endeared him to the rank and file. The army buried him with great ceremony near Perinthus, where he was killed, and lamented him as the saviour of Rome.

Aurelian's assassins quickly realized that whatever plans they may have had for the future were fated to founder on the opposition of the army. They withdrew temporarily to the deserts of Jordan, where pockets of resistance against the peace Aurelian had imposed on Palmyra still held out. Loyalist officers now fell to considering the question of who should succeed as emperor. Their candidate was a general by the name of Marcus Claudius Tacitus (*c.* AD 200–276; no relation to the famous historian), who proved incapable of resolving the tensions that still seethed within the high command. While the army was engaged on operations in central Turkey, Aurelian's assassins infiltrated its main camp and slew Tacitus too.

The period of turmoil did not end with the murder of Tacitus. It had been his intention that the throne would pass to his brother Florian; yet that too was unacceptable to the army in the east, which promptly proclaimed its own general Probus (AD 232–282) as emperor. Florian failed to suppress the revolt, and Probus assumed leadership of the whole empire. He duly summoned a 'reconciliation' meeting with Aurelian's assassins. The meeting ended with a dinner party at which Probus resolved the dispute that had divided the governing class for more than a year by murdering his guests. Having seized power in such a violent manner, Probus spent most of his reign trying to suppress uprisings in areas as diverse as southern Turkey, Egypt and Gaul. In each case, these revolts arose as a result of particular local tensions, but they all combined to undermine his authority in Rome. In AD 282, the praetorian prefect, Marcus Aurelius Carus, realized that he had sufficient support to overthrow Probus, and promptly did so.

Nefarious machinations

Carus decided that the best method of consolidating his rule was to embark upon a punitive military expedition against Rome's old enemy, the Persians. In the aftermath of the deaths of Shapur I of Persia in AD 272 and his successor Hormizd I the following year, the Sassanian empire found itself weakened and fraught with discord. Claiming that he was avenging Valerian's disgrace, Carus was able to invade Iraq with relative ease. Then something went terribly wrong. Tradition has it that Carus' tent was struck by lightning. This may indeed have been the case, or perhaps the historical sources used the phrase as a euphemism for mutiny. Whatever the truth, it is clear that Carus' younger son, who had accompanied him east with the title of Caesar, now became Numerian Augustus, while his elder brother, who had remained at home, became Carinus Augustus.

Carinus' and Numerian's succession incurred the displeasure of powerful elements in the eastern army. Numerian was murdered after the army left Antioch in the summer of AD 284. However, it appears that the only thing that his assassins could agree upon was that it was time for him to go; unable to decide on a successor, they concealed Numerian's dead body in a litter, claiming that an eye infection prevented him from appearing in public. Eventually, the stench of the decomposing body became intolerable, leaving everyone in no doubt that the emperor was dead. Forced to act, the general staff halted just outside Nicomedia in western Turkey and on 20 November, AD 284, selected a mid-grade officer named Gaius Aurelius Valerius Diocles as a compromise candidate. Standing on a high platform that had been erected some miles from the city, Diocles accepted the acclamation of the troops, drew his sword, and cleft the praetorian prefect Flavius Aper, whom he accused of having murdered Numerian, in two. Shortly afterwards, Diocles took the Latinized name Gaius Aurelius Valerius Diocletianus; he is known to history simply as Diocletian.

Stability at last

As Diocletian set out to contest the throne with Carinus in the spring of AD 285, few could have predicted that any great change would result. The contenders were typical third-century emperors who based their claims to power on the ability of their army to defeat those of their rivals. Whichever man won would be expected to spend the rest of his reign fighting on the frontiers until some northern barbarian, Persian or other Roman ended his life.

Alongside structural modifications to the army from the mid-third century onwards, the nature of imperial power had undergone a change over the 15 years prior to Diocletian taking office. Gallienus had been the last emperor to reside regularly at Rome. Aurelian, to be sure, had given the city new walls and a new god, but had spent most of his time on the march. So too had his successors, and that had important consequences for the composition of the governing class. The most obvious of these was that senators now only rarely enjoyed access to the emperor's charmed inner circle of advisers. As emperors spent increasingly less time at Rome, senators no longer had the ready social access that had been an important feature of the Antonine age. In consequence, while there were a few who still managed to achieve prominence under the new emperors, only one of the new emperors (Tacitus) had been a senator before taking office. Rather, the people who had chosen Claudius, Aurelian and Tacitus were all army generals, while Probus and Carus were both victors in civil wars. As the role of the senate declined, so too did that of the imperial court. With the emperor on the march, most courtiers were removed from regular contact with their master, which had the effect of concentrating power in the hands of those staff members whom the emperor chose to take with him.

One negative result of the extreme centralization of power in the emperor's camp became evident in the rebellions that dogged the reign of Probus: if people could not get access to the emperor, they took matters into their own hands. The new system of authority was in fact not worthy of the name, and it did not take Diocletian long to decide that, if he managed to defeat Carinus, major changes would need to be made. Diocletian did indeed win his victory, largely through treachery and desertions, and began to emerge from the shadow of more powerful men who had thought to install him as their placeman.

The new era began in the immediate aftermath of the victory over Carinus, when Diocletian married one of his daughters to a relatively junior officer named Maximian (*c.* AD 250–310), raised him to the position of deputy emperor, or Caesar, and dispatched him to show the eagle of the new regime to the western provinces. After initial success in quelling rebellions in Gaul, Maximian was made Augustus, with the proviso that important decisions would only be made in consultation with Diocletian. The relationship between the two men was presented to the empire through their symbolic association with the gods Jupiter and Hercules. As the chief emperor, Diocletian gave directions, while Maximian played the role of Hercules by wandering the earth to smash the foes of civilization. The association with these gods clearly expressed the nature of the *virtus* of the two emperors. Since the new relationship was also intrinsically familial – Hercules was the son of Jupiter – the *domus* was now intertwined once more with the concept of *virtus* in a way that had not been seen since the early days of the empire.

Devolving power

Diocletian was not content merely to reshape the outward image of government. Over the course of the next decade he replaced the ramshackle administrative system he had inherited with a bureaucracy unlike anything the Roman empire had seen before. Out went the notion that the emperor was a friend rather than a boss, and out too went the obsolete conceit that the empire had a single capital. Diocletian plainly did not find the city of Rome agreeable: in 21 years as emperor he only visited the capital twice, spending in total less than six months there. The centre of power would henceforth be wherever the emperor chose to reside. A quasi-imperial residence already existed at Sirmium in the Balkans, where Marcus had died; it was soon joined by similar sites at Aquileia and Milan in northern Italy and Trier in Germany. Other significant administrative complexes were established at Antioch (perhaps too close to the Persian frontier to be a primary residence), Carnuntum on the Danube, and Thessalonica in northern Greece. Most significantly, Diocletian decided that his main residence would be at Nicomedia in northwestern Turkey. Nicomedia, formerly the capital of the kingdom of Bithynia, controlled all the key routes running from east to west through Asia Minor. The establishment of the imperial seat here indicates that Diocletian deemed this area – from where he had easy access to either of the two main frontier armies – the optimal site for the new capital.

Diocletian's decision to govern away from Rome was

accompanied by a gradual, but thorough, reshuffling of the way in which government was organized. The tradition of dividing offices according to social class had largely ended in the middle of the third century. Most offices were now in the hands of men who, though technically equestrians, had little in common with the officials of the Antonine age. The hyperinflation that resulted from Aurelian's currency reform meant that the traditionally high salaries of these officers were now relatively modest. Although the annual pay of a legionary had been set at 1250 *denarii* in the period after Caracalla's reign, a lower-level equestrian, whose salary had not been increased, now made just 20 times the salary of a humble infantryman, as opposed to 60 times in the second century. The property valuations that had defined the equestrian and senatorial order in the Augustan age were likewise now meaningless. These changes had a levelling effect, placing the imperial office within the reach of men who would, in the past, have remained local dignitaries or have had little prospect of advancing beyond the level of a unit commander. People who disliked Diocletian would claim that he was little better than a barbarian of peasant background. This accusation, though false, reflects the fact that government was no longer the preserve of multimillionaires who would now have felt distinctly uncomfortable taking orders from people who were so unlike themselves.

The new civil administration had four main elements. Provincial governors reported through the praetorian prefects, and were henceforth to be responsible only for the administration of justice and the delivery of taxes in produce. The office of the *res privata*, the descendant of the old *patrimonium*, took over responsibility for the collection of all taxes paid in coin, the output from mines and the minting of coins. The equestrian secretariats of the old empire were now subsumed, along with the legal staff, under the authority of the *magister officiorum*, master of offices, while the operations of the various palaces continued to be under the control of *cubicularii*, now more numerous than ever before and more likely to be eunuchs.

Birth of the Tetrarchy

For the present, the army was under the direct command of each Augustus, with *comites* or *duces* commanding larger formations. The most momentous change in the system, however, came about as a result of a series of major setbacks suffered by Maximian in attempting to suppress a revolt that broke out along the Rhine and in Britain under Carausius, formerly the senior commander in the area.

Carausius' rebellion began in AD 288, but within three years Maximian had driven his forces out of most of northern Gaul. However, when he attempted to capitalize on this success by invading Britain, his fleet was destroyed in a storm. Carausius took advantage of this disaster to reoccupy parts of the Gaulish mainland. In AD 293 Maximian, whose authority was threatened by the difficulties he was experiencing, appointed a deputy emperor to take charge of the campaign. Diocletian followed suit, on the understanding that the two deputies, or Caesars, would one day succeed the current Augusti. This refined system of rule was known as the Tetrarchy ('rule of four'). The new Caesars were Flavius

Constantius (*c.* AD 250–306) and Gaius Galerius Valerius Maximianus (known simply in English as Galerius; *c.* AD 250–311). Both Constantius and Galerius were experienced soldiers, and their appointments relieved the Augusti of the need to take personal control of potentially risky military operations. To celebrate their new offices, the two men married into the families of their patrons: Constantius married Theodora, daughter of Maximian, while Galerius took Valeria, daughter of Diocletian, as his wife.

At the time of his promotion to the rank of Caesar, Constantius had one son by a woman named Helena – according to nasty gossip, a barmaid from the Balkans, though in fact she was a respectable woman from Drepanum in western Turkey – whom he continued to support. This son, whose name was Constantine, was around 11 years old in AD 293. A few years later he would serve in Diocletian's court, where he would ultimately be joined by Maximian's slightly younger son, Maxentius (*c.* AD 278–312). In time, both would become emperors.

Constantius soon proved his worth, driving Carausius' forces out of Gaul, invading Britain and bringing the breakaway state back under central government control. Galerius' record was initially more chequered. After years of internal turmoil, the Sassanian regime had recovered its sense of purpose under the leadership of Shapur I's son Narseh (r. AD 293–302), who had seized the throne in a coup d'état in AD 293. Narseh took great exception to Roman support for the restoration of an Arsacid ruler in parts of Armenia. In AD 297 he invaded Armenia and, pushing south, inflicted a serious defeat on Galerius, who had been lured into giving battle around Carrhae, which now had the unique distinction of being the only city to witness three major Roman defeats.

Diocletian was less than impressed with Galerius' performance. He came in person to Antioch, where he made Galerius march before his chariot for more than a mile before the assembled army, a powerful statement that emperors were responsible for military failure. Of more practical value was a new plan of campaign that drew Narseh into the Armenian mountains, where Galerius was able to win a decisive victory in AD 298, forcing the Persians to surrender five provinces east of the Tigris, and, with them, direct access to the Armenian highlands. It was perhaps the greatest victory won by a Roman army since the time of Marcus Aurelius.

The strength of the new collegial system of government was further demonstrated, even as Galerius advanced against Narseh, by the fact that Diocletian and Maximian were able to direct their energies towards quelling local disturbances in Egypt and Spain, while Constantius set up his headquarters at Trier to launch repeated assaults against the Franks, a loose federation of Germanic tribes along the Lower Rhine, and the Alamanni in southern Germany. It was with some justice that the propagandists of the regime trumpeted the restoration of the Roman world. It was also at this time that Diocletian turned his attention to domestic policy.

Domestic reforms

Throughout the AD 280s and 290s a pair of jurists named Gregorius and Hermogenianus had tried to systematize the huge corpus of Roman law. In AD 291 Gregorius produced a collection of the legal opinions of previous emperors that were still regarded as valid sources of law, while Hermogenianus updated the collection in AD 298 to include the rulings of Diocletian. The urge to set the legal record straight was just one part of a concerted effort to change the way in which the reformed imperial administration governed its subjects. In AD 296 Diocletian introduced a new tax system that aimed to create a coherent definition of the taxable units for the basic taxes across all the provinces (this reform is thought to have caused the revolts that engaged the two Augusti while Galerius was defeating the Persians). Prompted chiefly by complaints from the army about the dwindling purchasing power of their salaries, in AD 301 the emperor introduced a new system of coinage, followed by an edict fixing maximum prices for goods and services throughout the empire. The effort was a failure, but, like Diocletian's other fiscal measures, demonstrated his conviction that the government could reform the conduct of the empire's subjects to make them more efficient servants of the regime. Crucial to all of this was the view that the emperor no longer existed to serve the state but rather that the state, having been saved from its enemies, should serve the emperor.

By the end of AD 301, Diocletian had survived longer than any emperor since Septimius Severus, but he was also in his sixties. What would happen next? Diocletian was giving very clear indications that he did not intend to die in office; he had constructed a grand palace at Spalatum (Split), near his homeland of Salonae in modern Croatia, to which he intended to retire. But what of Maximian, and what of the Caesars? Constantius, who had been appointed a few weeks before Galerius, would naturally succeed to the position of Augustus that Diocletian intended to vacate, while Galerius might be expected to wait until Maximian, who had been in power for one year less than Diocletian, decided that it was time for him to leave as well. Long-term plans for the succession seem in any event to have been unformed. Who would be the next Caesars? In answering this question the key factor may have been a shortage of male children on the eastern side: Diocletian had only a daughter, and Galerius' son, Candidianus, was the child of his first marriage (nasty rumour held that he was actually the son of a concubine and thus illegitimate). Constantius and Maximian both had sons; Constantius had several, in fact, though the oldest, Constantine, was also the product of an earlier marriage. By 300, when Constantine was married to a woman whose parents were not members of the imperial college, a decision seems to have been made that the new Caesars would not be blood relatives of the existing ones (though they might be connected by marriage). As time passed, relations between the eastern and western courts grew strained. Diocletian had not seen Maximian in more than a decade, and there is no evidence that he had ever met Constantius as Caesar. Moreover, neither of the western emperors enforced the edict on maximum prices, which they may rightly have regarded as wholly unworkable.

A late spasm of persecution

On 24 February, AD 303, Diocletian introduced a further strain into the relationship between east and west. It was on this day that he posted an edict at Nicomedia ordering all Christians to sacrifice to the traditional gods. Their communal property was seized, and those who refused to recant their faith faced the loss of their civil rights and even capital punishment. It was now more than forty years since Gallienus had brought the persecution instituted by his father to an end, and some 30 years since Aurelian had referred the decision of a dispute among the Christians of Antioch to the bishops of Italy – and the question of the relationship between Christians and non-Christians in the empire had ceased to be a burning issue. By this stage, Christians were well represented in the army and the court. Most significantly, many were also employed in the higher-education establishment at Nicomedia, where the seminal early Christian teacher Lactantius (*c.* AD 240–320) may first have met Constantine.

The result of Diocletian's edict was to fuel the fire of Christian fundamentalism in some areas and alienate men like Lactantius. The rationale behind the edict, which upset long-established relationships, is hard to fathom. The fact that the edict ceased to be enforced within 18 months of its promulgation – only to be renewed with especial vigour by Galerius when he stepped into the role of Augustus – suggests indeed that Lactantius was right to explain it as a matter of politics more than of faith, and that the bigotry which was the driving force behind the measure was a particular hallmark of Galerius. Certainly, the responses of the Tetrarchs varied greatly; Constantius largely ignored the edict, while Maximian's enforcement of it was less than enthusiastic. The measure served to highlight sharply differences between the eastern and western rulers on the very eve of an important journey that Diocletian planned to make to Rome in AD 304 to celebrate his and Maximian's 20 years of shared power.

In ordering this joint celebration, Diocletian unilaterally took it upon himself to add a year to the period that Maximian had actually spent in office. At their meeting in Rome, Diocletian spelt out the intention behind his deliberate miscounting to his fellow senior member of the Tetrarchy: now that he and Maximian had the 'same' number of years in power, he expected them both to abdicate on the same day. Concurrently, he announced that he had already chosen the new Caesars, one of whom was a general named Flavius Valerius Severus (d. AD 307), and the other the nephew of Galerius, Maximinus Daia (*c.* AD 270–313). The principle enshrined in this pronouncement was that emperors made emperors; inheritance was not to be considered a decisive factor in the succession.

Renouncing the purple

Maximian and Constantius must have been infuriated by Diocletian's decision, but there was little they could do about it. As was only fitting after a 20-year reign in which he had effectively restored Rome to a position of dominance not seen since the time of Septimius Severus, Diocletian's personal authority was unbounded. Although not all of his actions could be regarded as prudent – the edicts on maximum prices and Christian persecution being cases in point – he possessed genuine wisdom. He was modest enough to realize that he could not govern on his own, and willing to entrust great power to a man (Constantius) who was plainly not part of his inner circle; and he was consistent enough in his belief that the nature of the imperial office needed to be changed that he did what no other emperor had ever dared do – he voluntarily renounced the most powerful position in the world.

On 1 May, AD 305, Diocletian removed the purple cloak that symbolized his authority and draped it around the shoulders of Maximinus Daia. Galerius ascended to the rank of Augustus at Sirmium. Maximian handed over power to Severus outside Milan, probably in the presence of Constantius, who now became the senior Augustus.

Withdrawing to his retirement palace, Diocletian spent his time growing cabbages. When asked later to resume office, he allegedly replied, 'If only you could see the vegetables planted by my own hand . . . you'd never think of asking such a thing.'

Beginnings of the Christian Empire: The Reign of Constantine

(AD 305–337)

Even as Diocletian set off on the long journey that would end at his retirement palace, and Maximian retired to a villa outside Rome, the succession plan began to fall apart. The reason was simple: although Constantius was now senior Augustus, he was far from content in his new role. He also saw a way to take advantage of new administrative structures that came into force just as he acceded to the highest office.

Although the Tetrarchic system established four separate imperial courts, under Diocletian the empire was not formally divided into administrative districts. The likely reason for this was that an informal arrangement was deemed perfectly adequate in a situation where no one challenged Diocletian's authority over the empire as a whole. Now, as a result of the tensions surrounding the succession, the empire was split into four praetorian prefectures, with each prefect controlling three dioceses. Each of these was under the control of a *vicarius* – so called because the office-holder acted 'in lieu of' (*vice*) the praetorian prefect for the purposes of day-to-day administration.

Sowing the seeds of destruction

Under this new administrative system, Galerius and his prefect administered the three dioceses comprising the Balkan provinces, Maximinus ruled the three from the Dardanelles to Egypt, Severus controlled Italy, Africa and Spain, while Constantius held sway in Gaul and Britain. All of them, theoretically at least, were subordinate to Constantius. The four prefectures roughly mirrored the natural tax distribution zones of the second-century empire, with one major exception: the inclusion of Egypt with the east rather than with Italy marked a significant redistribution of resources towards Syria and the new capital district in northern Turkey. This is not to say that Rome did not still get grain from Egypt, and was not still a major market for the trade in luxury goods from the Far East via Egypt, but it did signify that other areas had grown in importance. The administrative joining of Egypt to the east reflects the fact that the natural economic and cultural divisions of the empire were beginning to shape the formal administrative structure in ways that would, in the long run, contribute to the downfall of the empire in the west.

However, any idea of the collapse of the western empire – or any inkling that the empire was now less than a century away from permanent division and partial occupation of its territories by barbarians – would have been far from the minds of Diocletian's successors. There was no shortage of more immediate concerns to occupy them. No sooner had he come to power as the western Augustus than Constantius demanded the return of his son Constantine, who was effectively a hostage at the court of Galerius. He had other children, several of them boys, but they were all young, and it seems that the offspring of his early marriage with Helena held a special place in his affections. Constantius now had firm designs on his oldest son becoming emperor. Even if Galerius had guessed his colleague's intentions, he was in no position to refuse him. Since Maxentius had been handed back to Maximian, there was no justification for keeping Constantine from his father. And so, having secured the return of his son by the end of AD 305, Constantius left to campaign in northern England. On 25 July, AD 306, he died at York, and, evidently at his behest, the army declared Constantine emperor.

Galerius was furious, but was powerless to act, especially since Maxentius, inspired by developments in Britain, claimed the throne in Rome. His father Maximian came out of retirement to support him, and when Severus tried to quell the revolt he found that the loyalty of the army, which had served for years under Maximian, was suspect. Before the end of the year, he was imprisoned in a villa near Rome, and subsequently killed. Both factions now courted Constantine, who was recognized as Caesar by Galerius even as he contracted a formal marriage with Maximian's prepubescent daughter, Fausta (as she was still a child, marital relations were postponed for the better part of a decade).

The empire fragments

In the summer of AD 307 Galerius invaded Italy. Constantine remained formally neutral, which probably guaranteed the failure of the expedition. With the limited forces at his disposal, and Constantine the only potential source of reinforcements, Galerius simply did not have enough manpower to lay siege to the capital (now surrounded by Aurelian's massive defensive wall). Maximian, who plainly anticipated this turn of events, refused to engage in open battle. Faced with an impossible siege and a shortage of supplies, Galerius was forced to withdraw. The fact that he got out of Italy alive is testimony both to his own force of character and to the loyalty of the troops he had led for many years in the Balkans. It also testified to the fact that Diocletian's reforms had only reinforced the tendency for the Roman army to divide along regional lines. This had occurred once before, in AD 193 – in the power struggle following the death of Commodus – and now it was patently obvious that the four main armies were essentially separate entities. The paradox of Diocletian's reforms was that, while he sought to concentrate all power in the college of emperors, he actually succeeded in creating a number of separate governments that could operate independently of one another. Diocletian's dominant personality had held the system together, and it is significant that, in the wake of his failure to defeat Maxentius, Galerius turned again to his mentor for help.

Diocletian came out of retirement in AD 308, but made it clear that he was only doing so to aid Galerius. Given the great support he still commanded and the potential for enormous bloodshed, it is fortunate for all involved that Diocletian had a real abhorrence of civil war. After a confusing spring in which Constantine and Galerius squared up to one another, while Maximian tried to remove Maxentius from power, failed and fled to Gaul, a meeting was summoned at Carnuntum in Lower Austria, from which Maxentius was excluded. The outcome of the conference was that Galerius agreed that Constantine could call himself Augustus in the regions he controlled already, and Caesar elsewhere. This made it possible for Galerius to appoint a new Augustus, an experienced general named Licinius (*c.* AD 250–325), to replace the fallen Severus. With the principle of collegiate government re-established, and with Galerius clearly recognized as the senior member of the college, Diocletian retired once more to his palace, where he lived in peace for the final three years of his life, tending his vegetable garden.

It is one of the ironies of this period that Galerius, who tried so hard to uphold Diocletian's system, even constructing a massive retirement palace of his own at Roumaliana (Gamzigrad) in the Balkans, was fated to succumb to a malignant disease, possibly bowel cancer, a few months before his former mentor. His principal achievement had been to keep the peace between his fractious colleagues. During this uneasy peace, Constantine took advantage of the lull to hone his skills as a general, while Maximinus did nothing more constructive than work up a profound loathing for Licinius, who had effectively been promoted over his head. Maximian lived with Constantine until AD 310, when he suddenly tried to seize power for himself in southern France while Constantine was away campaigning on the Rhine. The attempt failed, and Maximian committed suicide (it is unclear whether he did so with or without the active collusion of his son-in-law).

Immediately after the death of Galerius, the surviving Augusti and Caesars split into two factions: Maximinus allied himself with Maxentius, and Constantine with Licinius. The war that loomed in AD 312 looked ominous indeed; the two sides had roughly equivalent armies, and neither had a clear strategic advantage. The threat of Maximinus constrained Licinius from lending significant aid to Constantine, while Constantine could not help Licinius until he had dealt with Maxentius.

Showdown with Maxentius

The invasion of Italy was a daunting task. Maxentius' army was supplemented by a series of fortified cities in the north, while Rome itself had so far proved unassailable. Constantine was plainly worried, and now set out upon a spiritual odyssey that would transform the history of Europe. While in Gaul, he had followed what was by now the traditional practice of letting it be known that he had a guardian divinity – in his case Sol Invictus. This may have been more than just self-aggrandizement on Constantine's part, since he was evidently a deeply pious person. But what if his faith in the gods was misplaced? It would not have escaped his attention that Galerius had been a devoted follower of the traditional gods yet had still failed utterly. In the spring of AD 312, Constantine suddenly announced that he placed all his confidence in *mens divina*, the 'Divine Mind'. It is not clear what he meant to signify by this term, and contemporary polytheistic propagandists writing immediately before and after the invasion supply no clue. It is altogether likely that, with an army that consisted of traditional believers behind him, Constantine did not wish to be more specific. He may well have speculated that the one deity that Galerius despised, the Christian God, now held the key to his fate. Later commentators are in no doubt that this was the point when Constantine became convinced he had been given signs that the God of the Christians would be on his side.

The uncertainty over the precise nature of his conversion is fully in accordance with Constantine's generally enigmatic character: he could be rash yet patient; he had the ability to listen and to change course when he realized he had made an error, yet placed enormous confidence in his own judgement; although no intellectual, he was extremely bright. He could be both compassionate and utterly ruthless. But what was beyond all dispute was Constantine's genius as a military commander, possibly the greatest general Rome had seen since the time of Julius Caesar.

Constantine's invasion of Italy was one of the most brilliant military operations in ancient history. Sweeping aside Maxentius' northern armies, and drawing them into battle before they could take refuge behind their fortifications, by the early autumn he was already advancing on Rome. The effect of the defeats in the north was that Maxentius could not retire behind the walls of Rome and wait for Constantine to exhaust his supplies. His reputation in tatters, he had to risk all in one final encounter. So it was that Maxentius led his army out of Rome on 28 October to a place near the Milvian Bridge called Saxa Rubra, north of the Tiber, to challenge Constantine. The final battle was swift and decisive. Maxentius was killed in the rout, and Constantine entered Rome in triumph.

The alliance with Licinius

Within weeks of the victory over Maxentius, Constantine was on his way back north. Meeting Licinius at Milan, he spoke to him of the power of his new god, and cemented their alliance by giving him his half-sister, Constantia, in marriage. It was now up to Licinius to deal with Maxentius' ally Maximinus.

Maximinus proved an obliging enemy; his crossing of the Dardanelles at the head of his field army in April, AD 313, saved Licinius the trouble of waging war in hostile territory. So thorough was the victory that Licinius won near the city of Adrianople, some 150 miles (220 kilometres) west of modern Istanbul, that Maximinus could mount no serious resistance when Licinius pursued him back into his own territory. As Licinius closed in on his stronghold at Tarsus in Anatolia (southern Turkey), Maximinus realized that the game was up and committed suicide. During his retreat, one of Maximinus' last acts had been to issue an edict declaring that the Christians in his part of the empire, against whom he had staged a series of persecutions, were free to practise their religion in peace. Licinius, whose wife was a Christian, followed this with an edict of his own restoring property confiscated in the persecutions. The combination of these edicts with the earlier edicts of Constantine restored Christianity to the position of equality with other religions that it had enjoyed in the years after Gallienus.

Although Licinius and Constantine both believed that Christians should have the freedom to worship, there was little else upon which they agreed. While it was possible for decrees of one emperor to be recognized as legally binding in the territory of the other, in practice the tendency was increasingly for the two to go their separate ways. Key documents have survived showing that Licinius' army was granted slightly different benefits from that of Constantine, and the bureaucracies of the eastern and western empires had little interchange with one another. Although there were now effectively two Roman empires, each one consisting of six of the 12 dioceses, neither man yet dared to take a step that would signal a decisive break. Nor would either yet conceive a succession plan. Licinius' position was straightforward, since he, as yet, had no son. For Constantine, the situation was somewhat more complex. He had a son, Crispus, the offspring of his marriage, while he was in Diocletian's court, to a woman named Minervina, who had died before his marriage to Fausta. Initially, Constantine was equivocal in promoting the claims of this boy, whose circumstances were reminiscent of his own. However, the situation changed radically between AD 315 and 316, when first Constantia and then Fausta produced sons. Between the birth of the two boys, Constantine and Licinius concluded an agreement that their sons should not be placed in the line of succession, and arrived at a compromise whereby Bassianus, the husband of Constantine's half-sister Anastasia, would be declared Caesar. Yet shortly after the birth of Fausta's first son – which meant that, if he stuck to the compromise, Constantine would now be sacrificing two of his children's hopes for one of Licinius' – Constantine executed Bassianus on a charge of treason. Anticipating conflict, both emperors had already prepared for war.

Constantine attacked in the autumn of AD 316 and succeeded in driving Licinius out of most of his territory in the Balkans, but then overreached himself. Manoeuvring with great skill, Licinius cut his adversary's supply lines, forcing Constantine to make peace on far less advantageous terms than might otherwise have been the case. The result was that Constantine gained just one of the three Balkan dioceses on a permanent basis and was obliged to recognize three Caesars: Constantine's eldest son, Crispus, the infant Constantine and the infant Licinius. The treaty was concluded on 1 March, AD 317, and remained in force for seven years.

Although Constantine spent much of his time after signing the treaty with Licinius commanding his army in the Balkans, he still found time to sire three more children with Fausta, two daughters and a son. By AD 324, with a household full of potential heirs, Constantine decided to be rid of Licinius for good. Declaring war in the summer, he drove his enemy out of the Balkans by the early autumn and forced him to surrender at Nicomedia in November. The defeated Licinius was granted clemency and sent into exile in Thessalonica. But shortly thereafter, Constantine 'discovered' that he was at the centre of a conspiracy and ordered his death.

Constantinople

No sooner had he defeated Licinius than a new problem arose for Constantine regarding the Christians of the eastern empire. Adherents of the faith were engaged in a bitter dispute over the true nature of God, arising from ideas developed by Arius (*c.* AD 250–336), a theologian from Alexandria. The

Arian controversy, as it became known, had caused a deep rift in Christian communities, which were split between rival leaders. Constantine had some experience of such disputes, having already tried to resolve an extremely unpleasant schism that developed in the Christian community of North Africa soon after he defeated Maxentius. On that occasion, the schism had resulted not from doctrinal differences but from practical disagreements over whether it was better to appease persecutors of the faith or to resist and run the risk of greater violence. When Constantine's officials arrived in North Africa to restore property seized in the persecution, they found themselves confronted by two diametrically opposed factions that had adopted entrenched positions. To determine which had the better claim, Constantine referred the matter to a series of church councils, all of which ruled against the party which claimed that resistance to the authorities was in accord with God's will. The defeated faction refused to abide by the decisions of the councils, and after a brief bout of persecution, Constantine washed his hands of the whole affair. Yet although his intervention in this dispute was unsuccessful, Constantine had learned a valuable lesson: third-party arbitration would not stop Christians from fighting with each other. He would need to intervene personally to get the warring parties around the negotiating table.

Thus it was that in AD 325, Constantine summoned the bishops of the east to a grand council at Nicaea, a town on the coast of Anatolia. After a show of listening to both sides in the dispute, the emperor offered a compromise formula that delivered a new creed expounding the nature of God.

This was a seminal event in the history of the Christian Church. Since not only eastern but also a few western bishops were present, the council of Nicaea was the first conference that claimed jurisdiction over the Christian community as a whole. It was also an important moment in relations between the secular and religious leaderships. Constantine's action showed that the emperor could exert authority in spiritual matters, thus setting a precedent for later emperors who would regard such intervention as part of their remit.

Even before Licinius surrendered, Constantine conceived the idea of building a new capital in the east. Perhaps because of its association with earlier regimes, Nicomedia was deemed unsuitable, and so his choice finally came to rest on the ancient city of Byzantium on the Bosphorus. This settlement, which was ideally placed to give the emperor easy access to Rome's northern frontier on the Danube and its eastern frontier on the Euphrates, was now to be refounded as Constantinople. The design of the new capital was intended to mirror Constantine's attitudes towards both government and religion.

The new city arose with remarkable speed. The centrepiece of the building programme was the imperial palace, with a massive Hippodrome attached, seating 80,000 people, as a venue where the emperor could meet his subjects. In addition, he ordered construction of a vast new church, while retaining the city's older temples. Christianity was to be presented as a faith that could supplement and enhance the regime without requiring that the old ways be repudiated. The same principle was applied to the way in which the new city was populated. Constantine did not force people to come to the city, but instead rewarded those who chose to move. Likewise, rather than create a new senate, an act that would have offended senators in Rome, he simply accorded privileges to senior officials who chose to relocate to his capital. To beautify the new capital, cities throughout the east were invited to send famous monuments of antiquity to adorn its public spaces.

Turmoil and divisions

Although Constantinople was never meant to replace Rome, but rather to augment it, its founding did nevertheless raise the question of how the western empire would now be run. Constantine was personally committed to the east, but his son Crispus, who had distinguished himself during the war with Licinius, had long been based at Trier. However, before the end of AD 326, the peace of the imperial household was shattered, with Crispus arrested, tried for treason and executed, and Fausta banished into internal exile, where she died within a couple of years. The reason for this dramatic turn of events is shrouded in mystery. A later pagan writer concocted a lurid tale of how Fausta had lusted after her stepson, and when he refused her advances, claimed that he had attempted to rape her, which led to his execution. According to this same author, Fausta's plot had been exposed by the emperor's mother, causing an enraged Constantine to lock his wife in an overheated bath house until she died. Nothing in this story is borne out by the facts as we know them. A more likely explanation was that a major rift had occurred between father and son regarding the future direction of government, and that Fausta had objected to the treatment of her stepson. Constantine seems to have interpreted Crispus' disagreement as potentially treasonous and acted precipitately. Perhaps a sign that he came to regret what happened was the fact that Fausta's sons remained in line for the succession, and that he never remarried.

Now lacking an empress, Constantine was forced to turn to his mother for help. The aged Helena was sent on a grand tour of the east, where she visited Palestine and was present as a massive new programme of church building was inaugurated in the Holy Land. The sacred sites of the Christian religion were honoured with their own churches, such as the Church of the Holy Sepulchre in Jerusalem, built over the supposed tomb of Christ, as well as churches at the site of the Ascension and the Nativity. Her participation in these events later gave rise to the legend that she found the fragments of the True Cross – on which Christ was crucified at Golgotha – in Jerusalem.

While Constantine's guiding principle was that religion should act as a unifying force in the empire, the exercise of secular authority during his reign caused ever-deepening divisions. As the central government asserted more control over local affairs – an inevitable consequence of Diocletian's policy of smaller, more numerous provinces – each region found that it had increasingly less freedom to define its own relationship to the centre. Conversely, the more extensive governing structures generated regional bureaucracies that were perfectly capable of functioning on their own. Constantine's empire was still split into multiple prefectures (though usually five, with one praetorian prefect assigned to the area north of the Alps, another to Italy, a third to Africa, a fourth to the Balkans and the fifth in the eastern provinces), while his army was now firmly divided between frontier units, the *limitanei*, and units attached to mobile reserve formations, the *comitatenses*, a system begun by Diocletian. In addition to this functional compartmentalization, the army was also divided into three main commands – the West, the Balkans and the East – with each front under its own *magister peditum* (master of infantry) and *magister equitum* (master of cavalry). The different parts of the army, like the different bureaucracies, were increasingly regional in character, with the western sector being heavily recruited from Franks and Alamanni as well as people from within the frontier zone, while the Balkan army increasingly included large numbers of Goths, who had replaced the earlier tribes north of the Danube over the course of the third century. It was only in the east, where the central Anatolian plateau offered a seemingly endless supply of hardy recruits to serve alongside Syrian and Armenian troops, that the imperial army could still broadly be described as 'Roman' (though many of these soldiers were only acclimatized to Roman ways after they had enlisted).

In the late 330s, as Constantinople expanded into a major city, Constantine confronted the need for a firm plan of succession. He still had three sons and two daughters by Fausta, and a number of nephews, the children of his half-brothers and sisters. Although much of his adult life had been spent eliminating rivals, Constantine felt that there was no intrinsic reason why the empire should have only one emperor. Indeed, the fact that a man who had ruled the entire empire on his own for 13 years should feel that collegial government would work best when he passed on speaks volumes about how deeply divided along regional lines the empire now was. Considering his succession, Constantine even looked beyond his immediate family, elevating his nephew Dalmatius (d. AD 337) to a position equal to that of his own sons as Caesar and making another nephew, Hannibalianus (d. AD 337), king of Armenia, with the evident intent that he should rule a fifth prefecture as soon as it could be acquired. This prefecture would be in Iraq, and in AD 337 Constantine began to plan a massive invasion to bring this region finally under Roman control.

The legacy of Constantine

Yet Constantine, whose first spell of military service is thought to have been as a junior officer in Galerius' successful campaign against Narseh some 40 years earlier, was fated never to return to Iraq. In the spring of AD 337 he fell dangerously ill, and died on 22 May after having himself baptized. His body was taken to Constantinople, where it was interred in the great mausoleum he had built for himself in his new city. Although he died a Christian, he intended to be buried as a Roman emperor in the tradition of Diocletian or Galerius. It was only later that his son, Constantius, transformed the mausoleum into the Church of the Twelve Apostles. This was just one of many indications that Constantius failed to appreciate the importance of Constantine's conviction that a person could be both a Roman emperor and a Christian concurrently, rather than simply a Christian emperor.

Constantine was a very dangerous person to be related to: his execution of a son, a wife, a father-in-law and two brothers-in-law is a record of domestic carnage unequalled in the annals of Roman history. Yet he reigned for nearly 31 years after his seizure of power in Britain. His longevity as emperor may in part be attributed to his great personal ability, yet it also highlights radical changes in the way that the imperial office was now perceived at Rome. While the emperor might now have colleagues in the imperial office, the position was inherently less collegial than it had been when Commodus succeeded Marcus. Commodus had been surrounded by men whose personal status was independent of their position at court. By contrast, in the empire of Diocletian and Constantine status at court defined status beyond the walls of the palaces. Although the post of senator was still highly attractive – ensuring a person great wealth (while also rendering him liable to new taxes) – the mere fact of sitting in the senate no longer guaranteed access to power at the imperial level.

The imperial role changes

In the course of his 20-year reign, Diocletian had fundamentally changed the landscape of power, driving home the point, time and again, that emperors could be created only by other emperors. When the army assembled to watch him retire it was not being invited to the ceremony in order to choose a successor, as it had done in the murky hours after the death of Pertinax or in the Danubian camp of Severus. It had gathered to pay homage to the man whom Diocletian had already marked out as the new Caesar. The emperor would still be presented, and, indeed, present himself through his edicts to the public as a creature of *virtus*, but as the community of Romans had extended far beyond Rome, the *virtus* of the emperor was an increasingly artificial construct, detached from the *domus*, which was now on a grander scale, and definitely off limits to the average person. If, as Diocletian realized, the emperor could only rule effectively if he was distanced from his subjects, then he could no longer be the ideal dinner companion. The Severans had fatally compromised the old system by courting only one element of the empire – the army – and offering no viable alternative. As the successors of Septimius Severus failed in the collective exercise of *virtus*, their conduct within the *domus*, ranging from the ghastly to the bizarre, undermined their authority.

However, internal factors alone cannot explain the transformation of the imperial office from one that depended upon the collective action of members of the aristocracy in Rome to one of mastery over an imperial bureaucracy. For much of the trouble that followed the reign of Alexander Severus, due measure of blame must be apportioned to failures by the military. While the inability of the army to defeat either the Sassanians under Ardashir and Shapur or the northern tribes was partly due to the sheer skill of these adversaries, the major role played by the inflexibility of Roman generals cannot be ignored. It was only after the disasters of the AD 250s that new, more professional, fighting soldiers came to the fore and built a new, more flexible army.

One key question remained: now that the emperor controlled an imperial rather than a Roman bureaucracy, could the empire survive with just one emperor? The bureaucracy naturally divided along the major economic lines of the empire, suggesting that multiple emperors would provide a better focus for regional administrations. Diocletian had believed as much, and at the end of his life it appears that Constantine thought so too.

FOUR

Losing Caesar

Carving up the Empire: From Constantine's Sons to Valens

(AD 337–375)

In the century and a half after the death of Constantine, the western empire ceased altogether to be governed by Rome, while the east continued to assert its essential Roman ancestry for almost a millennium. These momentous developments occurred under a system of governance that had first seen the light of day in the late second century. Yet key differences distinguish earlier attempts to find a more practical way of administering the empire from the modus operandi of Constantine and his successors.

Towards the end of a life spent unifying the empire, Constantine clearly concluded that it should be carved up into four prefectures and run by a college of emperors. The division of the monolithic empire into more manageable administrative units had already been foreshadowed in the reign of Marcus Aurelius, when Marcus authorized the creation of large military commands encompassing several provinces in both the east and the Balkans. The tripartite division of the empire that began under Gallienus in AD 260 was a later variation on this same theme. Yet Constantine's scheme, while preserving the naturally self-contained units of the Balkans and the east, further split the western Mediterranean away from Europe north of the Pyrenees and the Alps. Geopolitically, this represented a natural division; the two regions had been separate entities before the advent of the Augustan empire and continue to be thought of as essentially distinct from one another to the present day.

A sprawling bureaucracy

The prefectural model also harked back to Diocletian's dispersal of power in the AD 290s. The only difference was that in Constantine's system the college was made up of blood relatives, whereas Diocletian's had ultimately placed more of a premium on experience, supported by marriage into the imperial family. Hand in hand with their conviction that the empire needed collegiate government went the firm belief that it was in the empire's best interests not to be governed from Rome. This particular aspect is what distinguishes the shared governance schemes of the fourth century from those of earlier periods.

With the benefit of hindsight, it is tempting to regard the empire that Augustus created as an anomaly that was inevitably doomed to failure. Yet hindsight, as we know, is always twenty-twenty. The more remarkable fact is how long the Roman empire in this guise managed to sustain its precarious balancing act – 290 years all told, from Augustus' seizure of Alexandria to Shapur's capture of Valerian, the final death knell of unitary rule.

The empire had always been defined by its systems of taxation and provincial administration; as the style of government changed, then so too did the empire. The system of governance that Augustus put in place was surprisingly decentralized, as were the modes of provincial government that operated in the centuries that followed his reign. One consequence of this decentralization was that the emperor was obliged to negotiate with different groups and balance the interests of one against another. Under the Augustan and Antonine system, personal status determined the broad outlines of a career, as emperors were constrained to recruit their senior officials from people who were usually important in their own right. By contrast, after the death of Diocletian, all power flowed outwards from the palace; personal status was determined by the offices that a person held rather than the other way round. As central government expanded, the pressure to obtain these offices became ever greater, and official power was increasingly defined by a person's ability to secure jobs within the government for his clients. It is one of the great paradoxes of imperial history that as the struggle for status became ever more focused on the palace, the emperor actually lost power rather than gained it. Before a century had elapsed after the death of Constantine the bitterest partisan battles would be fought not over who should be emperor, but rather over who should control the offices that gave access to him. In other words, Caesar was by now little more than a figurehead.

The fractious sons of Constantine

Constantine had hoped that his sons and nephews would manage to govern the empire among themselves. These hopes foundered on the ambitions of Constantius II (AD 317–361), the second of his sons by Fausta, and, quite likely, on those of a number of senior officials that had been held in check during the last decade of Constantine's life. Young men of twenty, as Constantius was in the summer of 337, are not usually able to organize major changes in government on their own; and it is presumably not accidental that both of the long-serving praetorian prefects who were still in office when Constantine died on May 22 were both out of office very soon afterwards, and one was killed shortly after that. Although the cause of the subsequent discord between Constantine's heirs is lost in the mists of time, it is likely connected with the fact that, in the late summer of AD 337, Constantius suddenly ordered the arrest and execution of Dalmatius and Hannibalianus, as well as that of every other male descendant of Constantius I and Theodora, with the exception of the sons of his wife's brother Julius Constantius. These boys, Gallus and Julian, were taken away to Nicomedia, where they were confined in Diocletian's former palace. The three sons of Fausta now assumed the title of Augustus, though it appears that the eldest, Constantine II (AD 316–340), was made regent for the youngest, Constans (*c.* AD 323–350), who was still a minor.

Relations between the brothers soon proved to be as little imbued with Christian charity as their actions towards their cousins had been. Animosity between Constantine II and Constans – or perhaps more accurately the staff of Constans – reached boiling point by the spring of AD 340. Constantine II led an army from his domain (the western empire) into his younger brother's territory (Italy and Illyricum), claiming that he was on the way to help Constantius II, who was then engaged in a tough struggle against the Persian king Shapur

II (r. AD 309–379). As he did so, Constantine was ambushed and killed. And so, no military help ever arrived for Constantius from the west; the court of Constans, which annexed all Constantine II's lands after his death, apparently harboured a deep suspicion of the eastern establishment. The hostility of the western court was a genuine problem for Constantius, since his resources for the war against the Persians – a conflict his father had been planning just before his death – were limited. Unlike earlier rulers, he could not draw troops from the entire empire. It is therefore to his credit that the defensive strategy he employed succeeded in keeping Shapur II's forces in check for the next two decades, despite some bitter criticism from within his own staff.

A would-be theologian

Constantius was far less quiescent on the matter of his subjects' faith. The point at issue was not that he had been raised as a Christian; the same was true of Constans, yet he turned out to be far less dogmatic in his attitudes than his elder brother. Constantius' unyielding stance was the source of many quarrels with powerful opposing forces in the Eastern Church, notably those in Alexandria led by Bishop Athanasius (*c.* AD 293–373). Constantius convened council after council in an attempt to arrive at a modified version of the Nicene Creed that would restore church unity – but without much success.

Although he spent much of his career in exile from his see in his hometown of Alexandria in Egypt, Athanasius' career shows how important the model that Constantine set for relations between Church and state at Nicaea proved to be, and how the Church was injecting a powerful new dynamic into imperial politics as a whole. Emperors were finding that Constantine had created a structure that could challenge their own power. The key was the fact that at Nicaea Constantine had allowed the Church to be self-governing, albeit with guidance from the imperial government. Bishops who defied that council (or later ones) could be exiled, but they were not executed, and other bishops could be involved in determining their fate.

Although Christian bishops were not inclined to treat fellow bishops with whose doctrines they disagreed with great charity, they were not remotely interested in creating new martyrs of their enemies. This was a crucial change, and one need not have a great deal of imagination to feel certain what an emperor like Septimius Severus would have done with a subject who proved as recalcitrant as Athanasius. In part because Constantius could not have him executed, Athanasius could become a symbol for those who would assert that when spiritual values did not accord with the demands of government, conscience should triumph over expediency. Athanasius was able to achieve this status because he was his own best publicist, whose voluminous writings in defence of his position hide the fact that he authorized violent attacks on his ecclesiastical enemies, and that his own election as bishop was scandalous.

In addition to managing to keep himself at the forefront of ecclesiastical opposition to Constantius, Athanasius' major contributions to the development of Christian thought were two. One was his division of emperors into two categories:

'true believers' – that is to say, Trinitarians who followed the Nicene Creed – and Arians, which is what he accused his rivals of being, a gross distortion of their actual positions). The other was his promotion of an ascetic lifestyle, which he popularized through his biography of St Anthony (AD 251–356), the Egyptian founder of the monastic movement.

The influence of Athanasius extended beyond the realm of theology and church politics, making it plain that disputes about the nature of God masked deeper concerns about the nature of imperial authority. As early as AD 341, differences between Constans and Constantius emerged in their attitude to polytheism. Constantius made moves to abolish public sacrifice, which Constans initially went along with. However, he then chose to reinterpret the proscription as applying only to secret sacrifices that involved casting spells to distress one's neighbours or seeking information about the health of the emperor (practices that had always been illegal). The following year, when yet another council of eastern and western bishops was summoned, this time at Serdica (modern Sofia, Bulgaria), to discuss proposed 'improvements' to the Nicene Creed, matters came to a head. The western churchmen, sensing that they enjoyed strong support at the court of Constans, rejected the eastern document and demanded that Athanasius be permitted to attend. In AD 344, and for most of AD 345, the storm clouds of civil war appeared to be gathering, as different consuls were recognized in the two parts of the empire. Then, quite suddenly, Constantius, who was hard pressed by the Sassanians, gave in and allowed Athanasius to return to Alexandria.

The challenge of Magnentius

Though Constans had emerged victorious from this clash, major problems were looming for him elsewhere. He had been forced to spend the bulk of the AD 340s in the Danubian lands. The bureaucracy that had once served his brother Constantine in Gaul began to resent the lack of attention it was receiving, with results that would ultimately prove fatal to Constans when he decided to visit there in AD 349. On 18 January, AD 350, Flavius Magnentius (AD 303–353), the commander of the Gallic armies, declared himself emperor and hired assassins to murder Constans. Meanwhile, Constantius' rule teetered on a knife-edge, as Shapur II once again attacked his eastern frontier.

Constantius recognized that the problem he faced in the former realm of Constans would take years to sort out, and that nothing could be done about it until the Persian threat had abated. Thus it was that Constantius delayed his response until Shapur withdrew after a failed siege of the key stronghold of Nisibis in Mesopotamia in the summer of AD 350. Even then, before venturing west to take on Magnentius, Constantius saw that he would need to appoint a reliable deputy – someone who could show the dynastic flag during his absence but not do anything rash to put his realm at risk. Having no son, he called his oldest cousin, Gallus, out of the enforced seclusion in which he and his half-brother Julian (AD 331–363) had been living for the past decade and appointed him Caesar. At the same time, he released Julian from house arrest, allowing this keen scholar to resume his education at Constantinople and other cities along the Aegean seaboard.

Advancing into the Balkans during the winter of AD 350, Constantius first received the submission of the army under Vetranio and then prepared to deal with Magnentius. Diplomatic negotiations brought some significant desertions from Magnentius' camp before the two emperors met in battle at Mursa, a city near Sirmium on the Danube (modern Osijek in Croatia), in AD 351. The outcome was a bloody disaster for both sides, with Magnentius losing some two-thirds of his force while Constantius allegedly sacrificed nearly 40 per cent of his own army. This horrific casualty rate was a sign of just how great could be the difficulties any emperor would face if he tried to insist upon unified government. But insist Constantius must, for he could not possibly share power with a rival as determined as Magnentius. Constantius completed the destruction of the western regime at the battle of Mons Seleucus in Gaul in the spring of AD 353.

The victory over Magnentius gave Constantius only temporary respite from governmental crisis. Gallus forgot that his appointed role was merely to act as a figurehead for the regime, and began to quarrel with senior officials in the east, who refused to report to him. In the west, an effort to reward an officer named Silvanus for betraying Magnentius backfired when members of the court conspired against him, whereupon he declared himself emperor. Constantius ordered Gallus to leave Antioch and executed him for treason at the end of AD 354, then arranged Silvanus' assassination in AD 355. Yet these crises convinced him that he needed more help. For this he turned to Julian, who was appointed

Caesar in Gaul, with express instructions to prevent a recurrence of the troubles that had doomed Gallus.

In the course of his extensive education, Julian had secretly converted from Christianity to paganism under the tutelage of Maximus of Ephesus, a Neoplatonic philosopher, who had shown him how to make special contact with the gods through the theurgic arts. The central tenet of theurgy was the belief that humans could control the action of the gods through intense study of the divine world. The doctrine was based on the Chaldaean Oracles, texts allegedly written by a man named Julianus in the time of Marcus Aurelius (some historians now believe that they were composed much later). These writings disclosed 'secret' knowledge about the gods, imparted to mortals by the gods themselves. The actual practice of theurgy in the eastern empire was introduced at the end of the third century by Iamblichus (*c.* AD 245–325), a native of Syria, and promoted by certain philosophers who traced their ideas to those of Plotinus, the third-century AD founder of Neoplatonism. A great deal of magical ritual, sacrifice and invocation was involved in theurgical practice, and Maximus, who had been a student of Iamblichus, was a master of the art.

It seems to have been after Maximus introduced him to the flaming – and talking – statue of the goddess Hecate that he kept at his house, that Julian crossed the spiritual frontier and became a follower of the ancient gods. In another person, such a move might merely have been a local scandal, involving a certain amount of tutting by neighbours and the like. In the case of a man who was Constantine's nephew and the emperor's cousin, the move was tantamount to high treason. Maximus, Julian and a few others knew to keep the secret to themselves, but for how long would Julian be able to hide his true self from others?

Julian the schemer

Julian may have been eccentric, but he was by no means stupid. He understood the personal risks that he was taking and recognized that Constantius governed by sowing fear and suspicion among senior officials, who looked to him as the ultimate arbiter of all their affairs. One of the most telling anecdotes from Constantius' reign concerns the general Ursicinus, who was sent to murder Silvanus. When he arrived at Silvanus' headquarters, Silvanus greeted him as an old friend, assuming that Ursicinus was as disillusioned with Constantius' reign as he was. Indeed, this was a fair appraisal of Ursicinus' state of mind – Ammianus Marcellinus (*c.* AD 330–395), one of his staff officers, meticulously documented his incessant moaning about how badly treated he felt. Even so, he still feared Constantius enough that he thought it better to assassinate his friend than defy his emperor. In such circumstances, then, if Julian were to survive, he would need to find a way to exploit Constantius' tyrannical style of rule to his own advantage.

In the wake of Silvanus' murder, Ursicinus and an officer named Marcellus were put in command of military forces in Gaul. In AD 356 they were ordered to conduct manoeuvres to intimidate the Alamanni, an operation that went off tolerably well, while Julian played his role as imperial figurehead in the campaign. In the winter, however, Julian was cut off, well within Roman territory, by a band of Frankish raiders. He escaped, but thereafter histrionically dramatized the incident, suggesting that his near-death experience was the result of a dereliction of duty by his senior military commanders. Ursicinus and Marcellus were duly replaced by an officer named Barbatio, who was ordered to coordinate an operation with Julian in AD 357 similar to that of the previous year. Julian did as little as he could to help, perhaps hoping that Barbatio would run into trouble and retreat, which is indeed what happened. Julian, however, had reckoned without the consequences of his own subterfuge, and suddenly found himself confronted by an army of Alamanni near Strasbourg.

Even allowing for the fact that most of what we know comes from Ammianus, whose critical faculties were occasionally impaired by his partiality for Julian, the result of this encounter exceeded Julian's wildest hopes. His victory was total, including the capture of the king of the Alamanni, and established his reputation as a commander to be reckoned with. Even Constantius, who was in the Balkans at the time, seemed genuinely impressed, and began to entrust Julian with real authority.

Watch, learn and strike

Over the course of the winter, Julian won further credit, this time at the expense of the praetorian prefect in Gaul in a dispute over tax collection. This matter was dealt with by correspondence. In his dealings in Gaul, Julian emulated his cousin in avoiding personal entanglements with senior officials. Constantius had come to realize that maintaining a certain aloofness bred exactly the kind of constructive fear that was needed to keep officials in line. Julian did likewise, surrounding himself with a few close friends and staying clear of day-to-day administration.

All the while, as he built his own group of supporters and won the loyalty of select units of the army, Julian knew that he only had a limited amount of time to play with. Dreams revealed to him that he was destined to overthrow his cousin, and he entered into treasonous correspondence with his spiritual gurus. Constantius grew suspicious and so, in AD 358, he replaced a number of Julian's closest advisers with his own placemen. But then larger problems obtruded and demanded his attention, as Shapur II once again threatened war in the east. At the same time, he became embroiled again in doctrinal debate. In these circumstances, it would have been counterproductive to remove Julian, who was at least efficient and, as far as Constantius knew, not openly disloyal.

The Persian invasion ground to a halt before the city of Amida in the summer of AD 359. Ammianus, who was present, recorded the scene as the enemy carefully prepared his siege lines around the fortress for over two months. Meanwhile, Constantius was idle, awaiting the outcome of discussions on the Holy Trinity at Sirmium. Even when Amida fell, Constantius did not act. Yet the garrison's courageous stand had so seriously delayed the Persians' timetable for a summer offensive that they now withdrew. This would only be a temporary reprieve, however. If Constantius was to defeat Shapur, he would need more men, and the only person who was in a position to supply troops, having successfully pacified the Rhine frontier, was Julian.

Julian saw his chance. Antipathy to Constantius ran high both in the western army and among influential opinion-makers in Gallic society. Mainstream Christians in particular – now rejoined once more by Athanasius, who had been exiled from Alexandria for a third time in AD 355 – had come to regard the emperor as the Antichrist. Western troops were all too aware that units transferred east as a penalty for supporting Magnentius never came home – five were wiped out at Amida alone – and so refused point-blank to leave Gaul. These were disciplined soldiers, but they saw their loyalty as being primarily to the areas from which they came. Julian exploited their discontent, and in March AD 360 allowed himself to be proclaimed Augustus by troops who were in transit to the eastern front. Constantius' authority in Gaul collapsed and the new Augustus wrote saying that he would be content to split the empire with his cousin, who had no choice but to concede while Shapur threatened his borders.

Julian did not wait for Constantius to regroup. In the summer of AD 361 he invaded the Balkans and reached Naissus, where he stopped to gather his strength and bombard the cities of the east with propaganda leaflets justifying his rebellion. He now began to worship the old gods openly, and after 3 November had even more reason to put his faith in them. It was on that day that Constantius suddenly died of a fever in southern Turkey.

Desperate ploys

The brief reign of Julian is most noteworthy for his abortive attempts to revive traditional cult. If he had not combined this effort with a spectacularly ill-advised invasion of Iraq, it is conceivable that he might even have reversed the steady trend towards Christianization begun by Constantine. On the other hand, Julian's brand of religious fundamentalism was as distasteful to thinking pagans as it was to Christians. In dealing with the Christians, he held back from conducting persecutions, and tried instead to foment discord within their communities. He did this by recalling various bishops to the sees from which Constantius had exiled them for doctrinal nonconformity. Thus it was that Athanasius returned as archbishop of Alexandria after a pagan mob there had murdered the former incumbent (and Julian's former guardian) George of Cappadocia. Julian did not punish the Alexandrians for their act, but in various other places, when violence broke out between Christian communities, his response was to impose heavy sanctions upon them. Julian also created new provincial priesthoods to raise the profile of traditional pagan worship by engaging in lavish public sacrifices. The intention was that his new priests should mount a challenge to the Christian establishment, which, for all its internal divisions, had won genuine credit for dispensing charity to widows and the sick. This initiative failed; not only were aristocratic pagan priests totally unused to doing charitable works, but they also simply lacked the infrastructure to compete.

Equally problematic was Julian's attempt to encourage the Jews to restore the Temple at Jerusalem, destroyed in the revolt of AD 70. His sole motivation was to disprove Jesus' prophecy, as reported in the gospels, that the Temple would remain a ruin. All of Julian's plans ultimately turned to dust; in AD 362 work in Jerusalem was halted by an earthquake.

That same year, Athanasius was again evicted from Alexandria when he dared to convert several prominent pagans to Christianity. Worse still, the people of Antioch, where Julian overwintered, displayed open contempt for him after he controversially removed the bones of a Christian martyr from the site of an oracular shrine he planned to reopen. He also tried to blame the Christians of Antioch when a famous local temple was consumed by an accidental fire. Ultimately, he concluded that the only way out of the impasse he had got himself into was to undertake a massive assault against Persia.

Outflanked in Iraq

Julian launched his invasion of Iraq in the spring of AD 363. His strategy was to force the Persian king to negotiate by threatening his capital at Ctesiphon. The ultimate plan was to install Shapur's relative Hormizd (son of the former ruler Hormizd II), who was accompanying Julian, as a puppet ruler of some part of the realm. This was a foolish plan bedevilled by slapdash preparation. Julian brought with him no siege train, and was totally wrong-footed when Shapur refused to engage in a risky set-piece battle. Shapur had the luxury of being able to play a waiting game and win the war by exploiting Julian's woeful logistics. And so, as Julian advanced down the Euphrates, the Persians flooded the irrigation canals behind him, making it impossible for him to withdraw the same way that he had come.

Things went from bad to worse. Ctesiphon refused to surrender to a general who lacked the proper equipment to lay siege to it. Julian was forced to beat an ignominious retreat up the Tigris, harassed all the while by Persian delaying tactics designed to slow his withdrawal as he ran desperately short of food and other supplies. On 26 June, Julian was mortally wounded during a Persian attack on his rearguard. A relatively junior officer, Jovian (*c.* AD 332–364), was chosen by the general staff to serve as emperor and continue the retreat. On 1 July, he reached an agreement with Shapur, whereby the starving remnant of his army would be granted safe conduct to Roman territory in return for certain concessions. These included restoring to Persia the provinces seized by Diocletian and surrender of the fortress of Nisibis, which Shapur had failed to capture three times in the reign of Constantius. The emotions of the people of Nisibis, who seem to have been mostly Christian, when they saw Julian's body coming back and learned that their city would be turned over to the enemy, are powerfully reflected in the words of a Christian leader named Ephraim. He wrote:

> A wonder! By chance the corpse of the accursed one,
> Crossing over towards the rampart, met me near the city!
> And the Magus took and fastened on a tower
> The standard sent from the east. So that this standard-bearer would declare to the onlookers
> That the city was slave to the lords of that standard.

Brothers in power

Jovian might not have been a bad emperor. The surrender to Shapur was hardly his fault, and in his short reign he tried to bring confessional peace to the empire. Athanasius, the symbol of ecclesiastical resistance to imperial control, was permitted to return to Alexandria. At the same time, Jovian took only limited action against former supporters of Julian, and recognized that he could only secure power through negotiation with various entrenched interests in the bureaucracy.

Before he had a chance to get a firm grasp on the reins of power, however, he died on 17 February, AD 364. The official line was that a coal fire asphyxiated him in his bedroom. The fact that there was no investigation of his death hinted at murder. But if this were the case, those responsible had no clear plan for the future. It was not until 26 February that another comparatively junior officer, Valentinian (AD 321–375), was presented to the army as the general staff's candidate. The soldiers duly proclaimed him emperor, and, a few weeks later, as Valentinian realized that he would be spending a great deal of time in the west, he requested that they proclaim his brother, Valens (AD 328–378), as his co-emperor.

Constantius and Julian were strong personalities who had constantly reassigned senior officials to prevent the formation of powerful patronage networks. Yet, like the rank-and-file soldiers, senior bureaucrats tended to come from the regions where they served. Imperial authority simply set the seal on the power they had already acquired by cultivating connections within each bureau of government. All power was now centralized within the palace and was no longer based on the principle of collegiality. This meant that emperors were now obliged to negotiate with various diverse local power structures masquerading as representatives of a central government. The men who surrounded the throne had a vested interest in preventing effective imperial interference in their fiefdoms. They got exactly the emperors they wanted in Valentinian and Valens.

The nature of the new regime became apparent in September AD 365 when Procopius, a distant relative of Julian, whom Julian had allegedly designated as his successor before invading Iraq, staged a coup in Constantinople. In line with his lenient treatment of Julian's former confederates, Jovian had allowed Procopius, who did not press his claim, to retire to his estates in central Turkey. Valens now stirred things up by ordering Procopius' arrest. Procopius evaded capture and reappeared in the capital to win control of two legions. For several months, it looked as though he would unseat Valens. When Valentinian learned of the revolt, his advisers dissuaded him from intervening, emphasizing that it was vital he should remain in Gaul to repel any barbarian invasion. If Procopius prevailed, they would work out a way to deal with him later.

In the end, though, Valens was saved by the intervention of Arbitio, a member of Constantius' inner circle whom Julian had cashiered. Arbitio, whose personal authority was plainly far greater than that of Valens, convinced many of Procopius' men to switch sides prior to the battle that would decide who became emperor. In the course of the battle even more of Procopius' men deserted his ranks, and he was captured and executed.

The message of Procopius' coup was loud and clear. Valens and Valentinian were welcome to rule, but if they wanted to stay in power, it was essential that they respect the interests of their top civil servants. Valens' success was largely due to the fact that, once the western armies had returned home, most eastern officials were still Constantius' appointees, who hated Procopius for his links with Julian.

Corrupt sinecures

Valentinian remained on the throne for 11 years, and Valens for 14. In the west, Valentinian ruled through a small circle of associates who had supported his rise to power. Many abused their privileged position for years. In North Africa, for instance, a major scandal erupted at the start of Valentinian's reign, when the region's long-serving military commander, Romanus, arrived in the city of Leptis Magna to deal with the problem of ongoing attacks by desert raiders. After remaining there for 40 days, he suddenly demanded 4000 camels from the city's long-suffering inhabitants and, when these were not forthcoming, simply abandoned them to their fate. The people of Leptis Magna protested, but Romanus exploited his connections at court to ensure that no action was taken against him, even as the nomads resumed their raids. The issue dragged on for years, and Romanus continued all the while to feather his own nest. Indeed, Romanus' corruption only became the subject of scrutiny in a massive shake-up of government after Valentinian's death.

Similar corrupt practices flourished in Rome, where members of the senatorial aristocracy were charged with a range of offences of a largely personal nature (e.g. consulting magicians and adultery). Senators lodged vigorous protests, but were delivered a rude snub, as the official they most detested was promoted to the praetorian prefecture. The most significant feature of this incident is not that the representations of the senate failed to achieve their desired effect, but that this body now clearly saw itself as quite separate from the imperial court. The Roman senate had once been the pool from which future emperors were drawn, and a partner in the governance of the realm. Now, with only limited access to key posts, and the emperor living far away in Constantinople, it was reduced to acting as just another civic petitioner.

The senatorial prosecutions and the tribulations of the people of Leptis Magna, which were symptomatic of a court that exercised arbitrary power, help explain an event that was not only the most extraordinary of the reign of Valentinian, but also one of the most remarkable in the entire history of Rome. Valentinian fell seriously ill in AD 367, and the two principal factions at the court, described simply by Ammianus Marcellinus as the 'Gauls' and 'those with better aims', met to decide whom they should choose as his successor in the event of the emperor's death. There was evidently no question of consulting Valens, or even Valentinian himself. When Valentinian recovered, he punished none of those responsible but instead had his son, Gratian, declared Augustus. The bureaucracy allowed him to have his way, but it was clear from what had gone before that the government of the west felt no responsibility to the emperor in the east, nor to the dynastic principle. The situation in the east was no different.

Casting the runes

In AD 371 a group of officials consulted a bizarre prophetic device (an ancient form of ouija board) to determine who the next emperor should be. Details of the ceremony, which became well known as a result of the subsequent treason trial, suggest that the event unfolded as follows, in the words Ammianus places in the mouth of one of the participants:

> 'My lords, in an unlucky moment we put together out of laurel twigs in the shape of the Delphic tripod the hapless little table before you. We consecrated it with cryptic spells and a long series of magical rites, and at last made it work. The way in which it did so . . . was this. It was placed in the middle of a room thoroughly fumigated with spices from Arabia, and was covered with a round dish made from the alloys of various metals. The outer rim of the dish was cunningly engraved with the twenty-four letters of the alphabet separated by accurate intervals. A man dressed in linen garments and wearing linen sandals . . . officiated as priest. After uttering a set prayer to invoke the divine power which presides over prophecy, he took his place above the tripod as his knowledge of the proper ritual had taught him, and set swinging a ring suspended by a very fine

> cotton thread which had been consecrated by a mystic formula. The ring, moving in a series of jumps over the marked spaces, came to rest on particular letters.'

The answer it gave consisted of the Greek letters theta (th), epsilon (e) and omicron (o), which the consultants understood to indicate Theodorus, a Gaulish official in Valens' court. Even more curiously, when Theodorus was informed of his selection, Ammianus claims that he planned to tell Valens. Yet he was pre-empted by the praetorian prefect Modestus, who wanted to secure the succession for an easterner, and launched an investigation into treasonous magical practices. Many senior officials were brutally executed. Since Valens had no son yet, the matter of the succession was left open for the time being.

Valentinian, who had a ferocious temper, died of an apoplectic seizure in AD 375. Gratian stepped in as Augustus in Gaul, and his supporters immediately set about purging all of Valentinian's former confederates. The Balkan commander Merobaudes, who was one such ally, saw the writing on the wall if he failed to interpose some new titular authority between himself and the new ruler. Indeed, he seems to have planned for just this eventuality with the collusion of Valentinian's second wife, Justina. She had a son, also named Valentinian, and within five days of the announcement of the elder Valentinian's death, the younger Valentinian was proclaimed Augustus, with authority over Illyricum. Gratian and Valens accepted the proclamation as a fait accompli.

Whatever Valens thought of the proclamation of Valentinian, he soon found himself beset by far more urgent problems. As Valentinian II came to power, he was engaged in a fierce struggle with the Persians over control of Armenia. As if this were not serious enough, news reached him the following year in Antioch of a massive movement of peoples north of the Balkan frontier. The Goths were coming.

Enemies at the Gate: The Barbarian Invasions

(AD 376–411)

The Goths were not exactly an unknown quantity to the Romans. Having first arrived in the region to the north of Rome's border along the Danube around the end of the second century AD, they took part in the extensive raids that kept much of the Roman army tied down in the 250s and 260s. During the course of the next century, they divided into two main groups, the Tervingi, who inhabited the region around the Dneister River, and the Greuthingi, who occupied the lands bordering the Danube.

Over time, many Goths were recruited into the Roman army, while Constantine sponsored an effort to spread Christianity among them. The main agent of conversion was a Goth priest named Ulfilas (*c.* AD 311–383), who was ordained a bishop by Athanasius' great enemy, Eusebius of Nicomedia. The effects of his missionary work were deeply ambivalent, both at the time and later. From the Roman point of view, when Athanasius' brand of Christianity finally triumphed at the end of the century, Goths were regarded as heretics. In Ulfilas' own time, Gothic leaders who did not convert regarded him as an agent of the imperial government and persecuted his flock. As a result, Constantius II was forced to grant Ulfilas and some of his followers permission to move into Moesia Inferior (northern Bulgaria). Otherwise, contacts between the Romans and the Goths were regulated through Roman border posts. This was an uneasy coexistence, with occasional upsurges of violence, the most recent of which had been sparked by the Goths' alleged support for Procopius. A truce was concluded in AD 369, in which both parties agreed to maintain the status quo.

Invaders from the north

The Huns – a semi-nomadic people from the Eurasian steppes – shattered the peace. Although Roman sources describe in great detail the sudden irruption of these fearsome barbarians into northeastern Europe in the years immediately before AD 376, the truth about their appearance is probably somewhat more prosaic. As semi-nomads, the Huns would have long depended to some degree on neighbouring settled communities of Goths for their subsistence. It is not known what soured this relationship, but it is apparent that the Huns began to carry out massive raids against the Tervingi from the mid-370s onwards.

The Huns' success was due in large part to their adoption of a devastatingly effective piece of military hardware: a powerful form of recurved bow that enabled them to take down their opponents at long range. This weapon instantly rendered useless traditional Gothic tactics that relied on spear-armed cavalry engaging in close combat. A series of defeats threw the Tervingi into political turmoil, causing many to leave their lands and seek refuge among the Greuthingi, who also now began to suffer raids from the

Huns. A large number of Greuthingi decided to abandon their traditional territory and, like the Tervingi, seek refuge within the empire. As Ulfilas' flight shows, the empire was seen as a safe haven for Goths who could no longer live as they wished north of the border. This time, however, the sheer numbers involved made old models of accommodation unworkable.

Valens saw the displaced Goths as a potential source of recruits, and hoped to regulate the flow of refugees by allowing only the Greuthingi to enter Roman territory. Although this was a perfectly measured response, it would have required a great deal more advance planning than Valens had given it to make it work. The total number of Greuthingi is thought to have been in the region of 30,000–40,000 people, some 10,000 of whom were men of fighting age. With most of Valens' field army deployed in the east, there were not enough troops to control the situation. Moreover, even if it had been properly managed, the supply network was wholly inadequate for catering to such a huge influx of hungry people. Relations with the immigrants swiftly deteriorated and, after a botched Roman effort to seize the leaders of the Greuthingi at a banquet in AD 377, they broke down completely.

The outbreak of war with the Greuthingi opened the frontier to other tribes, and by the summer of AD 377 the number of new arrivals had swollen to around 80,000. When set against the overall population of the empire – still probably in the range of 60 million – this figure might appear negligible. Yet it represented a huge number of people concentrated in one area, and it would have required close coordination on the part of the three governments of the empire to bring the situation under control. As Valens made peace with Persia, neither the government of Valentinian II nor that of Gratian sent reinforcements to help the eastern emperor. Gratian, who was at least willing to help, was held up by insurrrection among his forces on the Lower Rhine. The Balkan commander Merobaudes, who was closer, did nothing except secure his own territory against Goth incursion. In AD 378, Gratian finally advanced east. Meanwhile Valens marshalled his forces, but still hoped that a diplomatic solution might be found.

In August, AD 378, the main Goth force encamped near Adrianople (the Turkish city of Edirne, in Thrace). Valens could delay no longer, and on 9 August made his move. The battle, fought on 9 August AD 378, pitted Valens' field army of the east, numbering between 30,000 and 40,000 men, against a Gothic force that was likely about the same size. After marching eight miles from their camp, the Romans deployed in line against the Goths, who had taken up defensive positions in front of their wagon laager. Following a parley between Valens and the Goth commanders, some units on the Roman left launched an attack on the Goths (quite possibly without orders). The Gothic cavalry, which had been away from the camp, then attacked and routed the Roman left, and subsequently encircled and destroyed the centre of the Roman force. Two-thirds of the Roman army are said to have perished. Valens was among the casualties, but his body was never found (perhaps because the Goths set fire to a farmhouse where he was taken after being wounded). This defeat changed the balance of power in the

Balkans for good, as the Romans would not thereafter be able to eliminate an independent Gothic presence south of the Danube.

The Goths, after realizing that they could not take Constantinople, and heeding the famous words of one of their leaders that they should try to attack walled cities, moved on to the hitherto unravaged lands of central Bulgaria and Serbia. Gratian was in something of a quandary. As senior surviving emperor, he could simply claim sovereignty over the east, but could not be sure that the eastern bureaucracy would accept him. Instead of doing battle with the Goths, he appointed two senior military commanders, one for the eastern frontier, the other for Illyricum, a rather ill-defined title that probably comprehended authority over the idle armies of Valentinian II as well as the remnants of Valens' forces in the Balkans. As commander in the east he selected a man with the portentous name of Shapur (evidently a Persian who had entered Roman service), while the man he chose to take military control of Illyricum was Theodosius.

Striking a deal

Theodosius was the son of the man who had been Valentinian I's *magister militum* (literally 'master of the soldiers'). This post was created in the early AD 370s, establishing a new level of command above those held by the master of infantry (*magister peditum*) and master of cavalry (*magister equitum*). Over time, it would become the most prestigious post within the military bureaucracy. Yet when Theodosius the Elder took on the role in AD 373, his position was precarious, to say the least. Dispatched to North Africa to suppress a minor revolt, he uncovered the corrupt conduct of Romanus and sent him for trial in Italy. The trial was conducted by Merobaudes, who promptly found Romanus innocent, and in addition ensured that his cronies at the court of Valentinian I charged Theodosius himself with treason. He was executed in AD 376.

It is probable that the scandalous death of the elder Theodosius sparked the violent reaction against Valentinian's inner circle, whose members now fell from power. This event would doubtless also have had repercussions at the court of Valentinian II. Certainly, Gratian's choice of the younger Theodosius – now in his 30s and with no experience of such a senior command – was more a message to the regime of Merobaudes than it was a threat to the Goths. Even at moments of extreme crisis, it seemed, internal bureaucratic politics were of prime importance.

Perhaps Theodosius' chief quality was that he was a fast learner. After defeating Sarmatian raiders, he promptly allowed himself to be proclaimed emperor in January, AD 379. This may all have been part of Gratian's plan; certainly the outcome was not unwelcome to Gratian's retinue of officials, who lent Theodosius vital support over the next couple of years, and the young Gratian recognized Theodosius' claim to the throne without demur. Perhaps he and his advisers felt that anyone who wanted to be Augustus in the east under the circumstances that obtained in AD 379 was welcome to the job. Theodosius knew that he needed to tread carefully, for he could not really claim the throne, or indeed show himself in Constantinople, until the problem of the Goths had been resolved. He therefore set up court at Thessalonica.

The shared experience of victory and pillage was gradually shaping the Goths who had ventured south from their original homeland into a cohesive new community. More than anything they now wanted a place that they could call home, and sought it within the bounds of the Roman empire. Theodosius was initially hostile, but after suffering a defeat at their hands in AD 380, made peace with the Goths. They were granted autonomous lands in the Balkans under the control of their own chiefs in return for service, when required, with the army of the east. Such subsidized barbarian tribes were known as *foederati* ('confederates').

Blueprint for break-up

Although the treaty of AD 382 might appear to hark back to a happier age when the emperor controlled a multi-ethnic state through careful diplomacy and overt displays of personal *virtus*, it was in fact a blueprint for the break-up of the Roman empire. The idea of client states and independent allies was nothing new; in the past Rome had allowed Palmyra to raise a powerful army, and fostered a variety of relationships with its subjects as a way of strengthening the empire. But this treaty was fundamentally different, inasmuch as there was now no apparatus for interaction between Rome's confederates and the central government that was not dictated (and tainted) by the vested interests of the bureaucratic élite. In other words, instead of becoming staunch and valued allies of the Roman people or the Roman empire, the Goths were to be mere pawns in the endless internal power struggle between different parts of the Roman bureaucracy.

Another reason for the incipient dissolution of the empire was the growing gap in prosperity that opened up between the east on the one hand and the centre and west on the other. Not only did the treaty with the Goths mean that no more tax revenues would flow to the western empire from the regions they occupied, but the foregoing years of war had also done terrible damage to the empire's infrastructure in the Balkans. Large swathes of countryside took years to recover from such depredations. By contrast, improving relations with Persia after the death of Shapur II in AD 379 meant that no such devastation was visited on the eastern empire. In consequence, there developed a substantial difference between the logistical capacity of the empire to the east of the Bosphorus and that of the empire to the west. To further exacerbate the problem, the inability of the eastern, western and central bureaucracies to unite behind a common set of objectives meant that deterioration in one area was now unlikely to be repaired through the altruistic cooperation of the others.

The interventions by Gratian, whose generals continued to help Theodosius up until the treaty of AD 382, stand as an honourable exception to the general rule that each region was left to fend for itself. Certainly, Theodosius did not reciprocate Gratian's loyalty. In AD 383, Magnus Maximus, the commander of the British garrison, took advantage of serious discontent with Gratian's management of affairs in Gaul by invading the province. Encouraged by Merobaudes, the

Gallic army deserted Gratian, and Theodosius responded by recognizing Maximus as a member of the imperial college. It was only when Maximus launched a sudden invasion of Italy in AD 386, driving Valentinian II into exile in Theodosius' part of the empire, that the relationship between the two men broke down. In AD 388, Theodosius invaded Maximus' realm. Caught off guard by the speed of the invasion, Maximus was captured outside Aquileia and summarily put to death. Valentinian was restored to power, but in name only. In fact, Theodosius' marshals began to exert an iron grip over the region. Prominent among them was his *magister militum*, the Frankish general Arbogast (d. AD 394), who ruthlessly mopped up any remaining sympathizers of Maximus and placed Valentinian under virtual house arrest in Vienne after Theodosius returned to Constantinople. In AD 392, Valentinian tried to depose Arbogast and paid with his life.

Showdown in the west

The fact that Arbogast was not a pure-blooded Roman effectively disqualified him from taking the throne himself; no such official sanction existed, but there was enough residual anti-German sentiment in the empire to make it impossible. Instead, he selected a senator named Eugenius to play the role, thereby assuring himself of the loyal backing of the senate. In all of this, there were also unmistakable signs of tensions that had been growing in the past few years between the court and the Roman aristocracy. Eugenius and some of his most prominent supporters were Roman aristocrats, and they seem to have been thoroughly tired of taking orders from Milan – and, indeed, from Milanese figures such as its bishop, Ambrose, who seemed to them to have been excessively powerful in recent years.

Ambrose, the son of a praetorian prefect, had first asserted his power against the court in a dispute with Valentinian II about where his soldiers could pray (like other Romans, he held that Goths were not orthodox believers). After a tense standoff and the miraculous discovery of the relics of two martyrs, Ambrose got his way. A few years later he played a leading role in removing the altar of Victory from the senate (this was a pure power-play on his part, as even the bishop of Rome was willing to leave the altar in place and the majority of senators were Christians). Finally, he had quarrelled with Theodosius on two occasions, once excommunicating the emperor and forcing him to submit to ecclesiastical authority in order to be readmitted to communion. In light of this history, we need not assume that Arbogast's well advertised hatred of the man stemmed merely from the fact that he was a pagan; rather, he was tired of Ambrose's meddling in secular affairs.

The civil war that broke out between Arbogast and Theodosius in AD 394, although later presented as a religious conflict between pagans and Christians, was really nothing more than a repeat of earlier conflicts between eastern and western bureaucracies. The one difference from earlier struggles was that Theodosius' propagandists decided to dress the conflict in virtually mythic terms, suggesting that Arbogast openly placed his faith in the power of the old gods while Theodosius made much of his devotion to his God

When the two sides met at the Battle of the Frigidus on 6 September, Theodosius attributed his eventual victory to the intervention of a violent storm, which he proclaimed a divine miracle. Arbogast and Eugenius were executed and Theodosius moved into Italy to re-establish his authority. Before leaving on campaign, Theodosius had elevated his teenaged son, Arcadius (AD 377–408), to the rank of Augustus in the east, a sign perhaps that he intended to remain in the west for some time. That was not to be; in January, AD 395, he died at the age of 49 in Milan. Theodosius was the last emperor who could claim to rule the bureaucracies of both east and west. Following his death, these were divided into two equal parts, with the Balkan dioceses of Illyricum and Macedonia going to the west, and Moesia and Thrace going to the east. With Illyricum went the land settled by the Goths after AD 382. The specifics of this division determined the future course of Roman history, for the Goths now became an exclusively western rather than an eastern problem.

Stilicho and Alaric

Theodosius' *magister militum* during the campaign against Arbogast was a man called Stilicho (*c.* AD 359–408), the son of a German officer and a Roman mother. At Theodosius' deathbed, Stilicho announced that he had been appointed guardian to the emperor's successors Arcadius and his brother Honorius (AD 384–423). Also serving in the army that invaded Italy was Alaric, a leader of the Gothic community that Theodosius had settled in the Balkans after the treaty of AD 382. On the first day of the Battle of the Frigidus,

Theodosius is said to have ordered these Gothic commanders to launch a series of attacks on their compatriots' defensive works that cost the lives of 10,000 Goths all told. Theodosius allegedly boasted that he had simultaneously destroyed two enemies of Rome – the Goths and Arbogast. However, this story was greatly exaggerated – the number cited was in fact the entire number of warriors deployed by the Goths. Even so, the result seems to have displeased Alaric, even as Arcadius' government recognized him as leader of the Goths who returned to Lower Moesia.

Meanwhile, following the death of Theodosius the next year, Stilicho travelled with the eastern army as far as Thessalonica, where messengers from the eastern government, then dominated by the praetorian prefect Rufinus, sent word that if he personally came any closer to Constantinople, his force would be regarded as a threat and attacked. Stilicho handed control of the eastern army over to Gainas, a Goth who had risen to high command under Theodosius. When the army reached Constantinople, Gainas promptly arranged for Rufinus to be assassinated at a military review. With a loyal supporter now in charge of the eastern army, Stilicho might well have imagined that he had succeeded, at minimal cost, in making himself effective master of the empire. However, this would not turn out to be the case; Gainas allied himself with Eutropius, the eunuch who dominated the court of Arcadius. At their prompting, Arcadius refused to acknowledge Stilicho's claim to be his guardian.

The complete lack of cooperation between the two governments in the face of a series of crises over the next seven years demonstrated that the empire was more firmly divided than ever. In AD 397–398, Stilicho received no assistance from the east in quelling a major uprising in North Africa, nor when Alaric burst forth from his enclave to raid the Greek peninsula. Stilicho caught Alaric's forces in a potentially fatal trap in the northern Peloponnese in AD 399, but in allowing him to slip away, Stilicho may have had at the back of his mind the idea that Alaric might one day prove useful in the event of a war with the east. In Constantinople, Gainas now gave further evidence of his treacherous nature, though this time he overplayed his hand. Sent to suppress a serious revolt against the eastern empire by a group of Goths in Phrygia under the leadership of the chieftain Tribigild, Gainas apparently cut a secret deal with his Gothic counterpart. His aim was to deflect blame for the failure of his campaign onto his erstwhile ally Eutropius; this tactic succeeded, and Eutropius was dismissed and executed. A year later, Gainas again blackmailed the imperial government, forcing the resignation of Eutropius' successor, Aurelian. But he immediately overplayed his hand by demanding a special church for his men to practise their Ulfilan brand of Christianity in the capital, and higher office for himself. The people of Constantinople rose up, slaughtering thousands of his men and driving the rest from the city. When Gainas tried to lead his surviving men back across the Hellespont, naval forces destroyed their transports, and Gainas fled into Thrace where he, and his surviving followers, were caught and slaughtered by Uldin, king of the Huns, who had recently joined forces with Arcadius. Uldin sent Gainas' head to the emperor as a gift.

In AD 401 Alaric launched an invasion of Italy; with no

Roman army in his way, he advanced easily into northern Italy, drove Honorius from his palace at Milan to the city of Asta, and besieged the emperor for several months until Stilicho arrived with a portion of the field army from Gaul. On Easter Sunday, AD 402, Stilicho attacked the now largely Christian Goths as they prepared for their religious observances near Pollentia. Despite being caught by surprise, Alaric managed to withdraw with the bulk of his army intact and fought a running war with Stilicho until the following summer, when Stilicho pinned him down and defeated him near Verona. Yet although Alaric had staged two uprisings in under a decade, Stilicho regarded him as more useful alive than dead, signing a pact with him and allowing him to return to his Balkan lands. He evidently still took the view that Alaric could play a useful role in furthering his own ambitions.

Stilicho's lenient treatment of Alaric contrasts sharply with his handling of the next group of invaders to cross his path. In the summer of AD 406, Radagaisus led an armed migration of the Alamanni from the Upper Rhine into Italy. So huge was this displacement of people that Stilicho judged the western field army unequal to the task of defeating his new foe. Accordingly, he turned then to the accomplished mercenary leader, King Uldin of the Huns. Uldin's appearance at the head of a large cavalry force enabled Stilicho to force the surrender of his enemies. Around 10,000 of Radagaisus' men were taken into imperial service for use in the defence of Italy, while many thousands of others were sold into slavery.

Invaders cross the Rhine

Disaster followed hard on the heels of victory. On 31 December, AD 406, the Rhine froze over, allowing a second massive invasion wave to crash down upon Gaul. This time the invaders were relatively new arrivals – the Vandals, Alans and Sueves, all of whom came from central Europe. The bulk of Stilicho's field army was still caught up further south and there was nothing he could do to prevent the destruction of the Rhine frontier. The tribes that crossed the frontier on this occasion would never leave Roman territory; the integrity of the frontier first established by Augustus, and stabilized by Tiberius, would never be fully restored. Around the same time, the commander of the Roman army in Britain, Constantine, declared himself emperor and moved into Gaul. Driving the recent invaders south and west, he rapidly took control of the Gallic dioceses.

Stilicho was in a genuine quandary. Uldin had gone home, and he was unwilling to commit his own army to open battle against Constantine. Instead, he contented himself with garrisoning the passes over the Alps. Stilicho also faced a number of other difficulties. The western emperor Honorius, now in his early 20s, had taken Stilicho's daughter as his wife but had come to detest her. He was also surrounded with courtiers who wanted to be rid of Stilicho. Moreover, there remained among the Romans a deep-seated dislike of Germans. While it was the case that most of the army was now German, the same was not true of the civil administration. Tensions between civil servants and German soldiers had played a large part in the upheaval in Constantinople that led to the downfall of Gainas. There had also been occasional violent attacks on Germanic units in other imperial cities. In the wake of Adrianople the *magister militum* of the east ordered the massacre of Goths serving in the Roman army there. Now, with what could not have been worse timing, Arcadius died. The eastern regime replaced him with his seven-year-old son, Theodosius II, on 8 May, AD 408.

Stilicho's first instinct was to lead an army east, but at the same time he had to watch Constantine and find some way of dealing with the renegade Alaric. Breaking his parole, Alaric had in the meantime advanced on northern Italy and was demanding a huge tribute in return for a promise of good behaviour. Stilicho's response was to buy off Alaric and suggest that he should go to Gaul to fight Constantine. This stratagem proved to be Stilicho's downfall; the anti-German prejudice in the western imperial establishment now reached fever pitch. On 13 August, soldiers mutinied as Honorius reviewed them in Pavia and murdered a number of Stilicho's generals; eight days later, Stilicho himself was killed in Ravenna. The new leader of the government, Olympius, then ordered a massacre of the 'Germans' in the army – in this case former followers of Radagaisus – who were thought to be loyal to Stilicho. The survivors fled to join Alaric. Realizing that there was now no Roman army of any strength between himself and Rome, Alaric bypassed the emperor and made straight for the city. The senate voted to pay him a massive bribe and to negotiate a fresh deal with Honorius that would give Alaric new status within the Roman hierarchy. When Honorius refused to go along with this, Alaric returned to Rome with an even longer list of demands. These included a homeland for his people in Switzerland and southern Austria, and the rank of *magister militum* for himself. Though Honorius' officials were willing to accede to this demand – to do so would give them a decisive edge against Constantine in Gaul – Honorius refused outright.

New thinking was needed to find ways of assimilating immigrants into imperial society. With many Germans serving in the army, even after the massacre of AD 408, and many still in the officer corps, a pragmatic solution should have been possible. With this in mind, in AD 409, after another siege of Rome, the senate proclaimed a new emperor, Priscus Attalus, who with its blessing made common cause with Alaric.

The fall of Rome

Alaric seems genuinely to have believed that the empire would last for ever and that the imperial government alone could grant security to his people. The problem was that he still lacked the wherewithal to realize these goals. Attalus had little influence with the bureaucracy, and Alaric's army had no siege equipment. These two shortcomings meant that Alaric would still have to treat with Honorius; however, having recently gained reinforcements from the east, Honorius refused to deal with him. Betrayed at every turn, Alaric deposed his puppet emperor and appeared once more before the walls of Rome. On 24 August, AD 410, the Goths found that a sympathizer had left the Salarian Gate open. For the first time in 800 years, a man who was not part of the Roman hierarchy took control of the capital.

The fall of Rome revealed many things. In terms of political power, it demonstrated just how little the city now mattered: Honorius and his government were still secure in Ravenna, as was Theodosius II in Constantinople, while the field army remained encamped on the border with Gaul. In terms of Roman culture, the sack of Rome was more momentous. Jerome, the great Christian theologian who had moved from his home in the west to Palestine – where he was engaged in creating the Latin translation of the Bible that would be the basis of expressions of Christian faith in the west until the Reformation of the sixteenth century – lamented the event as an unsurpassed catastrophe. When the bright light of all the world was put out, or, rather, when the Roman empire was decapitated, and, to speak more correctly, the whole world perished in one city, 'I became dumb and humbled myself.' Augustine, the bishop of Hippo in North Africa, responded to pagan claims that the sack of the city was the result of the conversion of the state to Christianity by writing his massive treatise *City of God*, in which he argued that political history was of little consequence when compared with the history of God's relationship with humanity. After all, he contested, far worse things had happened in the past, before the rise of Christianity.

In support of Augustine's argument, a Christian from Spain named Orosius wrote a seven-volume work entitled *History against the Pagans*, the bulk of which recounts disasters before the birth of Christ. The city of Rome was a symbol of a world that was past, rather than of the world that was to come. It was eminently possible for there to be a civilized world that was both Christian and Roman and that did not depend on any specific political order. For the Goths, the situation was even more problematic. Alaric had played his last card, and still not gained the office that he wanted or a homeland for his people. He died a year later in southern Italy.

Final Decline and Fall: The Collapse of the Western Empire

(AD 411–476)

At the start of the fourth century AD the governments of the eastern and western Roman empires faced essentially the same problem – the movement of peoples from central Europe towards the central tax-generating zones around the Mediterranean. One of the most intriguing questions of European history is why the western regime failed within 70 years of Alaric's sack of Rome, while the eastern continued, in varying forms, until the Ottoman capture of Constantinople in 1453.

Certainly, Asia Minor had the geographical advantage of being protected from attack by the Bosphorus, yet this fact alone is not as decisive as it might at first appear. This narrow body of water was no real barrier to a determined enemy, and the walls of Constantinople, mighty though they were, still needed to be manned by large and well-led defensive forces. The main reason that the eastern empire survived the movement of peoples and the western empire did not is that in the crucial decades of the early fifth century the government of the east was far more efficient than its western counterpart.

Wasted opportunities

The western empire lacked coherent direction during the period between the death of Stilicho and the advent of a new regime led by Theodosius' daughter Galla Placidia in the AD 430s. By then, there was no salvaging anything that resembled the western empire of the past. Too much territory had already fallen under the political control of immigrants who could have been peacefully assimilated into the power structure of the empire if Honorius' court had not been staffed by bigoted incompetents. The primary interest of these officials was self-advancement, and their ways of securing it conspiracy and murder. In addition, the emperor himself was hamstrung by his pathological prejudice against 'Germans'. In the end, German communities that could not be assimilated were set upon each other in a destructive cycle of violence that saw ever more territory prised from the direct control of the emperor, and ever more land in the provinces laid waste. Tribes that had already decamped once to move into the empire were not so attached to the districts where they settled that they were unwilling to move on to some other area they had not yet ravaged. Ultimately, this led to the catastrophic passage of the Vandals from Spain to North Africa in AD 429, and the loss of North Africa to the Vandal king Geiseric in AD 439. Thereafter, the western government simply lacked the resources to govern alone, while its bureaucrats were unwilling to surrender their authority to the only government with the power to help, the regime in Constantinople.

The government of the east, by contrast, functioned relatively smoothly in the 30 years after the revolt of Gainas, largely due to the immensely able stewardship of the empresses Pulcheria (AD 399–453) and Eudoxia (AD 401–460), who were able to construct a coherent regime with reasonably orderly patterns of advancement despite their personal antipathy to one another. When the violent incursion of the Huns under Attila occurred in the AD 440s and 450s, the eastern government was strong enough to survive. It did so by adopting the policy of diverting potential enemies to the west, whose failed regimes it had only limited interest in supporting.

Around this time, an important change occurs in the language that Roman writers use to refer to the empire. As late as the AD 430s, the historian Olympiodorus, the principal source for later accounts of the period, was still writing in terms of the eastern and western parts of the empire. Yet the younger Priscus of Panium – an immensely gifted historian who also played a minor role in the government of the period, serving on an embassy to Attila – wrote instead of the 'western' and 'eastern Romans'. Ostensibly a linguistic quibble, Priscus' terminology in fact indicates that the two states were now distinct entities, pursuing quite different policies when it suited them. Shortly after Priscus brought his history to an end in the early AD 470s, the western empire collapsed completely, leading to the abolition of the imperial office after AD 476, and, within a decade, to the creation of a new Gothic state in Italy. This polity joined the other successor states that had already developed in Rome's western provinces.

Ensuring the dynastic succession

The story of the decline of the western empire is initially that of two empresses: Galla Placidia (*c.* AD 388–450), the long-suffering daughter of Theodosius I, and Pulcheria, the sister of the emperor Theodosius II. Galla Placidia was one of the prizes abducted from Rome by Alaric in AD 410. In the years after the sack of Rome she accompanied the Goths, now led by Athaulf, the half-brother of Alaric, as they moved to Gaul. There then ensued a highly complex series of events culminating in the collapse of the regime of the usurper Constantine III. At the same time, the Vandals and Sueves, the invaders of AD 407, occupied Spain, wreaking havoc on its inhabitants, and Athaulf's Goths, now called the Visigoths, took over territory along the southern coast of Gaul. In AD 414, Athaulf married Galla and proclaimed Priscus Attalus – the emperor installed and deposed by Alaric who had remained with the Goths throughout the intervening years – as his own emperor. Athaulf's ultimate ambition is revealed by the fact that when Galla bore him a son at the end of AD 414, the child was named Theodosius. Since Honorius was childless, the boy would have been an obvious candidate for the succession at Ravenna if he had lived, but he did not survive infancy. A year later, Athaulf was murdered, and his successor returned Galla to Constantius, the *magister militum* of Honorius' regime, and acceded to the Roman request to attack the tribes in Spain. In AD 418, after years of wanton slaughter in Spain, the Visigoths were rewarded with land of their own around Toulouse.

The empire in the west was by now a shambles. Britain, which had expelled the representatives of Constantine III in AD 410, was barely part of the empire any longer. Its tiny garrison was fully occupied defending the country against raids by the tribes north of Hadrian's Wall (the Picts and Scots) as well as raiders from across the North Sea (Angles, from Schleswig, and Saxons). The Burgundians, a tribe that had taken advantage of the collapse of the Rhine frontier to establish themselves in Roman territory, occupied a substantial portion of northwestern France. Southwestern France was now the home of the Visigoths; and most of Spain was Roman in name only. The regime in the east was largely untroubled by these reverses. After all, the west yielded no revenue, and was obviously in no position to provide military support should any be needed. As long as Honorius was alive, the government of Theodosius II rested easy in the knowledge that there was a representative of the dynasty in place. But if that dynasty were to continue, the key figure would be Galla Placidia.

Constantius could fairly claim that he had rescued Galla from the hands of the barbarians, and that she should show him due gratitude by accepting his generous offer of marriage. Galla, however, found him abhorrent and the prospect of becoming his wife deeply distasteful. Ever since his defeat of Constantine, the ambitious Constantius had successfully inveigled himself into ever more influential positions within the regime. His self-appointment as a patrician was designed to advance his career still further. Galla was the key to the future of the western empire, for any offspring she bore would guarantee that western officialdom avoided potential take-over by representatives of the dynasty from the east, or another civil war. Although she managed to resist what was essentially a political act of rape for three years, her brother finally forced her to take Constantius' hand on 1 January, AD 418. Their son Valentinian III (AD 418–455) was born before the end of that year, with a second child, Honoria, following shortly thereafter. In early AD 421, having finally achieved his aim of being named Augustus (a title which the eastern court refused to recognize), Constantius suddenly died. The tensions in government between the 'Germans' and 'Romans', which he had kept in check, resurfaced almost immediately. Even as Constantius, the de facto leader of the 'German' group, was rising to power, the court of Honorius had issued a remarkable edict forbidding anyone to wear German dress within the walls of Rome. Galla now became the focus of loyalty for the German soldiers with whom her late husband had surrounded himself. At the same time, Honorius began to hint that he wanted carnal relations with his sister, and Galla fled to the east by the end of AD 423.

Empresses at the helm

The government of the east was far less colourful than that of the west. Although Arcadius was as weak-willed and ineffectual as his brother, he had made a much better marriage. After the revolt of Gainas, his wife Eudoxia had forged an alliance with powerful factions at court, and had herself proclaimed Augusta. No woman had held an imperial title since the death of Helena; despite howls of protest from Christian traditionalists, foremost among whom was John Chrysostom, archbishop of Constantinople, Eudoxia made it abundantly clear that she intended to exercise real authority, especially given the shortcomings of her husband in exercising his regnal duties. She died in AD 404, but the precedent she set for strong female rule paved the way for her daughter Pulcheria to become effective regent for her brother, Theodosius II (AD 401–450), who was only eight years old when he ascended the throne in AD 408.

In AD 413, as Pulcheria turned 14 and began to be looked upon as potential marriage material by ambitious politicians, she took a momentous decision that ultimately assured her a unique position in imperial society. Turning down all bids by the praetorian prefect Anthemius – a former key ally of her mother – to arrange a union with one of his relatives, she publicly devoted her virginity to God. Pulcheria was doubtless influenced in her decision by her profound loathing of Anthemius.

Pulcheria subsequently led a reclusive existence in the palace in the company of her younger sisters, who were inspired to follow her example. Together, they created an aura of imperial power that was inextricably linked with the Church. Through her public proclamation of virginity (probably genuine) and her essentially ascetic lifestyle, Pulcheria also helped foster a growing interest in the figure of the Virgin Mary. Thus began the cult of the Virgin and the influential area of ecclesiastical scholarship known as Marian theology. At the same time, however, Pulcheria pandered to more distasteful elements in the early Christian Church. In trying to prevent inter-Christian violence, she consciously acted as a lightning-rod, conducting intolerance onto relatively defenceless scapegoats. Jews were persecuted and synagogues destroyed, while pagans were systematically debarred from serving in the administration. In this way, she made her position within Constantinople unassailable; one clear lesson that had emerged from Eudoxia's clash with St John Chrysostom was that whoever managed to harness the passions of fundamentalist Christians would wield enormous power in the capital. On 4 July, AD 414, Pulcheria was made Augusta by Theodosius II.

Even more significantly, the alliance that Pulcheria forged between the imperial office and the Church helped reconcile different groups within the bureaucracy. German generals now stood four-square with traditional aristocrats in the defence of the eastern empire. The institutionalized piety of the regime was clearly demonstrated in AD 415, when the supposed relics of the first Christian martyr, St Stephen, were discovered. The relics of Stephen were transported from Jerusalem to Constantinople with enormous pomp and ceremony before being deposited in the household of Pulcheria herself. Although the veneration of relics already had a long history in the early Church, the ever more prominent connection between political power and the possession of relics made their collection an important, and lucrative, aspect of Christian devotion and was eventually to become one of the principal bones of contention behind the Protestant Reformation. The dual meaning of the Latin term for the uncovering of relics (*inventio*) – 'discovery' or 'invention' – hints at the focus of later criticism.

On the positive side, the highly Christianized version of the imperial office that took shape in the eastern part of the empire did succeed in bringing the concept of emperorship back in line with contemporary social values. Disputes about doctrine were played out in massive church councils that assembled bishops from all over the empire. These synods were conducted in Greek rather than Latin, an important concession by an administration that still issued official proclamations in Latin, even though few people in the eastern empire used that language in their daily lives. People from outside the official power structure of the bureaucracy thus had an opportunity to meet with the emperor, and hear him declare his attachment to their values, in their own language. Even if there remained serious disagreements about the nature of God, and controversial rulings were not universally accepted, there was no question that the imperial government was now trying to address the concerns of its subjects. In the time of Augustus, the notion that the emperor represented the ideal of *virtus* had been essential in defining the purpose of the office. But as times changed, and the nature of the office with them, it needed to be imbued with new significance. An emperor who was the equal of the apostles was far more in tune with contemporary thought than one whose actions referenced the moral code of the Roman Republic.

From AD 421 onwards, Pulcheria had to share significant public space with her brother's new wife Eudocia, who was just as able as Pulcheria but also more accepting of doctrinal differences. Although she converted before her marriage, her background as the daughter of a pagan family predisposed her to greater tolerance for religious nonconformity. As Theodosius' wife, Eudocia enthusiastically espoused

Christianity and rivalled Pulcheria in her demonstrations of devotion. In AD 438–439, for example, she made a pilgrimage to Jerusalem and brought back precious relics. At least in the short term, personal rancour between the two women tended to manifest itself exclusively in the form of religious dispute. While the imperial office was now conceived of in terms of Christian piety, the contemporary definition of this virtue did not preclude a ruler from entertaining a lust for power or meting out vicious treatment to political rivals. As a new threat emerged on the frontiers of the eastern empire, Eudocia's position came under fire. In AD 443 her opponents at court succeeded in making a charge of adultery against her stick. She was exiled to Jerusalem, where she lived on until AD 460. Interestingly, she was allowed to retain her insignia as empress – an admission, perhaps, that the reason for her exile had had more to do with politics than sex.

The late western empire

Galla Placidia arrived in Constantinople at the very beginning of Eudocia's period of ascendancy, and the new empress seems to have seen in Galla a useful tool to assert her own supremacy. Eudocia had been granted the title of Augusta after giving birth to a daughter in AD 421, around the time that Galla fled the west. This infant was now betrothed to Galla's six-year-old son Valentinian III as a symbolic gesture of the eastern court's interest in the succession to Honorius. The issue of succession arose almost immediately, for Honorius died before the end of AD 423, whereupon western officials tried to assert their independence by proclaiming a palace functionary named John as Augustus. He was a poor choice; the Visigoths declared allegiance to the cause of their former queen and began to attack imperial territory in Gaul, and the eastern court made extensive plans for an invasion of the west. The result was a foregone conclusion. John was captured, mutilated and executed in the circus at Aquileia.

The armies of the east were not sent to occupy the west. Once John was dead, it was Galla's job to govern the west in the name of her son. To do so she had to balance the ambitions of three generals, Flavius, Boniface and Aetius, who had once served her late and unlamented husband, Constantius. These men had played various roles in the recent civil war. Flavius had been recalled from retirement; Boniface, who ruled Africa as a virtual principality, had openly sided with the invaders; while the third, Aetius (*c.* AD 396–454), had appeared at the head of an army of Huns just after John had been killed. Realizing that there was no point in defending a dead man, he paid off the Huns and accepted command of the army in Gaul. Having spent much of his youth as a hostage, first with the Goths of Alaric and Athaulf, and then with the Huns of Uldin, Aetius combined fierce ambition with a genuine knowledge of the people with whom he would have to deal. As an added bonus, he was also a genuinely talented officer. None of these qualities endeared him to the empress, however, who saw in him the image of Constantius, and her antipathy would prove disastrous. Thus it was that when Aetius arrested Flavius on a charge of conspiracy in AD 430, Galla summoned Boniface from Africa to bring him under control. Boniface died in the moment of victory, leaving control of Italy to his son-in-law, Sebastian, while Aetius sought aid from the Huns. With an army of Huns at his back, Aetius returned to Italy. Sebastian fled to Constantinople, and Aetius took control of the western empire, assuming the title of patrician in AD 435, just in time to face the loss of Africa.

Galla's recall of Boniface could not have come at a worse time. After years of warfare both among themselves and against sundry Roman forces, the Vandals, Alans and Sueves had been severely weakened, so much so that one of the two Vandal tribes had virtually ceased to exist, and the Alans had been forced to join with the Vandals to form a new nation. In AD 429, Geiseric (*c.* AD 389–477), the leader of this new confederacy, recognized that there was no future in Spain, where years of conflict had ruined much of the land. He also realized that there was nothing that passed for an effective Roman fleet in the western Mediterranean, and so transported his people across the straits of Gibraltar into Africa. Boniface's effort to organize resistance faltered in the face of his commitment in Italy, with the result that the Vandals gradually established themselves in the western provinces of Africa. Although their advance was halted in AD 435, when Aetius reinforced the African garrison with troops from the eastern empire, this interruption was only temporary. Geiseric captured Carthage in AD 439, and even as Aetius, aided again by forces from the east, assembled a fleet to invade Africa, the Huns appeared, with new leadership and new ambitions, to threaten the Balkan frontier. Eastern help evaporated, and Aetius had no choice but to negotiate a treaty recognizing Vandal control of the only remaining area from which the western empire could draw resources to support a significant army. To ensure the peace, Geiseric continued nominal tax payments from the region under his control in return for the betrothal of Valentinian's infant daughter to his young son, Huneric. Ever the astute observer, Geiseric wanted security for his people, and had perhaps noted that Athaulf's heir might have been a claimant to the throne. What was good for a Goth would be good for a Vandal, or so he may have thought.

The scourge of God

The new enemies that began to threaten the borders of the eastern empire from AD 443 onwards were the Huns. Ever since their emergence as a major force in the AD 370s the Huns who lived in the Balkans had more often assisted the empire than assailed it. With the exception of a brutal raid by Uldin in AD 407, the leaders of the Huns had chosen to accept large payments from the empire, either to keep the peace on their side of the frontier or to lend significant assistance at moments of crisis. This all changed shortly after the brothers Attila (*c.* AD 406–453) and Bleda (*c.* AD 390–445) came to power in AD 434. By far the dominant partner, Attila was a man whose vast ambition was matched by a propensity for ruthless savagery. Initially, Attila followed the traditional Hunnish policy of hiring out large mercenary armies to suppress Germanic enemies of the Roman empire.

Presently, however, Attila realized that his forces were more than a match for the moribund Roman empire. The change in Attila's policy towards Rome is most clearly evident in his demand that the Huns control the frontier. For centuries the Roman empire had regulated trade across the frontier through border crossings, and had maintained a cordon sanitaire north of the Danube as a buffer against incursions. Yet when the historian Priscus of Panium accompanied a Roman mission to Attila in AD 449, he reports that he and his fellow legates passed through a deserted zone south, not north, of the Danube that took five days to cross. There could be no more potent demonstration of the reversal of fortunes as between the two empires. Well might the Hunnish ambassador Eslas boast that Theodosius was now Attila's subject; by the time he did so, the annual tribute paid by the empire to the Huns had risen sixfold from 350 pounds of gold to 2,100 pounds. This great reversal in status resulted from two massive invasions of eastern Roman territory, the first in AD 441, and the second in AD 447. During these incursions, Roman armies had proved incapable of resisting Attila's armies and Attila had shown that he had the technology to capture fortified Roman cities – battering-rams and rolling siege towers. No other northern people had so mastered the techniques of siegecraft, which had hitherto been the preserve of Romans and Persians. Goths, Vandals and others relied on long blockades or sudden attacks on the rare occasions when they chose to 'make war on walls', and this had given the empire a measure of operational security.

There would be no such security in dealing with Attila, who made extensive use of engineers trained in Roman siege techniques in his army. The effects of Hunnish attacks can still be seen in the massive destruction layers evident at various archaeological sites throughout central Europe.

Defeat at the Catalaunian Fields

Even as Priscus' legation was making its way north to see the great Hun, ambassadors of the 'western Romans' were being browbeaten by Attila. The Hun ruler accused them of 'concealing stolen treasure and protecting the thief' – in other words, harbouring and giving succour to the Huns' enemies. In the past, when levelled at the eastern Romans, such an accusation had always been the prelude to an attack. Attila duly unleashed a massive army from the Balkans on Gaul in AD 451. Things looked bleak for the western empire. Geiseric controlled North Africa, and the only way that Valentinian III's regime could support an army was if it retained the tenuous control of Gaul that Aetius had spent the previous decade building up. But Aetius was a skilled diplomat as well as a good soldier. Recognizing that domination by the Huns was to be avoided at all costs, he forged an alliance with the Visigoths of south-central France and other tribes in the region.

At the height of summer in AD 451, on a vast expanse of flat land outside Orléans variously known as Châlons, or the Catalaunian or Mauriacan Fields, the army of Aetius met that of Attila. It was here that the western Roman army fought its last great set-piece battle, and it was on this day that the independent Visigoths played the decisive role – according to an admittedly pro-Gothic writer – in securing a Roman victory. Attila was driven back to his camp and allegedly planned to commit suicide if the Romans overran it the following day. However, this never came to pass, since Theodoric, the king of the Visigoths, had fallen in battle and Aetius chose not to chance his luck any further. Attila withdrew to the Balkans.

Attila had never before suffered a serious defeat. Aetius seems not to have appreciated the potential harm that such a setback could inflict on a ruler whose unlimited power depended solely upon others' terrified belief in his invincibility. If Attila was to maintain control of his empire, then, staying at home and licking his wounds was not an option. And so, in AD 452, while Aetius was still in Gaul, he returned, this time making straight for Italy. Aquileia was destroyed after a terrible siege, and Milan was taken. But then Attila's attack faltered. He did not have the logistical support to advance on Rome, and disease began to take its toll of his army. After receiving an embassy that included the bishop of Rome, now a leading figure in the Roman aristocracy, he agreed to withdraw. Within months he was dead. Legend recounts that, while attending a feast to celebrate his marriage to a woman named Ilico, he overindulged in wine, burst a blood vessel and suffocated. The kingdom of the Huns, dependent as it was upon his personal authority, collapsed in civil war the next year as the many Germanic peoples he had once held in thrall rose up against their masters and defeated them in a huge battle in the central Balkans (the site of which is now lost). The Huns withdrew to the north and resumed their role as occasional mercenaries in Roman service.

The last generation of western Romans

While the great battles had been raging between Attila and the 'western Romans', significant changes had taken place in the political structures of the two empires. Theodosius II died in Constantinople in July, AD 450, followed by Galla Placidia later that same year in Rome. With no eastern heir available from the house of Theodosius, a general named Marcian (*c.* AD 390–457) emerged as the consensus choice of generals and the palace (Pulcheria even agreed to marry him if he would respect her vow of chastity). Marcian was a different sort of emperor. A career soldier, he made common cause with others who resented the annual tribute payments to Attila. He immediately revoked the tributes and set about reclaiming Roman territory from the Huns while Attila was campaigning in the west.

Valentinian III was evidently furious that he was not consulted about Marcian's actions, but it wasn't his empire. Meanwhile, he had grown increasingly antagonistic towards Aetius, the man who had saved his realm from Attila. His antipathy was encouraged by Petronius Maximus, the most powerful senator of the time, and Heracleius, a eunuch who was the emperor's *cubicularius*. On 21 September, AD 454, Aetius met with Valentinian at Ravenna in the presence of Heracleius. Aetius anticipated that the agenda of the meeting would be the empire's parlous financial state; instead, Valentinian accused him of treason for allowing Marcian to take over in the east, and attacked him with a sword. Heracleius joined in the brutal assault with a meat cleaver. Valentinian then set about purging Aetius' senior supporters, but failed to reward Maximus sufficiently for his services. Maximus' response was to recruit two soldiers from Aetius' bodyguard as assassins. On 21 March, AD 455, they murdered Valentinian, and Maximus ascended the throne. He forced Valentinian's widow Eudocia to marry him, and madc Eudocia's daughter (another Eudocia) marry his son. This second marriage was a terrible mistake, and was the chief reason why Maximus' reign lasted a mere 11 weeks. The younger Eudocia had once been betrothed to Geiseric's son. No sooner did Geiseric hear of the marriages in Rome than he claimed that Eudocia had summoned him to her aid. The Vandal fleet sailed from Carthage and landed near Rome in May, AD 455. When Maximus tried to flee, a mob murdered him. The Vandals then sacked the city for over two weeks, causing terrible devastation.

Through his conquest of North Africa, Geiseric becomes the key figure in the destruction of the Roman empire in the west. What we know of him, aside from his record as a warrior, is that, according to a later historian, he was of moderate stature, and lame as the result of a fall from a horse; a deep thinker who spoke rarely and despised luxury, was fierce in anger, desirous of gain, skilled in negotiation, and ready to sow dissension so as to arouse hatred. Like Attila, he came to occupy a position roughly on a par with that of emperor; and, like Attila, he provided a model for post-Roman rulers, joining the traditions of their own peoples with those of Rome. Some of the actors in the last decades of the western empire made their debuts under Attila before the Hun empire imploded, while the continuing Vandal control of

North Africa deprived the western Roman state of the resources it needed to rally its strength.

The vandalizing of Rome opened the final act of the collapse of the western empire, a drama that had begun with Honorius' murder of Stilicho. In the power vacuum that ensued after the deaths of Aetius and Valentinian, a soldier of Germanic origin named Ricimer (*c.* AD 405– 472), *magister militum* of the west, took upon himself the role of official kingmaker when, shortly after the Vandals sacked Rome, a senator named Flavius Avitus had himself proclaimed emperor at Arles. Ricimer, who was based in Italy, opposed his accession. When Avitus invaded Italy in AD 456, his army was defeated near Placentia. Avitus surrendered and became bishop of Placentia, dying in office shortly thereafter. Ricimer declined to become emperor and installed an officer named Majorian on the throne. When Majorian failed to defeat the Vandals, Ricimer replaced him with Liberius Severus, in AD 461. The eastern emperor refused to recognize Severus, who died under suspicious circumstances in AD 465. Ricimer did without an emperor until AD 467, when he accepted the eastern general, Anthemius, as his ruler.

Ricimer's success in these years seems to have derived from his ability to deal with the eastern court, which was at that time dominated by another general of Germanic descent, Aspar (*c.* AD 400–471). Aspar had played a leading role in installing Marcian as emperor, and, after Marcian's death, in promoting an officer from southern Turkey named Leo to be Marcian's successor. Leo, however, had a mind of his own, and wished to be succeeded by a man from his own part of the empire. In AD 469 he overthrew Aspar, and, five years later, put his preferred candidate, Zeno, on the throne.

Cutting the west adrift

The accession of Zeno to the eastern throne effectively sealed the fate of the western empire, for it sparked an immediate revolt by a general named Basiliscus. The revolt lasted for two years and occupied the whole attention of Zeno. As he struggled with Basiliscus, there were growing signs that the office of emperor was losing whatever residual relevance it had in western politics. In the meantime, in AD 472 Ricimer replaced Anthemius with a one Olybrius. Ricimer died on 18 August, AD 472, then Olybrius on 2 November, leaving the Burgundian general Gundobad, who had assisted Ricimer in the overthrow of Anthemius, as the chief kingmaker. After ending a five-month interregnum by persuading a man named Glycerius to become emperor, Gundobad departed the scene, deeming developments in Gaul of greater importance. The effect of his departure was to leave Glycerius facing an insurrection by Julius Nepos, commander of the Balkan army. When Nepos learned that Orestes, commander of the army of Italy and formerly a high official in Attila's court, was hostile to his bid for power, he returned to his base in Illyricum.

Back in Italy, however, Orestes promptly exploited the volatile situation to install his young son, Romulus Augustulus, as emperor. A year later Orestes died in a mutiny led by another general, Odoacer (AD 435–493), who deposed Romulus and wrote to Zeno announcing that there was no longer any need for an emperor in the west. At the same time, Zeno received representations from Nepos asking the eastern emperor to recognize him. Zeno was sympathetic to Nepos, being related to him through marriage, but was in no position to champion his cause.

The decision to leave the west to its own devices made Zeno the first emperor of a new Roman world, long in formation, that no longer had any need of Rome. The Roman empire had ceased to exist, and the classical world was now supplanted by a new era, as the Middle Ages dawned.

Epilogue

Dido's Revenge

At the end of the fourth book of Virgil's *Aeneid*, Dido, the queen of Carthage, curses Aeneas as he sails away to found the city of Rome. Dido is pregnant with his child, but the Trojan hero insists on leaving; the gods have commanded him to establish his own city, a city that will one day rule the world. Dido is not convinced that commitment to an unknown future should be stronger than a sense of duty to the knowable present. The figure whom she dreams will avenge the injustice she has suffered is the great Hannibal, whose invasion of Italy at the end of the third century BC and whose crushing victories over the armies of Rome were to play a formative role in shaping the ancient Roman concept of *virtus*. It was the ability to survive such disasters that defined the greatness of the community of Rome.

This close intertwining of the histories of Rome and Carthage was not Virgil's invention. It was central to the first great original work of Latin literature, Naevius' poem on Rome's First Punic War, a conflict that raged for over 20 years in the mid-third century BC. There was a neat historical symmetry in the fact that, as Rome began its inexorable final decline, an important nail was driven into its coffin by a ruler from the same North African city. Certainly, when the Vandal king Geiseric set sail from Carthage for Aeneas' city in AD 455, the ghost of Dido would have wished him 'God Speed'.

Even so, when Geiseric landed in Italy, the western Roman state still controlled more land than it had when Rome declared war on Carthage in 264 BC. Rome won the earlier war because it was able to mobilize the resources of Italy with enormous efficiency. In the course of that struggle, Italy suffered far heavier casualties than in the war against the Goths in the AD 370s, or even in the bloody civil wars earlier that century. Simple loss of territory cannot therefore explain why Roman Italy in the fifth century AD was no longer able to muster a strong enough army to defend itself. The key difference between AD 455 and 264 BC was not to do with the Italian environment or its population figures, but rather with a fundamental change in the relationship between the state and the people. The armies and navies of the mid-third century BC comprised civilians called up from their farms to serve the state, while the civilians of the fifth century AD were bound by the imperial tax structure to their lands. The Romans and Italians who flocked to swell the ranks of the Republic's armies were motivated by a fierce loyalty to their communities, and expected to share in the rewards of victory. The Roman people voted for the Punic Wars, and repeated disasters only reinforced their desire for ultimate victory.

Not so the civilians of the fifth century, who had no say in the direction of their state and no reason to love either their emperor or the private armies with which his generals maintained their status at court. Very different too was the attitude of people in the eastern empire. The redefinition of the office of emperor to exploit the religious fervour of the eastern empire's populace meant that the average person there felt a far stronger sense of allegiance to the emperor than did the civilians of the west. Even though religious opinions were often difficult to control, giving rise to innumerable theological controversies that plagued the politics of the eastern empire, meetings summoned with the ostensible purpose of debating matters of faith offered a common forum for people to voice their concerns. Whether by design or accident, the yoking together of imperial and religious ideology lent the eastern government a cohesion that was lacking in the west. The notion that the imperial house existed to protect the faithful was a narrative that proved as potent as the Augustan discourse of *virtus* or Diocletian's discourse of victory. By contrast, the utter failure of governments of the west from Honorius to Valentinian to offer a coherent justification for their existence, together with the bigotry, jealousy and folly that often marked the actions of these rulers, doomed the western empire to decline and fall.

If there is a lesson to be learned from the history of the Caesars from Augustus to Romulus, it is that government must represent the collective moral wisdom of society. It is the duty of an administration not simply to ensure justice and peace for its people, but also to create a viable way for those people to make their voices heard. Government that withdraws from the realities of the world around it, or simply asserts banal 'truths' that have little resonance with the opinions of its people, ultimately only erodes the very foundations of society. The fall of the western Roman empire was not so much the result of barbarian invasion as of a failure of imagination in assimilating the new arrivals. Appeals to prejudice and fantasies about the nature of the world were then, and always will be, a recipe for disaster.

GLOSSARY

aerarium the Roman state treasury, as distinct from the *patrimonium*, which controlled the personal wealth and property portfolio of the emperor.

amphitheatre an elliptical arena surrounded by banked tiers of seating for staging public spectacles such as gladiatorial combats.

Arianism in Christian theology, a doctrine expounded by Arius of Alexandria in the third–fourth centuries AD, which maintained that the son of God, Jesus Christ, was not of the same 'substance' as God the Father; the Council of Nicaea affirmed that the Father and Son were coequal, coeternal and 'of one substance', thereby declaring Arianism a heresy.

Augustus (lit. 'exalted one') the name conferred by the senate on Octavian and adopted as the ruler's title by all subsequent emperors. Under the Tetrarchy, the title was used by the two senior imperial colleagues (and 'Caesar' by the two junior colleagues).

auxiliary supplementary troops supporting the legionaries of the regular Roman army, auxiliaries were drawn from across the empire. They often deployed specialist fighting skills, as horsemen, archers, slingshot-throwers, etc.

Caesar the family name (*nomen*) of Gaius Julius Caesar and his adoptive son Octavian (Augustus). 'Caesar' came to be used by all Roman emperors as an imperial title. When it was not used in conjunction with the title/name 'Augustus' it signified the heir apparent, a meaning that was strengthened under the Tetrarchy when it became the title of the two junior imperial colleagues.

Circus Maximus site of a large hippodrome in Ancient Rome, where various equestrian events and festivals were held. Chief among these were the popular chariot races, in which twelve chariots could race abreast around the oval track. The Circus has become a public park in modern Rome.

colonia a free city in a province of the Roman empire, whose inhabitants enjoyed full citizenship and which was exempt from any tribute payments to Rome.

consul the senior magistrate in the Roman administrative system. Prior to the time of Augustus there were ordinarily two consuls elected each year (additional consuls might be elected to replace those who died in office). From Augustus onwards, there were usually more than two consuls for each year, though the office still represented the high point of a senatorial career.

cubicularius a freedman who held the post of personal attendant to the emperor. Many *cubicularii* exerted great influence over particular emperors.

Dacia the area, roughly equivalent to modern Romania, north of the River Danube, which became a Roman province after Trajan's victorious campaigns against the tribes there in AD 106. Dacia was abandoned to the Germanic tribes after AD 272.

dictator in the Roman Republic, a magistrate granted absolute powers by the consuls for a term of six months during times of crisis. Dictators were the only Roman magistrates not to be elected.

diocese in the late Roman Christian empire, a group of provinces under the supervision of a *vicarius*.

domus the Roman household; a key concept in promoting the idea of stability and fidelity in the Roman world. The ability of the head of the household (*paterfamilias*) to maintain order and harmony in his domestic domain was regarded as mirroring the emperor's wise stewardship of the state as a whole.

donativum a 'gift', usually financial, made by an emperor. Major gifts were expected by members of the military, especially the Praetorian Guard, at the beginning of each reign and to mark other significant events.

equestrian a member of the second aristocratic rank, just below the senate in terms of prestige. From Augustus onwards the equestrian order was defined as being all Roman citizens of free birth who possessed property valued at 400,000 sesterces.

federates (Latin *foederati*) 'barbarian' peoples, such as the Goths, who settled in the Roman empire after being displaced by the Huns in the late fourth century AD in return for pledging to serve Rome militarily in time of crisis.

forum a market square or public space in Roman towns. Usually colonnaded and surrounded by temples and public buildings, *fora* were equivalent to *agora* in the Greek world.

Franks a confederation of Germanic peoples from the Lower

Rhine region. Emerging in the third century AD, the Franks settled in northern Gaul in the subsequent centuries.

freedman/freedwoman a slave who had been granted his/her freedom. Freedmen/women remained attached to the households of their former masters, and were often employed in positions of great trust. In the emperor's household, they performed many important functions in those aspects of government connected with the imperial household, and could exercise enormous power.

frieze a band of relief sculpture decorating the upper levels of stonework on a temple or other monument.

gladiator in public entertainments held at Rome's Colosseum and at other amphitheatres, a slave (or sometimes a volunteer) trained in combat. Different types of gladiator specialized in fighting with particular weapons.

Goths a Germanic people of central Europe. The Goths formed a number of different groups in the course of their years of contact with Rome; the most significant were perhaps the Visigoths, who developed out of the people led by Alaric in the early fifth century, and the Ostrogoths, a group that formed in the Balkans at the end of that century.

Huns a semi-nomadic people, who came to prominence as invaders in eastern Europe from the late fourth century AD onwards. Led by Attila in the mid-fifth century, they wrought havoc in the Balkans and the western empire but their empire broke up shortly after his death in AD 453.

imperator the Roman title from which our word 'emperor' derives. Signifying 'victorious general', it was adopted by

Augustus' successors as a standard feature of the imperial nomenclature.

imperium ('power') the authority to rule over the Roman people, once conferred on the kings of the city and after their deposition on magistrates, notably the consuls.

imperium maius ('greater power') one of two key powers upon which the legal foundations of the imperial system were based (the other being *tribunicia potestas*). *Imperium maius* was power that was 'greater' than that of other magistrates, who were therefore supposed to obey orders issued by one who held this power.

legionary a soldier in the regular Roman army; legions, which originally each numbered over 5000 men but whose strength was later reduced to 1000–2000, were made up of professionally trained, well-equipped heavy infantry.

lex maiestatis in Roman law, the charge of high treason, a capital offence.

magister equitum ('master of the horse') in the Roman army, the supreme commanding officer of the cavalry units on each war front.

magister militum ('master of the soldiers') a new level of command, created in the late fourth century, above master of infantry and master of cavalry.

magister peditum ('master of the footsoldiers') in the Roman army, the supreme commanding officer of the infantry units on each war front.

Mithraism cult of the sun-god Mithras. Originating in the eastern provinces of the Roman empire, it became increasingly popular during the second and third centuries AD.

municipium an urban centre that had been granted a civic constitution by Rome and whose citizens enjoyed the benefits of Roman citizenship. Compare *colonia*.

Neoplatonism a school of thought combining teachings based upon the writings of the fourth-century BC Greek philosopher Plato with those of other groups. The founding father of Neoplatonism was Plotinus, whose career spanned the middle of the third century AD.

optimates ('best men') men who tended to support the legacy of Sulla's dictatorship in the generation of Caesar; in other words, inherently conservative members of the senate. It was generally used in contrast to the term *popularis*, or 'supporter of the interests of the people as a whole'.

Pantheon temple built by Marcus Agrippa and repaired by the emperor Hadrian to honour all the gods in the Roman state cult. The building was circular in design and surmounted by a large dome; the term later came to be used figuratively to describe all the gods in any polytheistic belief system.

Parthia name used by the Romans for the territory, primarily in Iran and Iraq, controlled by the Iranian dynasty that preceded the Sassanid empire in the early third century AD.

paterfamilias the head of a Roman household (*domus*); Roman law granted the *paterfamilias* power of life and death (*patria potestas*) within his home over every member of his family and his servants.

patrician a member of a ruling élite of Rome. The aristocratic families who made up the patrician order claimed descent from the city's original senators, who according to legend were appointed by Romulus.

patrimonium the portfolio of land and other property holdings under personal imperial control (largely acquired through seizures and bequests from citizens) and handed down from one emperor to the next.

plebeian any Roman citizen who was not a patrician. Plebeians (or plebs for short) constituted the majority of the Roman populace.

pontifex maximus the high priest of the Roman state cult. Beginning with Julius Caesar, emperors held the post until AD 382.

praetor Roman magistrate, second in rank to the consul, responsible for civil jurisdiction.

praetorian guard élite imperial bodyguard, first formed under Augustus. Coming to prominence under the influence of their prefect Aelius Sejanus during the reign of Tiberius, the praetorians increasingly wielded political power in the appointment of emperors. Their power was curbed by later emperors from Diocletian onwards.

princeps (lit. 'leading man') the most common designation for the emperor from the first century AD onwards.

Punic Roman adjective for the people of Carthage in North Africa and their language. It derives from the Latin *Poeni*, meaning Phoenicians, from the area in the eastern Mediterranean around the ports of Tyre and Sidon, where the Carthaginians originally came from.

quaestor the lowest-ranking Roman magistrate. Quaestors had responsibilities for state finances and public works.

relief a form of sculpture in which the design is raised above a flat background surface.

saeculum a time period theoretically equivalent to the lifespan of the longest-lived person on earth, calculated at either 100 or 110 years. In Rome, the end of a *saeculum* was marked with extensive games and sacrifices.

Sassanid (or Sassanian) **empire** the state in Persia, established by the Sassanid dynasty, which succeeded the Parthian empire and ruled from AD 225 until Arab Muslims conquered the region in *c.* AD 636.

senate the governing body of the Roman Republic. Members of the senate had to possess significant property and, ordinarily, to have held the office of quaestor or tribune of the plebs.

Tetrarchy (lit. 'rule of four') the system, named by later historians, instituted by Diocletian to rule the empire. The responsibilities of government were shared by two senior emperors and two juniors.

tribune the main representative of the Roman plebeian class. Ten tribunes were elected annually by the 'council of the plebs', a body set up in fifth-century BC Rome. The tribune's powers, an important part of state authority in Rome, were known as the *tribunicia potestas*.

triumvirate in common usage, any group of three magistrates. The term was applied to the informal political alliance between Pompey, Crassus and Caesar in the fifties BC and, later, to the official board of three established in 43 BC 'to set the state in order' comprised Mark Antony, Octavian and Lepidus.

Vestal Virgin servant of Vesta, the patron goddess of the Roman hearth and home. The Vestals were charged with keeping alight the eternal flame, symbolizing the enduring strength of the state, at the Temple of Vesta in the forum.

vicarius (lit. 'substitute, stand-in') term used in the early Roman empire to denote a deputy to a provincial governor. Following Diocletian's administrative reforms in the third century AD, the term denoted an office-holder who was responsible for the day-to-day administration of one of the three dioceses under the jurisdiction of each of the empire's four praetorian prefects.

villa the buildings of a Roman country estate, traditionally comprising living quarters, storehouses, stables, workshops, farm buildings, and so on. Lavish villas became the preferred residence of many Roman emperors, who ran the business of empire from there, when not in the capital or on campaign.

virtus the manly quality of service to the state, much prized as a quintessential Roman characteristic that helped create social cohesion from the early days of the republic onwards.

INDEX

INDEX